1985

SECOND
EDITION

SPEAK
EASY

AN INTRODUCTION TO PUBLIC SPEAKING

SPEAK EASY

SECOND
EDITION

AN INTRODUCTION TO PUBLIC SPEAKING

BRENT D. PETERSON
BRIGHAM YOUNG UNIVERSITY

NOEL D. WHITE
EASTERN WASHINGTON STATE UNIVERSITY

ERIC G. STEPHAN
BRIGHAM YOUNG UNIVERSITY

WEST PUBLISHING COMPANY
ST. PAUL   NEW YORK   LOS ANGELES   SAN FRANCISCO

Text and cover design: Design Office / Peter Martin

Cover painting: MARK ROTHKO, *Number 22,* 1949.
Collection of the Museum of Modern Art, New York.

Credits appear on page 280.

Library of Congress Cataloging in Publication Data

Peterson, Brent D.
   Speak Easy

Includes bibliographies and index.
   1. Public speaking.   I. White, Noel D., joint
author.
II. Stephan, Eric. G., joint author.
III. Title.
PN4121.P43   1984   808.5'1   84-2233
ISBN 0-314-77783-0

CONTENTS

PART TWO

PLANNING, PREPARING, AND PRESENTING   45

CHAPTER 3   SELECTING A TOPIC AND A PURPOSE   47
OUTLINE   47

CHAPTER 4   SUPPORTING AND ILLUSTRATING YOUR IDEAS   69
OUTLINE   69

CHAPTER 5   ORGANIZING YOUR SPEECH INFORMATION   105

OUTLINE   105

CHAPTER 6   DELIVERING YOUR IDEAS   129

OUTLINE   129

PART THREE

SPEAKING WITH A PURPOSE   161

CHAPTER 7   INFORMATIVE SPEAKING   163
OUTLINE   163

PREFACE

We feel strongly that this is not just another book about giving a speech, but is a book about speaking publicly.

1. The text follows our conviction that the key to effective speaking is (a) getting the listener's attention, (b) keeping the listener interested and involved, and (c) stimulating a favorable response in the listener.

2. Further, we take the position that the roots of effective speaking exist in everyday conversing skills. Everyone already has a substantial experience base for speaking. In others words, public speaking instruction should not be seen as being at the opposite end of the communication continuum from two person/interpersonal interaction. Public speaking principles evolve and can be best understood by examining the principles of interpersonal exchanges and transactions.

3. The reader will find the text to be designed, organized, and illustrated to parallel what an effective presentation should be. This is a do-as-I-do, not a do-as-I-say, book. The text is simple, to the point, and highly illustrative—a speech should be no less.

If you will take a moment to glance over the table of contents and then flip through the pages, you will see that the book does not just talk about public speaking, but rather, models what it is teaching.

As speech-communication teachers, we have often discussed with each other what principles of traditional public speaking we actually use in our own professional lives. We discovered that mainly we adapt to the audience, develop the speech around a specific purpose or point, use plenty of examples and visual materials, and are enthusiastic about what we say.

We also noted that some of our personal discoveries regarding effective speaking do not appear consistently in other available texts. What do you do if your audience isn't responding after you have finished your introduction? How do you discover your own speaking style rather than just mimic someone else's? Why are some of the more effective speakers today using an informal delivery? How can speakers make themselves more credible as they speak?

We embrace the idea that public speaking cannot be separated or taught apart from everyday talking, conversing, making a point in a meeting, or answering or asking a question in class. The roots of public speaking are in our everyday interactions; basic speaking skills exist in social exchanges. And we strongly believe that how you say it can be as important as what you say.

Our own research suggests that we should explain further why physiologically and psychologically some traditional techniques for speaking work. For example, an explanation of the functioning of the right/left brain hemispheres helps in understanding why and how general and specific statements, verbal and nonverbal elements, abstract and visual points must be combined in a presentation. The reasons certain speaking formats or styles are effective have a lot to do with how the brain processes information.

In this book we also take the position that the instructor is a *coach*. The instructor may not have the time to model every single principle; neither does a coach. Various coaches have different approaches and sometimes can train people to do the activity better than they can do it themselves. So, many beginning public speakers allow anyone who has an opinion to be the coach. *Our belief is that the student can have only one coach at a time. In this case it is the instructor.* In addition, the student has to be willing to try out new skills even though doing so may be a bit uncomfortable. You should not expect high grades on every class presentation, but your reward will be that this course will make a difference in your life. More specifically when you, the student, complete this book and the course, you will find greater confidence and ability in:

- getting and holding a listener's attention
- responding to critical questions and comments
- being specific and to the point
- accepting and using constructive speaking criticism
- examining your credibility as a message source
- organizing information to obtain a specific speaking purpose
- speaking up in meetings and public situations
- influencing others' opinions and attitudes
- giving presentations in small or large groups
- speaking to inform on a controversial issue

And if you become addicted to speaking as we have, you may end up making a living by doing the very thing that scared you to death at one point.

For those readers who insist on a simple overview of the book, we should mention that the book is organized into three parts. The first, "Speaking with Others," includes an opening chapter, "Public Speaking and You." A speaking analysis test is offered here. Chapter 2, "The Process of Public Speaking: An Overview," focuses on listener-oriented speaking.

The second part, "Planning, Preparing, and Presenting the Speech," has four chapters. Chapter 3, "Selecting a Topic and a Purpose," emphasizes speaking about topics that interest you. Chapter 4, "Supporting and Illustrating Your Ideas," has a special section on visual supporting materials. Chapter 5, "Organizing Your Speech Information," and chapter 6, "Delivering Your Ideas," emphasize how to present yourself and the material.

The third part, "Speaking with a Purpose," has six chapters. Chapter 7, "Informative Speaking," covers the basics of informative speaking, including giving instructions to others. Chapter 8, "Persuasive Speaking," focuses on key persuasive techniques that have practical application. Chapter 9, "Special Speaking Occasions," chapter 10, "Speaking in Small Groups and Conferences," and chapter 11, "Responding to Questions and Comments," deal with the special speaking situations in which we find ourselves. Chapter 12 concludes the book on a high note of personal challenge.

We have gone through the same steps and materials in preparing this book that we would in preparing to speak for a large audience. We think the book reflects that practical flavor.

BRENT, NOEL, AND ERIC

NOTE TO THE READER: If you read the foregoing material, you probably have a better understanding of the writers, the book, and the subject of public speaking. In fact, you may even feel a bit warm and encouraged about some of the possibilities for being more effective and comfortable when speaking. At any rate, congratulations for "reading this first."

PART ONE

SPEAKING WITH OTHERS

Herein lies the tragedy of the age: not that men are poor—all men know something of poverty; not that men are wicked—who is good? Not that men are ignorant—what is truth? Nay, but that men know so little of men.

WILLIAM E. B. DU BOIS

PUBLIC SPEAKING
AND YOU

1

SPEAKING: COMMON MISCONCEPTIONS

You may have noticed by now a familiar experience related to speaking publicly. We tend to be "experts" in critiquing how others could have *obviously* improved their speaking effectiveness. This spectator expertise has been called "armchair quarterbacking" in relation to viewing football games. This confidence, which often comes in retrospect, tends to diminish and turn into outright humbleness when we are doing the speaking. Questions without apparent answers pop up uninvited in our mind. What would be the best approach to the subject? How should I organize what I want to say? For that matter, what do I want to say? Why am I so nervous? Does everyone else go through what I am going through?

Actually, most of us talk so much and have been talking so long that we fail to notice on the conscious level when we do it well and when we do it poorly. Somehow we have come to believe that giving a talk is completely different from talking with others. This is in fact not true. Only minor differences in technique exist between talking and "giving a talk." In fact we are likely to forget just how much time we spend giving talks or mini-speeches and expressing our opinions with others.

Before proceeding with the chapter, we want to give you an opportunity to assess working knowledge and concepts of speaking in public. Complete the following Public Speaking Inventory to see how well you commonly sense what might be considered, upon the completion of this book, as speaking common sense.

INVENTORY OF PUBLIC SPEAKING

Circle the response that you believe is *most* correct.

1. Delivery is more important in persuasive speaking than it is in informative speaking.
   True   False

2. Most public speaking today is informative.
   True   False

3. Visual aids should be shown to the audience for one to two minutes before the speaker actually refers to them.
   True   False

4. If you have speaking aids or samples that are too small to see, they should be passed around the audience during the speech.
   True   False

5. When a visual aid is being viewed or an aid is being handled by the audience, the speaker should remain silent until the audience can process the material.
   True   False

6. The organization of a speech is always dictated by the topic chosen.
   True   False

7. Eye contact means you scan all parts of the audience with your eyes while speaking.
   True   False

8. The primary place to research a presentation is in the library.
   True   False

9. The very best speeches are written out word for word or memorized to control precise wording.
   True   False

10. Transitions just link ideas, they should not change the meaning of the ideas.
    True   False

11. Public speaking can best be described as a speaker sending a message to a receiver and the receiver giving feedback.
    True   False

12. Delivery pertains to just the vocal aspects of speaking.
    True   False

13. The most important factor to discover in audience analysis is the age of the listeners.
    True   False

14. Speaker credibility is determined by how much the listeners like the speaker.
    True   False

15. Speaker credibility is always increased if the speaker refers to specific evidence.
    True   False

16. It is more important for a speaker to talk about a topic the audience is interested in than a topic he/she is interested in.
    True   False

17. The main purpose of visual aids is to highlight words or phrases important for the audience to remember.
    True   False

18. The number of words on a visual aid are not important as long as the words are easy to read.

    True   False

19. Good organization is the most important characteristic associated with effective speaking.

    True   False

20. It is not possible to inform on a controversial issue.

    True   False

21. The key to persuasive speaking is getting your audience to understand your point of view.

    True   False

22. In most cases the way a speaker handles questions and comments after the presentation does not affect the listeners' overall perception of the presentation.

    True   False

The best overall answer for each question is FALSE. The explanations for the answers appear in the text of the various chapters. Check the number of correct responses you had against the following scale:

Number Correct	Insight into Principles of Public Speaking
21–22	Outstanding
19–20	Very good
17–18	Adequate
below 16	Inadequate

Just in case you don't believe in inventories and quizzes, we include this cartoon. We hope the inventory wasn't a flop. If it was, think of all you will learn from this point on.

Public Communication Today

Roderick P. Hart, Gustav W. Friedrich, and William D. Brooks

Today, communication is not limited to face-to-face situations—we have worldwide electronic communication, television saturation, and packaged entertainment. And it is understandable why some have said that live, in-person public speaking is as extinct as the dodo bird. Nothing could be further from the truth! Not only is public speaking alive and well, but it is thriving as it never has before despite—and perhaps because of—the coming of the mass media. *Per person,* public speech consumption is higher today than ever before, including the era of the late 1800s. Even platform lecturing, one small aspect of non-mediated public communication, is a booming, million-dollar industry today. Political figures, journalists, authors, entertainers, business leaders, and proponents of all sorts of "isms" found the lecture circuit of the 1970s to be a virtual gold mine. More than one presidential loser has paid the campaign bills by going on the lecture circuit. We, as a people, have *not* lost our enthu-siasm for in-person public speaking as a significant social institution. Teddy Roosevelt once called the public speaking platform America's fourth great institution, surpassed only by the home, school, and church. This statement remains true today, no matter what has happened, or may be happening, to the other three institutions.

No one knows exactly how many speeches are given each year in the United States, but conservative estimates made by one group, the International Platform Association, run as high as 500,000. Speeches are given by persons representing literally thousands of organizations, groups that are large and small, governmental and private, commercial and philanthropic. . . .

If ever there was a fear that mass media extravaganzas would run public speaking out of town, that fear has now been buried. Indeed, public speakers are seemingly created and nurtured by the television screen. Instead of killing off the public platform as was at first predicted, TV has actually stimulated the demand for "live" speakers. . . . There were upwards of 25,000 professional speaking opportunities in the business and convention fields alone—ranging from closed seminars for a handful of top-echelon executives to the annual open meetings of the National Education Association, which brings out a whop-ping 10,000 registrants.

The second largest sponsor of paid lectures is education—from kindergarten assemblies to graduate school forums. About one in five of all elementary and secondary schools have at least one public program annually. The average number of speaking programs is running as high as five per institution. This totals up to 130,000 programs each year. Add to that another 200,000 programs on the junior college, college, and graduate levels, and it seems that the machinery of education is being lubricated by the juices of eloquence!

Such public speaking statistics are staggering. In one week, for example, there were 40,000 paid speaking engagements in New York and 30,000 in Chicago. In addition, some U.S. senators make as much as $35,000 per year on the lecture circuit.

SOURCE: Pages 11–12 in *Public Communication* by Roderick P. Hart, Gustav W. Friedrich, and William D. Brooks. Copyright © 1975 by Roderick P. Hart, Gustav W. Friedrich and William D. Brooks. Reprinted by permission of Harper & Row Publishers, Inc.

WHO IS SPEAKING?

Who is speaking and why are they doing it? People are speaking by the millions—citizens, public figures, scientists, doctors, generals, artists, engineers, architects, wives, husbands, children, managers, laborers, priests, evangelists, teachers, students, friends, you, me, everyone is speaking. And why are we speaking? Because speaking is the most direct way of getting understanding, acceptance, and actions from others.

THINGS TO LEARN ABOUT SPEAKING WELL

What is public speaking? The dictionary claims that public speaking is "the art or science of effective oral communication with an audience." We agree, but add that any public speaking situation is private as well as public. In other words, the speaking process is experienced between you and a single listener even though many others might be present. Just because there are several people in the audience does not take away from the fact that each listener processes the speaking/listening relationship as a personal experience to him/herself.

All of us spend much of our time informally talking to small groups of people. Sometimes we speak in more formal circumstances. In order to speak effectively in small or large groups, formal or informal situations, we must do at least four things:

1. Learn how to think through (prepare) a message.
2. Learn how to feel confident before a large or small group of listeners.
3. Learn how to spark attention and maintain the interest of the listener.
4. Win a favorable response.

During the last few years, hundreds of students have responded to the following two-stage self-evaluation to estimate their present awareness of standard public speaking factors. Fill in the answers and compare your results with those of other college students enrolled in an introductory course on public speaking (sec p. 13).

PUBLIC SPEAKING SELF-EVALUATION

First, evaluate your knowledge of the following items, on a continuum from 1 to 10 (1 is low, 10 is high). Circle a number for each item. Then, in the column on the right, rank the items listed from 1 through 19, in their order of importance to effective speaking (1 is most important, 19 is least important).

Present Knowledge of:											Priority Ranking
Listening	1	2	3	4	5	6	7	8	9	10	_____
Informative speaking	1	2	3	4	5	6	7	8	9	10	_____
Persuasive speaking	1	2	3	4	5	6	7	8	9	10	_____
Audiovisual aids	1	2	3	4	5	6	7	8	9	10	_____
Outlines	1	2	3	4	5	6	7	8	9	10	_____
Introductions	1	2	3	4	5	6	7	8	9	10	_____
Developing the body	1	2	3	4	5	6	7	8	9	10	_____
Conclusions	1	2	3	4	5	6	7	8	9	10	_____
Transitions	1	2	3	4	5	6	7	8	9	10	_____
Holding audiences	1	2	3	4	5	6	7	8	9	10	_____
Eye contact	1	2	3	4	5	6	7	8	9	10	_____
Bodily action	1	2	3	4	5	6	7	8	9	10	_____
Gestures	1	2	3	4	5	6	7	8	9	10	_____
Inflection	1	2	3	4	5	6	7	8	9	10	_____
Minimizing stage fright	1	2	3	4	5	6	7	8	9	10	_____
Emotional appeals	1	2	3	4	5	6	7	8	9	10	_____
Rate of delivery	1	2	3	4	5	6	7	8	9	10	_____
Anatomy of speech mechanisms	1	2	3	4	5	6	7	8	9	10	_____
Organization	1	2	3	4	5	6	7	8	9	10	_____

*Some untaught men have become good orators,
but the best orators are those who combine ability
with training.*

ISOCRATES

Students reported the least amount of knowledge concerning emotional appeals (3), rate of delivery (3), and anatomy of speech mechanisms (3). They knew only slightly more about audiovisual aids (4), outlines (4), transitions (4), inflection (4), and minimizing stage fright (4). They knew the most about eye contact (8), and just slightly less about listening (7) and introductions (7). But look at how they ranked on items of most importance—almost everyone ranked the ability to hold an audience as the most important ability. The other items they felt to be of most importance in effective public speaking were: developing the body (2), organization (3), minimizing stage fright (4), informative speaking (5), persuasive speaking (6), eye contact (7), and introductions (8). Thus, what students enrolling in a public-speaking class want to learn is, once again:

- how to prepare a message (introductions, organization, and developing the body)
- how to feel confident before an audience (minimizing stage fright)
- how to hold the attention of an audience and win a favorable response (persuasive and informative speaking, and eye contact)

We have also asked people who take our introductory public speaking class: "What do you hope to gain from this course? List any particular goals, interests, or problems you wish." A typical response appears here:

> I would really like to become a dynamic speaker!!! I would like to be able to select interesting topics and present my message in such a way that people will truly listen and learn. Nerves and emotions are a problem to me. It would sure be nice to enlarge my vocabulary and add some "spice" to my speech but on the other hand, not be a "show-boat." Being able to talk to everyone, from tiny tot to senior citizen and also listening to them is important to me. I guess, just being able to effectively communicate with people is my main objective.

AVERAGE STUDENT ANSWERS
TO THE PUBLIC SPEAKING SELF-EVALUATION

Present knowledge of:											Priority Ranking
Listening	1	2	3	4	5	6	⑦	8	9	10	9
Informative speaking	1	2	3	4	⑤	6	7	8	9	10	5
Persuasive speaking	1	2	3	4	⑤	6	7	8	9	10	6
Audiovisual aids	1	2	3	④	5	6	7	8	9	10	11
Outlines	1	2	3	④	5	6	7	8	9	10	14
Introductions	1	2	3	4	5	6	⑦	8	9	10	8
Developing the body	1	2	3	4	5	⑥	7	8	9	10	2
Conclusions	1	2	3	4	5	⑥	7	8	9	10	10
Transitions	1	2	3	④	5	6	7	8	9	10	17
Holding audiences	1	2	3	4	⑤	6	7	8	9	10	1
Eye contact	1	2	3	4	5	6	7	⑧	9	10	7
Bodily action	1	2	3	④	5	6	7	8	9	10	13
Gestures	1	2	3	4	⑤	6	7	8	9	10	12
Inflection	1	2	3	④	5	6	7	8	9	10	15
Minimizing stage fright	1	2	3	④	5	6	7	8	9	10	4
Emotional appeals	1	2	③	4	5	6	7	8	9	10	18
Rate of delivery	1	2	③	4	5	6	7	8	9	10	19
Anatomy of speech mechanisms	1	2	③	4	5	6	7	8	9	10	16
Organization	1	2	3	4	⑤	6	7	8	9	10	3

When participants complete the beginning speech course, we ask them what they gained from the course. Some typical responses follow:

I always felt that I had important ideas but no way to communicate them to people in a natural and honest way. I learned from this course skills necessary to accomplish my goal. I recently ran for the local school board and lost; however, as a result I was asked to serve on an influential study and planning committee.

I took this speech class because I have to teach this year and never felt I could really keep student attention. I'm impressed! My new ability to organize and illustrate ideas and speak in an enthusiastic way has changed my whole feeling about being a successful teacher.

I have been married twice and worked for the government 15 years on overages, shortages, damage shortages, and other transportational discrepancies. Better speaking and more confidence in presenting my ideas enabled me to change to higher pay and achieve more recognition.

It is often said that speakers aren't born, they are made, and that a speech communication course will not solve a personality problem. Interestingly, however, we all know people who seem to be "born" with a great natural ability to communicate and who develop quite nicely without a great deal of coaching. And yes, some minor personality problems can be overcome through a good course in effective speaking. What, however, is probably most discouraging to students are the lists of "things you must be" in order to be an effective speaker. For example, it has been stated that you must have knowledge, integrity, confidence, humbleness, self-esteem, responsiveness, communication skills, credibility, willingness, poise, fluency, sensitivity, organizational ability, and so on. Furthermore, you should be at once peaceful and forceful, simple and grand, listener and speaker, gentle and strong, creative yet thoroughly outlined. In short, it would be most helpful if you wear blue tights and an undershirt with an S on the front, if you speak faster than a speeding bullet, if you have vocal qualities more powerful than a locomotive, and if your voice can project over large audiences with a single resonating bound. Unfortunately, most of us will never have all these superhuman speaking skills. *Fortunately, we won't need to.*

"As I was saying . . ."

We are concerned that you don't become overwhelmed by complex sets of instructions on speaking well. And also that you do have great confidence in the many natural speaking abilities you already possess and use everyday. We all have things to say, so the important thing is to learn to say them well—to change our talking into successful speaking.

If all my talents and powers were to be taken from me by some inscrutable Providence, and I had my choice of keeping but one, I would unhesitatingly ask to be allowed to keep the Power of Speaking, for through it, I would quickly recover all the rest.

DANIEL WEBSTER

We all have special talents and attributes. Calvin Taylor, a creative-talent researcher for the last several decades, says that in a group of 5,000 people, one person can do at least one thing better than anyone else in the group; and in some special way of thinking about something or doing something, each person is literally a genius! Our university commu-

9,999 Out of Every 10,000 Speakers Have Something to Say

The Problem Is That No One Listens If You Don't Say It Well.

"I used to speak every day; now that I speak well, I've been speaking once a month!"

"Yesterday, when everybody was talking, I said it well instead of how I usually say it. I found it produced a broken lip."

"The only place you get criticized for saying it well is on your CB."

"Whenever I spot another "Say it Well" speaker, I always honk my horn and wave."

"I first tried to say it well on the Great Wall of China and didn't care for it. But that was before I met Chang."

"I never knew a secret agent who didn't speak well."

"I still haven't gotten Cindy to say it well, but I'm hopeful. Last month I got her to say maybe."

*"You should have seen me **before** I took this speaking class!"*

"I found out that saying it before dinner reduced the necessity of saying it well after dinner."

nication and self-concept research suggests that each one of us has the ability to become rather successful at something—even speaking. About the only important question that remains is how serious we are about changing our talking into successful speaking.

So, let's get on with our program for quick growth in public speaking: Continue to review the suggestions on the process of public speaking (chapter 2) and see if you can find your own best speaking style. Learn about selecting a topic and a purpose (chapter 3), supporting and illustrating your ideas (chapter 4), organizing your speech information (chapter 5), and delivering your ideas (chapter 6). Then sharpen your skills for informing (chapter 7), persuading (chapter 8), speaking on special occasions (chapter 9), and speaking in small groups (chapter 10). Learn to have fun by responding and interacting more easily with your audience (chapter 11). Then reflect on the course we have put together. Tough but exhilarating. Hard work but observable results. Common sense but not always commonly sensed (chapter 12). We spend so much of our time talking we might as well learn to have more fun doing it.

WHAT TO KNOW

We actually do more speaking in our daily lives than we suspect. Speaking ranges from informal conversation to formal public speech. We are all aware of what public speaking is, though we read to have more knowledge and skills of the various elements in the process in order to be more effective. This book is a planned program for helping you accomplish your goal of becoming a more effective speaker.

WHAT TO DO

Speaking Log for a Day   Design a log for recording every separate situation where you talk to others (express your opinion, make a comment in a class, interact in a conversation, tell someone how to do something, describe a recent movie, etc.). Look at your results:

1. Do you do one kind of speaking more than others?

2. Do you feel there is enough variety and challenge to you in the kinds of everyday speaking you do? If not, how could you improve?

3. Do you consider yourself to be more of an extrovert or more of an introvert? Are you comfortable with this? What will you do to improve?

Compare your results with other members of the class.

1. Could you predict what specific individuals have in their log results, based on your observation of them in class?

2. Did the results of a particular class member's speaking log surprise you? Why or why not?

Classroom Communicators

1. Make it a personal project to observe students who participate in the classes you are in. Pay particular attention to:
   a. The questions asked
   b. How an opinion is stated
   c. How a person disagrees subtly or openly with another
2. Look at classroom participation in relation to the instructor's communication style. How does the instructor respond to:
   a. Questions of inquiry
   b. Questions that challenge the instructor's points-of-view
   c. Various class members discussing a point

WHERE TO LEARN MORE

Ehninger, Douglas, Alan H. Monroe, and Bruce E. Gronbeck, *Principles and Types of Speech Communication*. 8th ed. Glenview, IL: Scott, Foresman, 1980.

Seiler, William J., E. Scott Baudheim, and L. David Schuelke. *Communication in Business and Professional Organizations*. Reading, Mass.: Addison-Wesley, 1982.

Verderber, Rudolf F. *Communicate*. 3rd ed. Belmont, CA: Wadsworth, 1980.

Walter, Otis M., and Robert L. Scott. *Thinking and Speaking*, chap. 1. New York: Macmillan, 1979.

Whitman, Richard F., and Paul H. Boase. *Speech Communication: Principles and Contexts*, chap. 1. New York: Macmillan, 1983.

Wilson, John F., and Carrol C. Arnold. *Public Speaking as a Liberal Art*. 4th ed. Boston: Allyn and Bacon, 1978.

THE PROCESS OF
PUBLIC SPEAKING:
AN OVERVIEW

2

THE PROCESS OF PUBLIC SPEAKING

A simplistic way of viewing the process of public speaking has been presented in several other texts. Speaking is said to be a stimulus-and-response process. The speaker offers the stimulus (message) and the audience responds (feedback). This perspective can be graphically represented as:

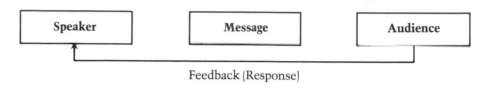

Feedback (Response)

DRAWING: FUTZIE NUTZLE

350 BC: To overcome a speech impediment, Demosthenes spoke with pebbles in his mouth, recited poetry while running, and practiced speeches before a mirror. He is still considered the world's greatest orator.

The focus of this perspective usually is on what the speaker says (content). The speaker is considered the primary entity in the event. The audience may be viewed as a group whose role is to respectfully attend to the message. The process which includes speaking and feedback (usually considered as only verbal) are part of a start-stop process. The speaker talks and the audience listens. The speaker stops talking. The people in the audience, through questions or comments, give feedback (responses) to the speaker about how they are perceiving the message.

The same communication book that describes public speaking as a start-stop process may, however, label two people conversing as interpersonal communication and offer a transactional perspective as a description of the process taking place between the two. A transactional process is one where simultaneous encoding/decoding and sending/receiving are taking place on multiple levels with both individuals experiencing changes in their perceptions to some degree. The following diagram depicts the key factors of the transactional perspective.

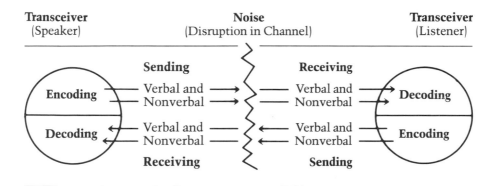

Encoding: *ideation; mentally creating the message.*
Decoding: *giving meaning; interpreting the received signals.*
Sending and receiving: *a physical activity involving signals (air compressions and light refractions).*

We believe that what takes place in the process of public speaking is more accurately described from the transactional prespective. The speaker and each individual listener are in fact simultaneously encoding cues and decoding cues while sending and receiving on both verbal and nonverbal levels. We do not believe that the speaker encodes a message and then sends it via air compressions (words) and light refractions (gestures and movement) while the receiver patiently waits to receive the signals and then decode them. We hold that the speaker and all the individual listeners are involved simultaneously in one-to-one transactions. The speaker personalizes the message with first one listener, then another, then another, and so on.

You may be asking, "What difference does all this about stimulus-response versus transactional communication make?" It makes a tremendous difference in terms of the speaking skills the speaker thinks are available, and how the speaker reacts to the listeners. Take eye contact, for example. A speaker who views public speaking as a stimulus-response (start-stop) process will usually scan the listeners as a whole, letting his/her eyes take in large anonymous sections of the audience at once. He/she is caught up in sending the message at this point. The speaker does not really see many individual behaviors or facial expressions among the listeners. The speaker may perceive the audience shifting in their chairs or making audible groans, if on a large scale. On the other hand, a speaker operating from the transactional perspective will tend to practice the skill of individualizing eye contact with the single listener for a second or two, then shifting to another section of the audience and establishing individual and momentary (personalized) eye contact with another listener, and so on throughout the speaking.

> I never had a policy that I could always apply. I've
> simply attempted to do what made the greatest
> amount of sense at the moment.
>
> ABRAHAM LINCOLN

There are several other direct implications from viewing public speaking as a transaction similar to conversing, but we will, for now, let our argument stand or fall on the brief example we have presented.

Though we believe most effective public speaking follows from a transactional perspective (whether the speaker knows it is called transactional or not), we will present for the purpose of analysis a more traditional examination of the key elements in a speaking transaction. In examining the parts we will learn the role that each plays in the process.

Key Elements of Public Speaking

- Speaker
- Message
- Delivery
- Listener(s)
- Feedback
- Situation

THE SPEAKER

Your success with the listeners depends heavily on what they think about you. If the listeners feel that:

- you know what you are talking about (are competent)
- you can be trusted (have integrity)
- you are friendly (sociable)
- you are composed (emotionally stable)
- you are outgoing (dynamic)
- you have their best interest at heart (have helpful intentions)

then the audience will listen more attentively to you and more readily accept what you have to say.

It is imperative that your listeners think well of you the speaker. Traditionally, these characteristics of the speaker were called ethos and constituted "ethical proof." Today we call these same qualities "source-credibility factors." Now, as well as in the past, researchers and practitioners in communication recognize the tremendous influence that these characteristics have on an audience. Successful speakers seem to have pertinent information and experience about their subject matter, are reputed to be reliable, seem friendly and cooperative, appear to be devoid of excessive fear and fidgeting, are very much alive and talkative, and appear to have helpful rather than selfish motives. Don't lose your audience by failing to consider these important speaker qualities.

THE MESSAGE

The message as delivered is a product of the encoding that takes place before the speech, and also the encoding that accompanies the actual speaking. The topic and the listeners who will make up your audience help focus your encoding process.

aah´

what a person's vocabulary is reduced to.

when you hold down their tongue with a stick.

Although you may be assigned a subject to speak about, you usually have the task of deciding what you are going to say about the given topic. Focusing on what you want to say is an easier task once you decide what your specific purpose is—what do you want to accomplish with your audience? What is your main objective in speaking? Then it is important for you to visualize and analyze your listeners. What are *their* problems and questions? What can you say that will be particularly rewarding to this audience? After careful consideration of how to best help your listeners, select ideas with which you are familiar or can quickly get information about so that you can speak from experience and with authority. Also, find something that excites you and that you really want to share with others. No speaking gimmicks can hide a lack of enthusiasm for an idea. For example, given the topic The Value of a College Education, you might focus on one or more of the following ideas that really interest you:

- College as a place to try out new social skills
- College as a place to learn how to learn
- College as a place to learn to adjust quickly to different "supervisors" and the standards they require—valuable adaptive skills for future jobs
- College as income-generating—compare the average annual income of a college graduate with the average annual income of a nongraduate

We remember a speaker who was invited to speak to a very fussy group of teenagers seven times in succession because he kept selecting topics that fit their needs and that he got excited about sharing. For instance, one evening he spoke about "love and parking." Another time he talked of "prestige and smoking." Take time to consider your specific audience, and search until you find ideas that you feel excited about sharing.

Rhetoric is an art, not a science.

ISOCRATES

Message Supports (That Prove or Illustrate)   A message becomes meaningful and gains power when it is well supported. A vivid, firsthand experience is usually much more effective than a vague generalization. Even in a very short talk, a speaker can include a visual aid, a quotation, a statistic, an analogy, or a specific example.

For example, a college student started his three-minute talk by holding up a pen and asking the audience to estimate its value. The audience responded with prices ranging from twenty-nine cents to three-and-a-half dollars. He then held up an ordinary lead pencil and asked his listeners to estimate the value of the pencil. Again, they responded with guesses, ranging from about four cents to seventy-nine cents. He next pointed out that they had all estimated the value of the pen and pencil in terms of dollars and cents rather than in terms of what could be accomplished with the pen and pencil. After using these simple supporting materials to involve his audience, the student continued to give a most effective speech.

A speaker can also get attention and hold interest by using suspense, presenting a novel idea, identifying conflict, using humor, or self-disclosing to the listeners. So don't be caught speaking without message supports to help develop your ideas.

THE SATURDAY EVENING POST

"I'm not going to bore you with a lot of words. . . ."

Curtsey while you're thinking what to say. It saves time.

LEWIS CARROLL
Through the Looking-Glass

Message Organizing Listeners like a speaker who begins quickly, marches forward steadily, and stops with a minute to spare. You will feel more secure as a speaker when you know that one idea will lead to the next in an orderly manner. Speaking material must be organized so that the main points are distinct and clear. The simplest organization consists of introducing an idea, developing the idea with supporting details, and concluding the idea. Alan H. Monroe, a speech teacher, offers one of the easiest and most effective plans for organizing a short talk; he calls it the "one-point plan." In this plan the speaker begins the talk with a brief story, example, illustration, quotation, testimony, or statistic, which has a point. Then the speaker states the point. Next, another short illustration, quotation, testimony, or story that has the same moral or point is added. Finally, the speaker simply repeats the point and sits down! For instance, a speaker might start with a brief story abut the happiness Albert Schweitzer received from rendering humanitarian service; state the idea that service brings joy; read a quotation from Schweitzer supporting the idea that service brings joy; and conclude by stating once again that service brings joy. This is a speech plan that is deceptively simple, yet effective. Remember, start right off with a good idea, develop it quickly, and stop on time! Be organized.

To follow these message-development steps does not take special talent or great intelligence, but it does mean you must look at each principle to see whether you are attending to the items that make great speaking great. Ask yourself these questions: Have I selected a subject I am interested in? Do I have a specific purpose? Am I using a variety of materials in my talk to make it interesting to the listener? Is my material organized?

Voice and assurance are necessary to success in oratory.

ISOCRATES

Exciting speakers select their messages carefully, speak with a purpose, use a variety of ways of illustrating their messages, and organize simply. But what happens when a speaker pays little attention to these message components?

First, the listeners become bored because the speaker talks about a subject with which they are familiar and develops it in a worn-out way— the same old thing in the same old dry way. Second, the audience is left hopelessly adrift because the speaker didn't plan for any end result. The speaker simply strings a number of ideas together and hopes the listeners will do something about them. But alas, the listeners change very little. Third, the audience usually becomes quickly disinterested and disbelieving when the speaker does nothing to prove or illustrate a point. The speaker assumes that his or her word is the final proof and understanding of the subject. Fourth, the audience becomes confused and rapidly forgets what the speaker is saying because ideas are not related.

Now, what can be done about changing all the things that bother listeners about the "puts me asleep" speaker? The next part of this chapter will present suggestions and helps so you will not be a "puts me asleep" speaker. A speaker's delivery of a speech can be an asset or a hindrance.

How Not to Speak at a Meeting

Few meetings produce, nor do they require, much golden-throated oratory. But the ability to stand up and talk—lucidly, convincingly, and sometimes persuasively—is a must at any meeting. The rambler, the mumbler, the person who doesn't really know what he or she is talking about or *how* to talk, how to communicate, is worse than a nuisance, he or she's a dead loss.

These visuals depict a few of the all too common mistakes unpracticed speakers are likely to make.

The Moving Target This fellow walks off his nervousness. Listening to him is like watching a tennis match. He detracts from his own talk and, more important, may well "walk himself" away from some of the principal points he planned to make.

The Musician This fellow accompanies his talk with a rendition on the change, keys, and so on in his trouser pockets . . . and in short order his audience is busy trying to recognize the tune he's playing instead of listening to him. Many practiced speakers take their change and keys out of their pockets before they approach the podium.

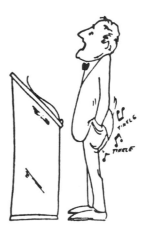

The Preening Peacock   He never gets his tie quite straight or his coat adjusted or his hair smoothed to his satisfaction. Chances are he's nervous. Chances are he doesn't know he's repeating these nervous gestures. But his audience knows it—and his audience is distracted.

The Nearsighted Note Nibbler   Most speakers use notes . . . but the best ones don't act like it. Usually, over-reliance on notes simply means the speaker is ill-prepared. But if she doesn't find her material important and interesting why should her audience?

The Deadly Sleeper   This man is simply dull. He sometimes looks as if he might drop off to sleep . . . and his audience does.

The Comedian   A joke is fine . . . but don't begin to mistake yourself for a scintillating night club comedian.

The Great Scientist He may be a brilliant speaker. Unquestionably, he's brilliant. Unfortunately, he's as abstruse as he is brilliant: there may be only nine other people in the world who fully understand him—and none of these are in the audience. Translating *technicalese* into lay language is one of the toughest problems many speakers face today.

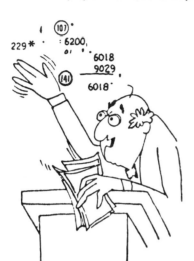

The Fumbler The Fumbler, at the podium, is about as popular as the fumbler on the football field. A good many speakers now use visual aids regularly. Their first rule is: Know thy equipment.

SOURCE: Reprinted from *Association and Society Manager,* Vol. 1, No. 3, August/September 1969. Copyright by Barrington Publications, Inc., 825 S. Barrington Ave., Los Angeles, Calif. 90049.

THE DELIVERY

Remember, listeners are not passive receptacles for your words. They are actively involved in the process of encoding/decoding and sending/receiving at the same time you are speaking. Listeners perceive, to some degree, both *what* is said and *how* it is said. When you do present a speech, *feel* what you are saying while you say it. Keep the ideas fresh, and speak with energy and conviction, allowing your voice and body to react to the importance of your ideas. Audiences quickly lose interest in a speaker who doesn't get into his or her speech enough to portray much vocal and physical activity. And, perhaps most important, focus your attention on the audience. When you step up to a counter and ask for a chocolate ice cream cone, do you worry about your hands or what your knees are doing? Usually not. You focus your attention on the clerk to be sure you are understood correctly.

> *It takes two to speak the truth—one to speak, and another to hear.*
>
> HENRY DAVID THOREAU

As you consider the delivery of your speech, four options or modes of presentation are available to you:

- *Manuscript:* write it out word for word and read it.
- *Memorize:* deliver it from memory.
- *Impromptu:* speak on the spur of the moment without any specific preparation.
- *Extemporaneous:* carefully select, organize, and outline your ideas, but allow the specific words and sentences to form themselves anew at the moment of delivery.

We prefer the extemporaneous method of delivery for most situations because it gives us some of the security of specific preparation yet a good deal of flexibility, allowing us to focus on the listeners. In this method, the speaker relies on notes rather than a manuscript or a memorized speech. A few notes together with a stimulating delivery should make speaking an enjoyable experience.

We do suggest that you practice speaking, especially when you use extemporaneous delivery. However, we do not mean you should practice aloud or that you have to practice the whole speech. Just running through the speech in your mind will be of great benefit when you speak later on. Mental practice can be as beneficial as physical practice. It may not be necessary to practice the whole speech. You may simply try out your ideas on friends. Use their comprehension and response to your subject to help you formally organize and present what you want to say.

THE LISTENERS

The ability of a speaker to help the listeners understand a complex idea or to change their beliefs about a matter seems to depend on the speaker's analysis of the listeners' present interests, values, and experiences. To communicate effectively, we must fire a message at a defined target—we must begin where the listeners generally are. To speak of choosing a career to a group of second graders misses the target. Or attempting to persuade someone to change a March of Dimes contribution from $5 to $50 per year, without first estimating the income or value system of the listener, might prove futile.

In analyzing the listeners, you must consider how they feel about your subject, what they already know about it, and how they perceive you and your credibility. From the moment you accept an opportunity to speak, you should begin to assess the audience. Such information as the number of people who will be present; whether they will be male or female or both; their average age; their educational, occupational, and ethnic backgrounds; and their knowledge about your subject can help you meet them where they are. *Remember, speeches are prepared for listeners, not for*

speakers. A speaker must adjust the content of the speech to the listeners, for maximum effectiveness. Find out all you can about your audience before you develop your speech.

FEEDBACK

The reaction (verbal and nonverbal) of the listeners during and after the speech is feedback. Feedback enables speakers to know whether they are being understood, heard, or even seen. An effective speaker uses feedback to monitor the communication effort. He or she watches the listeners to see whether they are getting the point. If the speaker notices that the audience is losing interest or becoming disturbed, she or he can alter the delivery of the message or modify the message so that it becomes more stimulating or acceptable. Listeners' responses fed back to the speaker thus influence the way the speaker will adjust the message while speaking.

THE SATURDAY EVENING POST

"Let's face it, Ralph, you're not as popular as we thought!"

As speakers, we want to be aware of the maximum amount of feedback that our speaking situation will allow. The better we monitor feedback from individual listeners or the audience as a whole, the better we can adapt how and what we planned to say to produce the results we intend. Unquestionably, feedback is essential for improvement in learning to speak effectively. Speakers who use this communication element are considered to be sensitive and good at understanding human relations.

SITUATION

Obviously, a speaker will do things a little differently when presenting a project in a marketing class than when presenting an advertising proposal to a financial corporation. Almost as important as analyzing the audience is the act of reviewing the situation or the occasion where you will be speaking. Surprises for the speaker arriving on the scene have been known to cause distress for both the speaker and the listeners. A mismatch between the speaker's preparation and the speaking occasion is one of those "rhetorical nightmares" that can be avoided if you take a moment to find out about the physical setting for your speech, the nature of the gathering, and the time limits. Thus, ask about the location, sound system, lighting, room, seating, lectern, distractions, and so on.

Ask also about the purpose of the meeting and the social setting in which the speech is to take place. Consider what expectations the occasion engenders in the minds of the listeners. Be sure to clearly understand what part you are playing in the total program. And, finally, be keenly aware of the amount of time given to your presentation. Quite often speakers do a poor job because they have prepared too much material for a limited amount of time.

REDUCING SPEAKING ANXIETY

Just in case you still feel uneasy or nervous about getting up in front of an audience—join us and thousands of others! You are definitely not alone!

One of the most frequent requests among students taking speech classes is for help in controlling or overcoming this tension when they communicate. Their self-evaluations contain such statements as:

- When I get up to give a talk, I'm so nervous I forget the things I'm going to say. My mouth gets so dry, it's hard to talk.

- Many times when I speak in front of people, I get embarrassed. It's hard for me to open up and express my feelings.

- I stumble over words and speak too fast. I fidget and can't make good eye contact.
- I get really self-conscious in front of groups. The larger the group, the more I worry.

The causes of speech anxiety are varied and complex. It is clear that those who have low self-esteem are apprehensive about speaking in front of people. They experience a fear of failure and of being negatively judged by those who listen. Yet even students with a positive feeling about themselves experience anxiety and tension. Professional speakers often complain of pre-speaking jitters. So first and last, being nervous or tense about speaking appears both normal and a natural state of emotional arousal to insure energy for the occasion. Similar emotional states precede and are useful in athletic competition. As in athletic competition, excessive anxiety may be described as that additional emotional arousal beyond the degree needed for alertness and energy in the activity.

Although the causes of speaking tension may be complex, helpful solutions have been developed and are being used with some exceptional results. Let us suggest two ways you might decrease or control anxiety about speaking in public.

Our first solution, and perhaps the more important, is that you learn to overcome excessive anxiety by speaking more often in informal as well as formal settings. One reason new speakers are fearful is that they are required to address groups before they have learned to speak to two or three individuals. They must address strangers when they are nervous even among friends. Speakers also experience more anxiety if they are not fully prepared.

We can overcome these obstacles in the following way: Choose a subject of great importance, one that you can be excited about and *want* to share with someone. Then prepare a little speech for your family or friends. As you collect ideas and support them, organize them as suggested earlier. This may seem a little difficult at first but if you are serious about overcoming a fear of speaking in public, you will be pleased with the results. As your ideas develop, try them out on your friends and family. Take advantage of relaxed and informal situations to share one of your ideas and to ask a question or two. There is something about a good question that helps dissolve fears. The pressure to communicate is lifted from your shoulders and placed on the listener; and yet the listener is often flattered that you consider him or her a resource, and is happy to answer your question. Find out what your ideas mean to others. If your first insights were shallow, enlarge them and adjust them to your listeners. Then try sharing your ideas again, only in a larger group or in a classroom. Notice the increased confidence you feel in hearing yourself speak your ideas and in receiving responses from your listeners. These informal opportunities for mini-speeches are your best preparation for a large audience—so speak as often as you can to gain experience and confidence. You will find your fear of speaking will turn into simple tension or nervousness as you gain more experience. And nervous energy can be used positively in speaking.

Our second suggestion for overcoming excessive anxiety has to do with a simple relaxation technique using imagery. This approach to reducing fear involves receiving information from your body about functions that are normally autonomic and nondiscernible. If a body process can be monitored and fed back to the conscious mind, it can be controlled.

Whenever we experience tension or fear, our body responds by restricting the flow of blood to the extremities and by increasing the flow to the heart, vital organs, and the brain. Our heartbeat increases, our respiration rate changes and our hands get cold.

When you feel your hands getting cold as you prepare to speak, or feel "butterflies in your stomach," use that feedback from your body as a sign to relax. Think of warming your hands and being relaxed. Words won't do. You must *see* pictures of warm, beautiful places. Imagine yourself on a warm beach in the sunshine or in a peaceful meadow on a summer day. If you see such pictures vividly, the autonomic nervous system will respond accordingly. Physiologically, it's the same as being there. Now, as you relax and defocus your mind from the concern of speaking, see yourself as a successful speaker. Watch yourself deliver a great speech and visualize a tremendous response of appreciation from the audience. After relaxing with pleasant and successful images for a few minutes, you will notice your body and mind becoming more comfortable and at ease. Your hands will warm and your heart will slow down. We use sophisticated electronic equipment to demonstrate to students that this relaxation technique works. But you don't need the equipment. If you experience "being there" in your mind, if you think in pictures, you will relax and become less fearful when you engage in public speaking.

The third approach to reducing speaking anxiety is a breathing technique. Breathing is a central focus in various types of relaxation methods, including forms of yoga. The key idea is that modifications in the breathing patterns associated with fear, stress, anxiety, and tension have direct effects on physiology and levels of emotional arousal. We describe the technique here in abbreviated fashion.

First sit in a firm chair that supports the body in an erect position. Place both feet flat on the floor and "center" your body in the chair so that you are comfortable yet erect (no slouching). Fold your hands in your lap or place them lightly on your upper legs. Begin taking deep breaths through your nose while extending your stomach. Push your stomach out in "beer belly" fashion as the air comes into your lungs. Your shoulders should be allowed to rise and possibly go back a bit. Take each deep inward breath through the nose slowly and methodically. You may find it comfortable to take five seconds to draw this deep breath in completely.

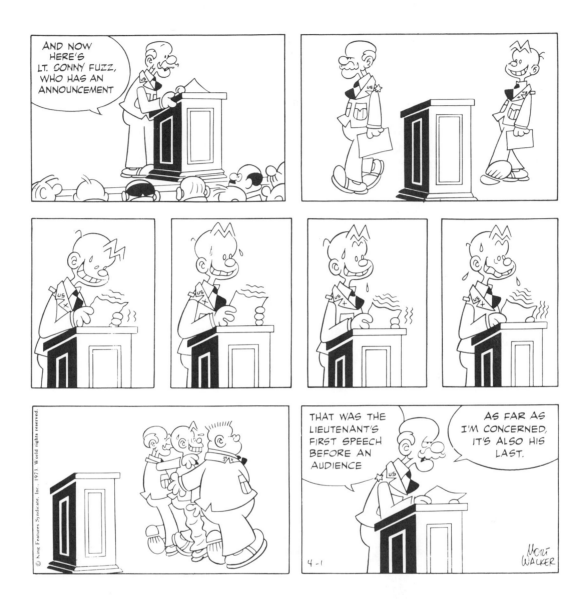

At the end of the intake phase, pause one or two seconds and just let the air escape naturally as if you were letting it out of a balloon. You will find that the shoulders will fall and the extended stomach will come back in if you let go, thus forcing a deep exhalation of used air. Do this inhalation-exhalation ten times while concentrating on the sound of the air going in and out of your nose; the cool sensation of the incoming air in the moist part of the nose; and the warm sensation of the body-heated, outgoing air.

If you complete this breathing technique with full concentration, you will modify your body physiology and your level of emotional arousal.

FINDING YOUR OWN SPEAKING STYLE

If all the preceding insights have started to intimidate you and made you wonder whether you will ever keep everything straight. Or worse, if at this point you are becoming an "unreal" speaking monster made of artificial gimmickry and everybody else's rules, please read "Kentucky Windage."

> *Buy a cigar and a pair of spectacles.*
>
> WINSTON CHURCHILL
> on how to become an effective speaker.*

*Reprinted with the permission of Houghton Mifflin Company.

The Veep's "Kentucky Windage"

William J. Buchanan

The late Vice President Alben Barkley once told me a fascinating little story. . . .

I was a senior at the University of Louisville that February in 1949, and failing miserably in a public-speaking course. When I learned that the newly elected Vice President would address the annual Jefferson-Jackson Day Democratic gathering on the 26th, I badgered my father, a longtime friend of Barkley's, into getting me an invitation. Here, I realized, was an opportunity to study one of the great speakers of all time. . . .

"When I was about your age . . . a friend of mine down in Paducah asked me to go skeet shooting with him. I'd never shot skeet, but I was pretty good with a shotgun, so I obliged. On the first round I powdered twenty-one of twenty-five clay birds. 'Good shooting!' my friend said. 'But there are a few things you should watch.' He then showed me the 'proper' stance, how to sight with both eyes open, and a whole slew of other things absolutely guaranteed to improve my style.

"Well, my friend was an expert, so I practiced his way. Only problem was, as my style improved my score went down. One afternoon, after I succeeded in breaking only eight birds, I asked a young lady watching from the sidelines how my form looked.

" 'Your form's fine, Alben,' she said, 'But aren't you supposed to break *all* those little black things?' Typical female reply, I thought. But her words bothered me; I found myself repeating them over and over. Was I really trying to "break all those little black things'? Or was I more concerned with trying to imitate a prima ballerina?"

He paused a chuckled softly. "Well, I realized right then that I'd never be much of a ballerina. I could hardly wait for the next round. I discarded all the fancy frills and went back and used my best Kentucky Windage.[1] I beat my friend that round—and he never outshot me again."

Barkley leaned forward in his chair, and looked directly at me. "What had I done wrong?" He paused to let the question soak in. "I had ignored my natural abilities, traded a way that worked well for me for one that didn't because I was overly impressed with my friend's criticism.

"Now don't mistake me. Expert advice can be a blessing. But only when it's used to sharpen your own instincts and talents—never as a substitute for them."

The Vice President held out his hand

---

[1]The term is derived from Kentucky frontiersmen's unique long-rifle shooting style: instead of relying solely on gunsights, they estimated wind conditions and offset aim accordingly. Among Kentucky hill people today, the expression means using one's own personal estimate and judgment in a situation as well as, and sometimes in spite of, precedent.

and said, "Next time you get up to speak, remember, use a little Kentucky Windage."

On my way to class next morning I threw away my carefully prepared notes with the marginal references to "pause briefly" and "emphasize here." I knew that never again would I try to imitate someone else's formula for success.

When my turn at the lectern came I made my point as simply as I could and sat down. The startled professor nodded his approval. I finished that semester in the top quarter of the class. . . .

SOURCE: Originally appeared in *Reader's Digest*. Copyright © 1968 by The Reader's Digest Assn., Inc.

WHAT TO KNOW

Public speaking can be described as a transactional process of communication similar in some ways to interpersonal communication. Both speaker and listener(s) are involved in simultaneously encoding/decoding and sending/receiving on multiple levels (verbal and nonverbal), which results in both the speaker and listener(s) experiencing a change in their perceptions.

Prior to speaking, the speaker needs to examine his or her credibility, analyze the audience, examine the nature of the situation, plan the message, choose and practice his or her best style of delivery, and plan for monitoring and using audience feedback. The origin of any fear of speaking is in the mind of the speaker—the control and elimination of this fear is thus the mental discipline the speaker puts into play prior to and during speaking.

WHAT TO DO

Question: Is an Instructor's Lecture a Speech? Analyze a lecture given by one of your teachers. Does it have all the elements of a speech? Would you consider it to be a speech?

Are some of your instructors better at one particular skill, such as adapting the material to the listeners or encouraging feedback, than others? Do you think this adapting is a conscious effort on the instructor's part?

Survey Ask ten students outside of class these questions and write their answers for use in class discussion.

1. What, if any, would be your fears of giving a public speech to a large group of students, instructors, and administrators on what you like and dislike about your school?

2. Would you be more nervous if you had to stand in front of a group to speak rather than sit down? Why or why not?

3. Would you find it easier to speak to a group of elementary school children than to a group of adults? Why or why not?

4. While speaking, would you rather the listeners interrupt you with their questions or wait until you finish your speech? Why?

5. If you had to speak to a local civic organization, what kind of delivery would you use?
   a. Write out and read the speech
   b. Memorize the speech
   c. Speak from outline notes
      Why?

Discussion Questions Why do you think young children immediately focus more on the television set the moment a commercial comes on?

What material covered in this chapter would help you analyze a television commercial as a message planned to elicit a particular response from the viewer?

WHERE TO LEARN MORE

Bradley, Bert E. *Fundamentals of Speech Communication: The Credibility of Ideas.* 3rd ed. Dubuque, IA: Wm. C. Brown, 1981

Carlson, Karen, and Alan Meyers. *Speaking with Confidence.* Glenview, IL: Scott, Foresman, 1977.

Rodman, George R. *Public Speaking: An Introduction to Message Preparation.* New York: Holt, 1978.

Ross, Raymond S. *Speech Communication: Fundamentals and Practice,* chap. 4. Englewood Cliffs, NJ: Prentice-Hall, 1977.

PART TWO

PLANNING, PREPARING, AND PRESENTING

Throughout history people have had an insatiable need to know. Unanswered questions stimulate research; research yields facts; and facts, when properly ordered and developed, yield understanding.

RUDOLPH F. VERDERBER

SELECTING
A TOPIC AND
A PURPOSE

3

SELECTING A SPEAKING TOPIC

In many of our communicating situations, we are assigned a speaking topic. For example, if a friend asks us about a certain person he or she would like to date, we have in effect been assigned to speak about this person. If we are asked how to change a tire, or why we like our brand of television set, we have been given a topic we know something about so we can usually give plenty of details about how to change a tire or plenty of reason why we like, or don't like, the quality of our set.

Thus, we have little difficulty responding or speaking in informal settings because the subject of our speech is chosen for us, and we already know quite a bit about the subject. Also, since our listeners "assigned" the topic, we know they are interested in it. However, in a formal speaking situation we often have to choose the subject, and we do not want to be embarrassed by selecting a topic that seems silly or unimportant to our audience. To help you over this hurdle, we would like to share our approach to selecting a topic on which to speak.

There are essentially three major questions to take into account when you are trying to select a speech topic:

1. Is the subject matter interesting to you?
2. Will the subject matter be interesting to the audience?
3. What general purpose are you trying to meet by giving the talk?

This chapter will be devoted to answering these three questions.

SPEAK ABOUT THINGS THAT INTEREST YOU

There is nothing more boring than speakers who talk about subjects they are not interested in. Speakers who speak about things they like can get excited and be very fascinating. For example, if you have just run the rapids of the Grand Canyon in a small boat, the experience will still be vivid and you will be able to speak with great detail and enthusiasm about floating the rapids. If a close friend has just died, you will be able to share details about the difficulty of adjusting to the loss of a friend. The experiences you have had will give you a special position from which to speak. What you say will be unique because no one else has experienced life exactly as you have.

So whenever possible, choose a real-life experience to speak about. This puts you in a position to speak about something you know well.

Most speakers, when asked to make a presentation, run immediately to the library, a magazine, or a friend. We believe the best source of information you have is yourself and your life experiences. Trust your own ideas and your own experiences. Even when your talk is assigned you can make it better by including information from the experiences you have had.

> *The gift of speech . . . is not often accompanied by the power of thought.*
>
> SOMERSET MAUGHAM

To determine if a subject interests you, ask yourself if you would go to hear someone else talk about it. If a subject does not pop immediately to mind, ask yourself the following questions:

1. What skills do you have? What do you do well and maybe even better than most people? What unusual things have you done?

2. What is your background? Where have you lived? What people have you known? What have you experienced with other people as you have grown up?

3. What are your special interests? What would you like to learn more about? What would you like to achieve? What seems to get you excited?

4. What knowledge do you have? What do you know a lot about? What do you know more about than most other people?

5. What special experiences have you had? What unusual things have happened to you that an audience might enjoy hearing about?

After you determine if the subject is interesting and important to you, you must then determine if the subject is important to your listening audience.

THE BORN LOSER   **By Art Sansom**

SPEAK ABOUT THINGS THAT INTEREST
THE AUDIENCE: AUDIENCE ANALYSIS

To be able to talk about things that are of interest to an audience, you must know the listeners who make up your audience. This necessitates evaluating the audience to determine their interests, needs and concerns. To effectively evaluate your listeners, you need to gain data about them. You can then determine to what degree your topic fits your audience.

When evaluating an audience, you can learn many things; however, we suggest always starting your analysis with the following variables:

1. **Age.** It is not necessary to know the exact age of each audience member but you should know the age range and average age of those who are present. The age characteristics of a group of students will obviously be considerably different from those of a Rotary Club.

2. **Sex.** Again, it does not matter that you know the exact number of males and females in the audience. However, it is important that you adapt your subject to the group if it is predominantly male or female.

3. **Occupation.** Is the audience mostly white-collar workers or blue-collar workers? Is it a mixture of both? Would the same topic interest an audience of physicians and an audience of lawyers? You must select a topic that will be understandable to the predominant occupations of an audience.

4. **Socioeconomic level.** Is your audience predominantly wealthy or predominantly poor? Do they come from a culturally deprived area? Are they high society?

When you can answer questions such as these, you will most likely know whether your topic fits your audience. Again, it is not necessary to make an in-depth scientific study of the audience, but the more information you have the greater the chance that you will be successful in selecting and adapting material.

GENERAL PURPOSE OF YOUR TOPIC

After determining whether you are interested in your topic and whether it fits your audience, determine the general purpose of your talk. The universal purpose of all speech is to win some kind of response. Most beginning speakers fail at this point because they do not consider what they want the audience to do as a result of their speech. Often the speech becomes aimless and never reaches a target. It seems to us that the following are the major purposes of speaking:

1. **To present information**—to increase an audience's knowledge and understanding about an issue or process.

2. **To persuade**—to cause the audience to think or behave in a different manner.

3. **To entertain**—to cause a pleasurable response in an audience.

Some presentations include all three purposes though one of these is usually the general (overall) purpose. Which of these purposes best fits your talk?

INFORMATIVE SPEAKING

The purpose of informative speaking is simply to give the audience new information. How lasers are used in surgery, how state government is organized, how to understand and translate the metric system—these are all examples of informative topics. In an informative speech, the main concern of the speaker is to help the audience learn and remember information. The best way to determine whether the speech has really met the purpose of informing an audience is to poll the listeners at the end of the speech to see what they now know about the subject.

PERSUASIVE SPEAKING

A persuasive speech is one that attempts to cause the audience to change its feelings or beliefs about something or to behave differently. Insurance salespeople use persuasive speech to get clients to purchase insurance. Football coaches give speeches at half-time to get the players to change their behavior and play differently. A mayor speaking about a new zoning

procedure to the city council is giving a persuasive speech to get the council to adopt the new system. Each of these examples shows someone trying to get other people to change their opinions or behave in a different way. If you are trying to get someone to believe differently or behave differently, then the purpose of your speech is persuasive.

ENTERTAINMENT SPEAKING

The entertainment speech is simply to give the audience a good time. The speech may also inform and persuade, but its main purpose is to have the audience feel good. The entertainment speech is often used in after-dinner speaking situations.

A speaker with a clear purpose can aim a talk in a definite direction, gain audience interest, and save time. Decide early in your speech preparation what kind of response you would like to have from your listeners so that they do not leave saying, "It was an interesting talk, but what was the point?"

> "The time has come," the Walrus said,
> "To talk of many things:
> Of shoes—and ships—and sealing-wax—
> Of cabbages—and kings . . ."
>
> LEWIS CARROLL
> *Through the Looking-Glass*

SPECIFIC PURPOSE OF YOUR TOPIC

We have indicated that the general purposes of speaking are to inform, to persuade, and to entertain. However, to really develop an effective speech you must strive to precisely form the general purpose into a specific purpose. The specific purpose should describe or indicate the exact type of response you expect or anticipate from your listening audience. It should state what you want the audience to know, feel, or do. A specific purpose should minimally do three things:

1. It should contain no more than one major or central idea.
2. It should be clear, concise, and to the point.
3. It should be stated in terms of what you want the audience to be able to do when you have finished speaking.

When the general purpose is **to inform,** some sample specific purposes might be: To have the audience know how to wax cross-country skis. To have the audience understand the methods of preparing natural foods. Or to have the audience understand how the United Way operates.

When the general purpose is **to persuade,** some sample specific purposes might be: To get the audience to contribute to Muscular Dystrophy. To get the audience to accept the use of nuclear energy. Or to get the audience to donate more money to your university.

When the general purpose is **to entertain,** some sample specific purposes might be: To have the audience laugh by telling about your ineptness as a golfer. To have the listeners laugh at hearing themselves described as animals. Or to have the audience enjoy hearing about the difficulties associated with the fear of giving speeches.

LEARNING FROM OTHER SPEAKERS

Listening to other people speak can help you learn a great deal about what to do, and what not to do, when working with your own topic and purpose. As you listen to other speakers pay particular attention to how the speaker limits and adapts the topic and purpose to the particular listeners. You may find some presentations appear to be "canned" because the speaker does not adjust the content of the speech to the specific audience being addressed. Sometimes students criticize teachers of large lecture classes of this shortsightedness. On the other hand, seasoned politicians are often polished at speaking from group to group using the same topic, general purpose and specific purpose while adjusting and adapting the content to each particular audience's interests and concerns. Thus, each separate group of listeners feels the speech was personally developed with them in mind.

To learn from other speakers takes more than hearing though. It takes more than just listening. To learn from other speakers, good and bad, requires effective listening.

DEVELOPING THE ABILITY TO LISTEN EFFECTIVELY

As we have implied, becoming an effective listener is an important step to becoming an effective speaker. you have to develop the ability to listen accurately and understand another person's speech. *It is difficult to speak with any more skill than your listening has allowed you to experience.* Dr. Lyman K. Steil, one of the foremost authorities on listening, along with co-workers developed the tests that follow on pages 56–58 to help people rate themselves as listeners. Complete the tests and see how you compare to others as a listener.

Speak About Yourself

You spend a good deal of time talking about yourself. You are quick to tell your friends what *you* think about a movie, a political figure, or a class. You will also jump at the chance to tell about how you were stopped for speeding, what you said to the cop, and so on—that was *your* experience. You may also talk at length to a person you have just met about how you came to choose this college or why you joined a particular group.

When we talk to others about what we know, what we own, what we like, or what we are capable of, we can exchange a lot of information with them and perhaps entertain and persuade them. It isn't even necessary to be an expert on a subject we talk about. For example, even if you have not won an Olympic ski medal, you can talk to a friend about the first time you put on skis and how you spent most of the day in the snow. You don't have to have made a hit record to talk about music with others.

However, when you begin to address a larger audience—more than just friends and acquaintances—about some of your experiences, it may be necessary to single out the ones with more flair, more impact, and more unusual qualities. You can't just say you have a pet dog; you ought to tell about the problems you had training it to count to five by barking. You can't just tell this bigger audience that you were born in Poughkeepsie; you should make some point about being the first baby born in the new year, about being born in a taxi on the way to the hospital, or about being delivered by the only midwife in upstate New York.

When you talk about yourself to a larger audience, you will select more dramatic things to say than you might in your day-to-day communication with your friends. For instance, you will want to talk about things the audience is interested in—probably things you have in common with them. If you want to talk about your hobbies, they should be either very unusual (collecting beer cans) or very outstanding (the best stamp collection in the city). For example, a collector of our acquaintance has pull handles from nearly fifty public toilets in France, which makes that person an unusual collector. Everybody has a name, but you can make a good story out of yours if it has given you trouble (being mistaken for a boy if you're a girl named Bruce, for example). Almost everyone has pets, but a python or an armadillo will make a better speech subject than a dog or cat.

SOURCE: E. E. Myers and M. T. Myers, *Communicating When We Speak* (New York: McGraw-Hill, 1975), pp. 206–207.

HOW WELL DO YOU LISTEN?
(A Personal Profile)

Here are three tests in which we'll ask you to rate yourself as a listener. There are no correct or incorrect answers. Your responses, however, will extend your understanding of yourself as a listener and highlight areas in which improvement might be welcome . . . to you and to those around you. When you've completed the tests, please turn to page 58 to see how your scores compare with those of thousands of others who've taken the same tests before you.

Quiz 1

A. Circle the term that best describes you as a listener.

Superior	Excellent	Above Average	Average
Below Average	Poor	Terrible	

B. On a scale of 0–100 (100 = highest), how would you rate yourself as a listener?

_____
(0–100)

Quiz 2

How do you think the following people would rate you as a listener?

Your Best Friend	_____
Your Boss	_____
Business Colleague	_____
A Job Subordinate	_____
Your Spouse	_____

NOTE: This Listening Profile (on pages 56–58) was prepared by Dr. Lyman K. Steil and appears in a Sperry pamphlet entitled "Your Personal Listening Profile." Sperry Corporation, © 1980.

Quiz 3

As a listener, how often do you find yourself engaging in these 10 bad listening habits? First, check the appropriate columns. Then tabulate your score using the key below.

Listening Habit	Almost Always	Usually	Some-times	Seldom	Almost Never	Score
1. Calling the subject untinteresting	____	____	____	____	____	____
2. Criticizing the speaker's delivery or mannerisms	____	____	____	____	____	____
3. Getting over-stimulated by something the speaker says	____	____	____	____	____	____
4. Listening primarily for facts	____	____	____	____	____	____
5. Trying to outline everything	____	____	____	____	____	____
6. Faking attention to the speaker	____	____	____	____	____	____
7. Allowing interfering distractions	____	____	____	____	____	____
8. Avoiding difficult material	____	____	____	____	____	____
9. Letting emotion-laden words arouse personal antagonism	____	____	____	____	____	____
10. Wasting the advantage of thought speed (daydreaming)	____	____	____	____	____	____

Total Score ____

KEY
For every "Almost Always" checked, give yourself a score of **2**
For every "Usually" checked, give yourself a score of **4**
For every "Sometimes" checked, give yourself a score of **6**
For every "Seldom" checked, give yourself a score of **8**
For every "Almost Never" checked, give yourself a score of **10**

PROFILE ANALYSIS

This is how other people have responded to the same questions that you've just answered.

Quiz 1

A. 85% of all listeners questioned rated themselves as *Average* or less. Fewer than 5% rate themselves as *Superior* or *Excellent*.
B. On the 0–100 scale, the extreme range is 10–90; the general range is 35–85; and the *average* rating is 55.

Quiz 2

When comparing the listening self-ratings and projected ratings of others, most respondents believe that their best friend would rate them highest as a listener. And that rating would be higher than the one they gave themselves in Quiz #1 . . . where the average was 55.

How come? We can only guess that best friend status is such an intimate, special kind of relationship that you can't imagine it ever happening unless you *were* a good listener. If you weren't, you and he or she wouldn't be best friends to begin with.

Going down the list, people who take this test usually think their bosses would rate them higher than they rated themselves. Now part of that is probably wishful thinking. And part of it is true. We *do* tend to listen to our bosses better . . . whether it's out of respect or fear or whatever doesn't matter.

The grades for colleague and job subordinate work out to be just about the same as the listener rated himself . . . that 55 figure again.

But when you get to spouse . . . husband or wife . . . something really dramatic happens. The score here is significantly lower than the 55 average that previous profile-takers gave themselves. And what's interesting is that the figure goes steadily downhill. While newlyweds tend to rate their spouse at the same high level as their best friend, as the marriage goes on . . . and on . . . the rating falls. So in a household where the couple has been married 50 years, there could be a lot of talk. But maybe nobody is *really* listening.

Quiz 3

The average score is a 62 . . . . 7 points higher than the 55 that the average test-taker gave himself in Quiz #1. Which suggests that when listening is broken down into specific areas of competence, we rate ourselves better than we do when listening is considered only as a generality.

Of course, the best way to discover how well you listen is to ask the people to whom you listen most frequently. Your spouse, boss, best friend, etc. They'll give you an earful.

You should now have a better understanding of yourself as a listener. It is hoped you will also better comprehend the importance of effective listening. The next section of this chapter will offer some aids for being more effective.

HELPS FOR BECOMING AN EFFECTIVE LISTENER

After reviewing a variety of textbooks that deal with listening and after analyzing the listening process in speaking situations, we have determined that there are at least ten helps that will enhance your ability to listen to speeches. Keep in mind that these aids are not sequential and that our order of presentation is random; however, each one can work to your benefit in a listening situation.

1. **Tune out distractions**—This aid stresses the importance of concentration. Force yourself to pay attention and keep your mind on what is being said.

2. **Get what you can get**—Be an opportunist. Do your best to find areas of interest between you and the speaker. Ask yourself, "What's in this for me? What can I get out of what is being said?" Try hard to get a message from each speaker. A good listener will always get a message from a speaker.

3. **Don't daydream**—Stay alert. Force yourself to stay alert even if the speaker is slow and boring. If your thoughts run ahead of the speaker, don't daydream; instead, anticipate and review what is being said.

4. **Identify and understand the speaker's purpose**—What is the speaker trying to do? Is the speaker informing, persuading, or entertaining? Whatever the speaker's purpose, identify it and adjust to it. Try your best to understand the purpose of the speech.

5. **Report the content of a speech to someone else**—This forces you to listen, concentrate, and remember. If you know you must report the contents of what you hear, you are more likely to pay attention. It is simply a good practice technique.

6. **Become a good note-taker**—There are many approaches to note taking. Whichever approach you use, the simple process of writing keypoints down as you hear them aids in your retaining what you hear even if you do not read the notes later.

7. **Don't blame the speaker**—As a listener, take primary responsibility for the success of two-way communication. Don't blame the

other person for your listening inadequacies. Listening is your responsibility, not the speaker's.

8. **Use spare listening time effectively**—Research has taught us that we can listen much faster than a speaker can speak. This causes us to be lazy. We find ourselves doodling on a piece of paper, or thinking about our evening date or what to do to pass the course. We can participate in all these activities and many more, and still listen to a speaker. However, the danger to effective listening is that when we tune out for any purpose we might not tune back in. Use the extra time to review and think about the speech.

9. **Don't become emotional**—There is a tendency to get too involved with a speech that we like or dislike to the extent that we get aroused and miss what is really being said. A good listener remains analytical and does not get caught up in the emotions of the speech.

THE WIZARD OF ID

10. **Don't let the speaker's personality and appearance get in your way**—Too often we are turned off by the appearance of speakers. Their hair is either too short or too long, their clothes are either too preppy or too mod, their makeup is either too heavy or too light, and so on. Don't get caught up in evaluating the speaker's looks and personality and not listening to what the speaker has to say.

These ten aids can be very helpful in your quest to be a better listener. In summary, if you wish to be a good listener your primary effort must be to *understand* rather than agree, disagree, judge, argue. etc. This does not mean that you should not have personal reactions to the speaker and the speech. It does mean that these personal reactions are controlled by you to allow for effective listening.

U.S. News and World Report interviewed Dr. Steil regarding how to sharpen listening skills. He had much to say about the need for better listening. The interview is presented here, on pages 63–65.

by Parker and Hart

TEN KEYS TO EFFECTIVE LISTENING

Lyman K. Steil lists these ten keys as a positive guideline to better listening. In fact, they're at the heart of developing better listening habits that could last a lifetime.

10 Keys to Effective Listening	The Bad Listener	The Good Listener
1. Find areas of interest	Tunes out dry subjects	Is an opportunist; asks "what's in it for me?"
2. Judge content, not delivery	Tunes out if delivery is poor	Judges content, skips over delivery errors
3. Hold your fire	Tends to enter into argument	Doesn't judge until comprehension complete
4. Listen for ideas	Listens for facts	Listens for central themes
5. Be flexible	Takes intensive notes using only one system	Takes fewer notes. Uses 4–5 different systems, depending on speaker
6. Work at listening	Shows no energy output. Fakes attention	Works hard, exhibits active body state
7. Resist distractions	Is easily distracted	Fights or avoids distractions, tolerates bad habits, knows how to concentrate
8. Exercise your mind	Resists difficult expository material; seeks light, recreational material	Uses heavier material as exercise for the mind
9. Keep your mind open	Reacts to emotional words	Interprets color words; does not get hung up on them
10. Capitalize on fact *thought* is faster than *speech*	Tends to daydream with slow speakers	Challenges, anticipates, mentally summarizes, weighs the evidence, listens between the lines to tone of voice

Secrets of Being a Better Listener

Interview with Lyman K. Steil

Dr. Steil, are people who are poor listeners a costly thing for business—and for the public in general?

Yes. With more than 100 million workers in this country, a simple $10 mistake by each of them, as a result of poor listening, would add up to a cost of a billion dollars. And most people make numerous listening mistakes every week

Because of listening mistakes, letters have to be retyped, appointments rescheduled, shipments rerouted. Productivity is affected and profits suffer.

Look at some of today's breakdowns in labor-management relations. Often you'll hear workers say: "Management isn't listening to us, so we'll fix them. We'll go on strike."

I'm convinced that a great many of the 3 million or more divorces in this country each year are related to the inability or the unwillingness of one or both partners to listen.

At its worst, bad listening can result in people being injured or killed. The sinking of the *Titanic,* Pearl Harbor, the Jonestown, Guyana incident and some recent airplane disasters are classic examples of a breakdown in communication and in judgment. A message was sent, and listening broke down.

On an airplane recently, I talked with the president of a small company. I asked whether his firm had experienced any problems because of his employees' inability or failure to listen.

The man's eyebrows went up, and he told how the company had recently lost a million-dollar sale: "Two of my employees were involved," he said. "One didn't hear the important message at all, and the other one misinterpreted it. The upshot was that we lost out on a bid that we should have won hands down."

What do you mean when you talk about "good" or "poor" listening?

It's more than merely *hearing* what someone else is saying. There are three other important components: *Interpretation* of what's said, which leads to understanding or misunderstanding; *evaluation,* which involves weighing the information and deciding how to use it, and, finally, *responding* based on what was heard, understood and evaluated.

When all four stages are taken together, our research indicates, people on average listen at an effective rate of only about 25 percent.

Is the ability to listen a trait that people are born with?

No. It's not inherent. It's learned behavior. It has to be taught. When we come into this world, we don't have built-in knowledge of how to listen well. That must be developed. And, unfortunately, it is not systematically developed well in our school systems. We teach reading, writing, speaking and numerous other abilities, but not listening.

Is that why you consider most people poor listeners?

Yes. They simply haven't been taught to listen well. Individuals spend 80 percent of their waking hours communicating in one way or another. Of that time, about 45 percent is spent listening. But the focus in our educational programs is upside down. We spend the greatest amount of time teaching people to do what they spend the least time doing—writing. And we spend the least amount of time teaching them what they do most in life—listening.

It's lamentable because listening is much more complex than reading. What we read is locked on the printed page. If people are distracted, they can put aside their reading and return to it later. If they don't understand the message right off, they have the means to repeat it. But in listening, the message is written on the wind. It's transient. If we don't get the message the first time, there's usually no going back.

Are school systems beginning to introduce courses in listening?

Yes, gradually. Until 1978, the basic competencies listed as determinants of literacy in this country were reading, writing and arithmetic. Then in 1978, the Primary-Secondary Education Act was amended, and two more competencies were added: Speaking and Listening. Unfortunately, there's a factor of realism that we have to recognize: Passing a law is one thing. Actually getting it implemented in school systems is something else. But schools ranging from New York State to Oregon and Minnesota to the Deep South are teaching listening. However, these programs are the exception and few in number.

How do you convince people that a listening course isn't a sort of transitory thing—like a course in speed reading or memory improvement that may be used for a period of time, then dropped?

You have to make it clear that listening is the predominant communication activity that we engage in day after day throughout a lifetime. It's at the heart of our success, whether in the family, in society, in business, in government,

in international affairs. And it must be taught in a systematic and focused manner.

In your opinion, how important is listening for managers?

The higher one advances in management, the more critical listening ability and skill become. The most common problems in business arise when management doesn't listen to something that their workers are trying to tell them.

In a recent study of the abilities managers considered to be most critical for their managerial success, they rated listening as the No. 1, most important competency to be developed. But, again, as most managers have not been taught how to listen well, they don't necessarily perform well.

Like others, managers often don't hear the messages of others—they're busy, preoccupied, distracted, etc.; or they misunderstand others—due to their expectations, preconceived notions, experiences, special perspectives, etc.; or they misevaluate or fail to respond to the messages of others.

Of course, these listening problems are not limited to managers, but they are of special concern to managers, due to the nature of the management task.

Most important, thousands of managers are recognizing this critical need and are working at improving their listening skills.

How can people tell whether they need to improve their listening?

It's not hard to show that individuals don't listen well, but we have to deal initially with an attitude of skepticism. Often a person will say: "Yes, I know a lot of people who need this kind of enhancement, but not me."

Prior to testing, we ask people to rate themselves as listeners, using a scale of 0 to 100. Most individuals give themselves a rating at the outset of about 55. None say they're superior, but neither do any say they're poor. They're all clustered in the average area. We then ask whether they think a rating of 55 out of 100 is good enough, and most answer, "Of course not."

We also challenge people to listen to short-duration messages as intently as possible. At the end of these messages, we ask questions to determine to what extent they heard and understood and to what extent they were able to make proper judgments and respond.

These exercises prove very quickly that the typical person is not as good a listener as at first thought.

The process is like exercising muscles. If we haven't been trained to listen productively or effectively, we cannot turn on our listening any more than we can say: I'm going to run 10 miles today even though I've never exercised a muscle."

Do people show improvement after completing a course in listening?

Yes. With the proper training, listening is improved. More than 85 percent of participants in professionally developed programs show significant measured imrpovement through training.

With extended, focused training, some participants more than double the listening efficiency and effectiveness. Listening can be improved with focused training and exercise.

How do you teach people to listen better?

It's done specifically and directly— the same way math, reading or physical education is taught. The most effective programs involve groups of people led by a trained instructor, using tests and listening exercises.

A common approach to our courses includes: No. 1, developing the nature, role, importance, problems and costs of listening; No. 2, aiding each participant

in analyzing his or her strengths and limitations in listening; No. 3, teaching, through practice, each individual how to develop specific skills and behaviors related to good listening, and eliminate behaviors related to poor listening.

The development and elimination of these behaviors are complex and require focused direction, effort and practice. But they can be accomplished and are certainly worth the effort.

Are companies increasingly giving listening courses to people at the management level?

Yes. The primary example is Sperry Corporation's revolutionary effort in developing the listening skills of their entire corporate body.

Hundreds of other companies, large to small, are focusing to some degree on developing this important skill. Some do it as part of a sales-training program, others as a separate group project. But it's still hard to convince many executives that they can see the results of a listening course on the bottom line of the profit-and-loss statement.

Let's go back to that company whose president I met on the plane. I asked him: "Knowing that you lost a million-dollar order as a result of poor listening, would you be willing to spend, say, $100,000 over a period of time to develop your employees' listening ability?" His response was typical: "I'm not sure."

So although there has been much gain in developing listening skills since Dr. Ralph G. Nichols's pioneering work at the University of Minnesota more than three decades ago, listening development is still a relatively new phenomenon. But it's something that I'm convinced is going to grow and spread as people realize its importance.

We can improve our listening, and the benefits far outweigh the cost.

Reprinted from "U.S. News and World Report"
© 1980 U.S. News and World Report.

WHAT TO KNOW

Selecting an appropriate subject and purpose for your speech can best be accomplished by speaking on a topic you are interested in. Make the talk yours by drawing on your own experiences. Analyzing the characteristics, interests and concerns of your listeners will allow you to adjust the material to them. Determining the general purpose of the speech (to inform, persuade, or entertain) is followed by formulating the specific purpose: the exact nature of the response you want from your audience. Applying your ability to listen to other speakers is one of the most direct ways to develop your own skills of limiting and adapting topics and speaking purposes to particular listeners.

WHAT TO DO

Topic Inventory

STEP 1: Write down eight things (topics, issues, subject areas, activities, beliefs, interests, or any combination) that interest you. For the moment, do not be at all concerned about whether anyone else is interested in them.

Topics	Audience Ranking	My Ranking
1. _____	_____	_____
2. _____	_____	_____
3. _____	_____	_____
4. _____	_____	_____
5. _____	_____	_____
6. _____	_____	_____
7. _____	_____	_____
8. _____	_____	_____

STEP 2: Now rank the topics from 1, the one that interests you the most, to 8, the one that interests you the least.

STEP 3: Now forget your interests. Look at the topics in Step 1 and guess which would be the most interesting to an audience similar to your speech-communication-class members. Now rank the topics again from 1 (the one that would interest the listeners the most) to 8, the one that would interest them the least.

STEP 4: You now have some rough data to use in selecting the speech topic you feel has the best chance of interesting you and your audience. How? Given the following example:

Topics	Audience Ranking	My Ranking
1. Government funding of abortion	7	8
2. Legalizing marijuana	3	7
3. Sports-car racing	5	3
4. Surfing	2	6
5. Stained glass	8	4
6. Summer in Alaska	6	1
7. Advertising	1	5
8. Special education	4	2

You should choose special education because it has the lowest (and thus best) total score (6), along with the lowest "my ranking" (2). Given the premise that the speaker's interest in the topic (my ranking) is more important to speech success than the audience's interest (audience ranking), you should choose special education rather than advertising which also totals to 6 but has a "my ranking" of 5. Now choose a topic from step 1.

STEP 5: At this point decide whether your general purpose will be to inform, persuade, or entertain. Finally, state clearly to yourself what specific response you want from your listeners.

WHERE TO LEARN MORE

Bryant, Donald C., and Karl R. Wallace. *Fundamentals of Public Speaking.* 4th ed. Englewood Cliffs, NJ: Prentice-Hall, 1976. Chapter 3.

Clevenger, Theodore, Jr. *Audience Analysis.* Indianapolis: Bobbs-Merrill, 1966.

Holtzman, Paul D. *The Psychology of Speaker's Audiences.* Glenview, IL: Scott, Foresman, 1970.

Reid, Loren. *Speaking Well.* 4th ed. New York: McGraw-Hill, 1982.

Wolvin, Andrew, D., and Carolyn Gwynn Coakley. *Listening.* Dubuque, Iowa Wm. C. Brown Company Publishers, 1982

SUPPORTING
AND ILLUSTRATING
YOUR IDEAS

4

MAKING YOURSELF A MORE BELIEVABLE SPEAKER

If you are not an expert on alternative energy sources, what would be the main difference in the expression of your thoughts: (1) to a group of friends in the student center, (2) in a discussion in a science class, or (3) to a group of thirty or forty members of the chamber of commerce in your community who have gathered to hear you speak on the topic?

What would be the main difference in the following situations: (1) a student trying to talk a friend into buying his motorcycle even though autumn has already arrived, (2) the same student attempting to sell the motorcycle to an unknown person who has phoned in response to a newspaper ad, and (3) the same student attempting to sell his motorcycle from the lot of a local Honda dealership, where the student is a part-time salesperson?

In both sets of circumstances, the main difference will most likely lie in the amount of supportive and illustrative materials the speaker uses. The closer the presentation of one's ideas comes to be what most people consider public speaking, the more use is usually made of these materials: testimony from experts, statistics, forms of reasoning, analogies, examples, and the like.

Why? The usual assumption of nonexpert speakers is that the credibility they lack as first-hand experts can be compensated for by demonstrating to listeners that they have become secondary experts. This is accomplished by quoting materials and facts that demonstrate a greater-than-average awareness of the subject.

We found an example of the credibility gap of a message source in *Reader's Digest*, where an unmarried person had written an article entitled "To Increase the Enjoyment of Sex in Marriage." Your authors had a bit of difficulty accepting the "expertness" of the article's recommendations of shoulds and should nots. Had the writer used surveys, interviews with married couples, or simply education in the field, his article would have been more credible to us as readers.

Similarly, picture yourself in a physician's office during a checkup. Your doctor is giving you advice about being out of shape and smoking too much. While he is talking, you happen to notice the roll of fat hanging four inches over his belt. As his voice wheezes, you look past him to a half-empty pack of cigarettes on his desk, and an ashtray full of butts. Since this is a situation where one person is trying to influence the thoughts and actions of another (persuasion), the credibility (believability) of the source is even more important than in a strictly informative presentation—although, as we have just seen, it is significant there, too.

What does the title of the chapter, "Supporting and Illustrating Your

Ideas," mean? In a communication sense, *to support* means to verify or to substantiate. In the same communication sense, *to illustrate* means to make clear, to shed light on. As you can see, there is an overlapping area between these two definitions. In the traditional approach, when you support your ideas you back them up with facts, evidence, statistics, logical reasoning, expert testimony, and the like. When you illustrate your ideas you paint a verbal picture with examples, stories, and specifics to help make your ideas live in the present. You create visual images for the minds of your listeners. You also may actually use visual or audio aids to be specific, clear and interesting.

> *You cannot deal with the most serious things in the world unless you understand the most amusing.*
>
> WINSTON CHURCHILL

The key to using what we have called supporting and illustrating materials is in understanding the role they play in what we call the *basic message unit*. The basic message unit is made up of two elements: (*a*) a general statement followed by (*b*) a specific, either a supporting or illustrating, point. (The order of *a* and *b* may be reversed.)

Example: Teachers forget what it is like to be a student studying for a major test (*general statement*). My instructor estimated that it would take only one or two hours to prepare for the test. It took me all evening to go through my notes. My roommate was up until 3:00 A.M. studying (*specific illustration*).

Example: Volkswagens generally get the best gas mileage of any of the compact cars (*general statement*). A recent study conducted by the EPA rated the the VW Rabbit as having the best all-around gas mileage for subcompacts with _____ mpg city and _____ mpg country driving (*specific research evidence*).

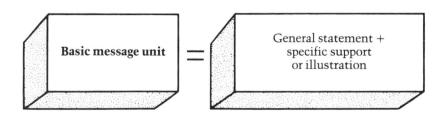

If you accept the notion that supportive and illustrative materials may be useful to you as a speaker, you need to know where to find materials related to the idea or topic you want to get across to others, and how to keep track of them once they are found. Also, you should examine some kinds of verbal illustrative and supportive materials, as well as visual aids, that can be used in typical speeches to create interest in and prove your ideas.

FINDING INFORMATION ABOUT YOUR IDEAS

The more public and formal your speaking, the greater the variety of sources of materials you will want to research or investigate in preparing the content of your talk. Gathering material for speaking is like shooting film for a television commercial. An advertising agency takes about ten times as many feet of film as it will actually use in the commercial. The agency looks at all the film and selects just the parts that will best accomplish the objective. The selected parts are then spliced together. And the rough print is tested for the full effect and finally edited down to a polished version. This whole process is parallel to gathering and evaluating material for a speech.

> *A fool uttereth all his mind.*
>
> PROVERBS 29:11

Professional speakers usually gather two or three times more material than they will actually be able to use. This extra material does not go to waste though. Often speakers can work in additional information when answering questions and comments after the main part of the presentation is over.

There are several ways to locate information about your topic. The greater the variety of sources of information you look into, the more knowledge you will gain in your attempt to become a secondary expert.

Some traditional and unique sources of information are interviewing, surveying, structured observations, experimental manipulation, and the library.

INTERVIEWING AND SURVEYING

Interviewing campus or local professionals and experts can be an interesting way to gather information and materials. But be careful not to get so carried away with a particular source's information that the speech becomes one continuous reference to that expert. When you decide to interview or gather information on the same questions from many people, whether they are peers, voters, teachers, lawyers, married couples, or third graders, you are doing a survey. When you conduct a survey in order to gather information on particular topics, do not be misled into believing that your information proves anything to be true or false. Your results may show a trend or tendency, but the survey would have to be done very scientifically to prove anything.

Surveys may take the form of printed questionnaires, face-to-face interviews, or telephone interviews. No matter what the surveying technique, you have to decide ahead of time how you will sample the people who represent the group about which you wish to discover something. You will also have to decide what questions will be asked of everyone, and how you will ask the questions.

There are several different types of questions:

1. **Open questions:** How do you feel about artificial conception? What do you think about the CIA scandal?
2. **Closed questions:** Do you like this course? Did you vote last year?
3. **Scaling questions:** How would you rate this class? Poor? Fair? Average? Good? Excellent?
4. **Multiple-choice questions:** How often do you openly argue with your spouse? ____ More than once a day. ____ About once a day. ____ Weekly. ____ Monthly. ____ Seldom. ____ Never.
5. **Directive questions:** Give me two reasons why you chose to attend this school.

In designing your survey, allow your instructor to examine and comment on the questions and interview technique you plan to use.

Next, pretest the survey on about ten people who are not familiar with what you are doing. Ask them to complete the survey in the manner you plan. After they have finished, you will see where your survey has rough spots in wording, directions, completion time, and so on. Smooth out these problems, and you are ready to administer the survey to your chosen sample.

STRUCTURED OBSERVATIONS

The purpose of structured observations is to witness first-hand how people behave (respond) in a particular situation, to learn more than you know now. Structured observing requires that nothing be manipulated by you and that the people are not aware they are being observed. When people are aware that "something is going on," it affects what they do and what you end up observing. To keep track of the behaviors, you have to record them on a tally sheet, sometimes called a tracking instrument. A simple example is the following:

Objective: To observe door-opening behavior of male/female (two-person) couples.

Procedure: Observe fifty couples approaching a closed door together, and record which person opens the door.

Results

Behavior	Total Number	Percentages
Male opened door	30	60%
Female opened door	12	24%
Both opened door together	8	16%

EXPERIMENTAL MANIPULATION

If you want to manipulate a situation to see how people will respond to a given stimulus, then you are setting up a mini-experiment. In most instances when you run an experiment, you need to record the behavior of people before you mainipulate anything (structured observation) to see what the "baseline" behavior is. For example, you could observe the average length of time students spend talking with an interviewer who is doing a survey on some subject. You would record the results the interviewer had in this normal circumstance. Then you could ask the interviewer to avoid eye contact with the interviewees as much as possible for the same number of interviews as conducted in the baseline observation. You would record the results. Then you could ask the interviewer to have good eye contact with the same number of interviewees. And you would record the results.

In some instances you might not need a baseline to see what people's responses to an experimental manipulation will be, because what you are doing is straightforward and simple. For example, you may want to see who can get more students to fill out a questionnaire—a male in sloppy and dirty clothes, the same male in clean and casual clothes, or the same male in a suit and tie. In each type of clothing, the interviewer would approach twenty-five (or some other set number) subjects. And you would keep track of the results.

A man should keep his little brain attic stocked with all the furniture that he is likely to use, and the rest he can put away in the lumber-room of his library, where he can get it if he wants it.

SIR ARTHUR CONAN DOYLE

THE LIBRARY

The library is the traditional place to locate books, articles, statistics, and other materials. You can use the encyclopedias for an overall view of your topic. The card catalogue will help you find books dealing with your subject. *The Guide to Periodical Literature* will lead you to articles on your topic or related topics in almost every published magazine in the United States. *The Statistical Abstract of the United States* will give you up-to-date statistics on a large range of subjects, from the number of women who are presidents of companies to the number of cars made in the United States last year.

Before you begin your work in the library, find the reference librarian and ask for assistance. Oh yes, don't overlook the deluge of popular magazines that surround us at the library as well as at home, work, school, and the dentists' and doctors' offices.

RECORDING YOUR INFORMATION

One thing an experienced speaker learns is that all the interesting ideas and facts found in research are not automatically remembered once it comes time to prepare the talk. This is why taking notes and jotting down ideas are important. It is a waste of time and energy to consult a piece of material only to forget it two days later when planning the speech. Take more notes than you will possibly need. Remember that the material will be refined and edited later. Make one notecard (3 × 5) for each source or major idea. Be sure to also note the title, author(s), date, issue, and page numbers, in case you need to consult the source again. Or sometimes a member of the audience will ask for documentation of a source if it is questioned, or if that person is interested in a particular point. The information can then be given from the card. A typical card might look like this:

> "It is commonly recognized that upwards of 60 percent of the people seeking employment do so by the seat of their pants with no flight plan."
>
> Amsden and White, *How to be Successful in the Employment Interview*, Kendall/Hunt, Publishers, 1977, page 60.

Keeping notecards of information is also an advantage when it comes to organizing the talk. The notes can simply be arranged into piles that will follow the opening, main body, and conclusion of the speech. The notecards can also be organized so as to put ideas in logical order.

USING VERBAL SUPPORTIVE MATERIALS THAT PROVE YOUR POINT

Now that we have discussed ways of gathering material, you may be wondering, "What difference does it make what individual items of my potential information are called—factual examples, testimony, or analogy?" Secondly, you may be thinking, "If there is a gray area where

The many magazines available at the library and at bookstores and newsstands are excellent source materials for researching speeches.

supportive materials and illustrative materials overlap, why worry about whether the items I use are supportive or illustrative as long as they are effective?"

The answer to the first question is simple. We name the kinds of informational materials so you can analyze the patterns or voids in their use in your speaking. Speakers tend to overuse favorite or habitual information types and ignore other types that could add more variety and interest to the speech. Maybe you can recall a persuasive speech where the speaker read one quote after another from supposed experts. How effective did you find this singular type of support in proving the point?

The answer to the second question ("Why worry about whether my material is supportive or illustrative?") is not as simple to answer. Illustrative and supportive materials are used to give a speech substance. They assist the speaker in developing the main points beyond abstract and general statements. When general statements of main points are given substance (specificity and vividness) by illustrative and supportive materials, we have what has been called the basic message unit in speaking.

In the literature on speaking, there is little consistent description as to what is an illustrative material and what is a supportive material. Generally, supportive materials are used to prove, to offer evidence, to substantiate. Speakers rely on supportive materials to build their own credibility, especially if they are a secondary source, and to develop the credibility of the information. Illustrative materials are used to give concreteness, clarity, and interest.

Both illustrative and supportive materials are found in informative and persuasive speaking. However, primary use of supportive materials fits persuasive speaking better, whereas primary use of illustrative materials is more appropriate to informative speaking. Now that we have generally described these two types of materials, let us move directly to the specific point via an exercise.

Here is a list of common materials. Your job is to identify each item. Put an *S* before each item you consider to be primarily a supportive material. Put an *I* before each item you consider to be primarily illustrative. Put a *B* before each item that can easily be used for *both* illustrative (informative) and supportive (persuasive) purposes.

_____ Reasoning   _____ Comparison and contrast

_____ Testimony   _____ Definition

_____ Statistics   _____ Personal experience

_____ Factual examples   _____ Analogy

_____ Hypothetical examples

If many of your responses were *B*, or if you had difficulty choosing *I* or *S*, then you are on the right track. Each item *could* be labeled *B*. These materials are not inherently supportive or illustrative by nature. The speaker determines whether they are supportive or illustrative by how he or she uses them. For example, an analogy may be used by one speaker to illustrate (inform) how the mind and computer are alike in some respects. Another speaker may use an analogy (as a support) to persuade the listener that the body needs the right fuel to operate smoothly.

In summary, it is important to be able to label materials, to see patterns in their use or misuse. It is also important to realize whether your materials have to prove something, or simply are meant to enlighten the listener. Now we are ready for a brief description of several of the supportive illustrative materials we listed in the exercise.

REASONING

Reasoning is the ability to interrelate perceptions—to recognize or create patterns among these perceptions. Reasoning is a process of using words to emphasize relationships among the objects, events, or ideas for which the words stand. Three types of reasoning we use everyday are causal, inductive, and deductive.

Causal Reasoning When something happens we assume that it had a cause. We infer the cause even when we are not sure of it. "The high divorce rate is the result of too many early marriages." "The use of drugs by youth is a result of their loss of personal identity in a society of manufactured images and numbers." "Students with good grades have efficient study habits."

In a similar sense, when we become aware of a process or event, we often speculate about what the end result will be. For example, your instructor comes to class without any materials except a pencil and notepad, and you speculate that today the class will be giving impromptu speeches. We reason from effect to inferred cause and from cause to what we think the effects will be.

Inductive Reasoning This is reasoning from specific examples to a general conclusion. The speaker will try to prove that a general rule or conclusion is warranted because several specific instances occur in some relationship. For example, an observant student would be using inductive reasoning in concluding a quiz was in store today because every time the class has a quiz the instructor, upon entering the room, does not establish eye contact with anyone, and today the instructor has entered the room and not established eye contact with anyone.

Deductive Reasoning This is reasoning from a generally accepted law or principle to a specific case. Sometimes, while generally accepted, the principle itself is questionable, as in the example: "Divorced women are loose women. Mary is divorced, therefore, she is a loose woman." Other examples of deductive reasoning are: "Volkswagens are good [whatever that might mean] cars. I bought a Volkswagen, therefore I have a good car." Or, "Religious speeches given in Snodbottom's communication class get As. Therefore I'm going to give a religious speech so I can get an A."

Checkpoints

- In causal reasoning, check to see whether there could be more than a single cause. Could the effects vary?
- In inductive reasoning, it is important to decide whether the examples are typical or representative.
- In deductive reasoning, it is important to examine the factual basis for the "law" or "principle."

TESTIMONY

Opinions and conclusions taken from others can add weight to the point you are trying to put forth if the audience makes the connection between your ideas and the ideas of other people. There are two commonly accepted kinds of testimony: expert testimony and peer testimony.

Expert Testimony   This is called for when the experience, knowledge, or insight of highly qualified people will be accepted as believable because of the complexity or sophistication of the material. For example, a ballistics expert is called into a trial to testify regarding the match-up between a bullet and a gun used in a crime. However, a problem in expert testimony can arise when "experts" claiming to be right are found on both sides of the topic.

Peer Testimony   This kind of testimony is helpful because listeners are interested in the opinions of people like themselves. Conducting a survey is a good way to arrive at peer testimony. Various television commercials have used this technique to sell products. We hear Bertha Grogen's advice on everything from cars to personal hygiene products because Bertha is one of us, a common everyday American with an opinion.

Checkpoints

- Choose your expert to be a source who is credible to your listeners, not necessarily the most credible source to you.
- Be aware of the expert's obvious biases (a biologist may not be seen as an objective expert if working for an environmental protection group).
- If your only expert is unknown to your audience, present credentials to the audience before giving that expert's opinion.

QUANTIFYING AND USING STATISTICS

When figures (numbers) are used to show relationships between specific items, we call these statistics. Statistics are summaries of facts. They can be effective proof if they are (1) understood by the listener, (2) meaningful to the listener, and (3) related to the point being made. For example, instead of saying "55,000 people are killed in needless traffic accidents every year," you could bring that large, abstract figure down to earth by adding, "that means one person dies in traffic accidents every ten minutes of every day." An example involving billions of dollars could be made more vivid by your stating that it would take a sixty-story pile of hundred-dollar bills to add up to a billion dollars.

The common reaction to the suggestion that a speaker use numbers or statistics to support (prove) or illustrate (add interest and concreteness) to the presentation is, "Numbers can be so confusing." This is correct if they are not used well. If you use many figures or comparisons, they should be put on visual aids. But if you want to make a single point that involves numbers or statistics, you can do this effectively by relating the numbers to something concrete and easily visualized. (This is similar to an analogy.) For example, "It is roughly 240,000 miles from the earth to the moon. Comparatively, that means if the earth were this softball (hold up softball) the moon would be about the size of this golf ball (hold up golf ball in other hand). Another example would be "The moon is 240,000 miles from the earth. This means that if you started driving your car toward the moon at fifty-five miles per hour and you could continue without stopping, you would get there in 182 days."

The use of calculators can be fun in figuring costs, time lost, and percentages, to add interest to a topic. The results can be unique to a listener who has never stopped to think about the idea in that way. An example could be figuring how many years of a lifetime a person spends sleeping: "If you sleep an average of eight hours a night for a life of seventy years, you will spend over twenty-three years sleeping. If you could get by with only six hours of sleep per night instead of eight, you would have over five and one-half more years awake to be active in your life." Or: "A person who drinks at least one six-pack of beer a week will drink about 390 cases of beer in a thirty-year span. At $2.50 per six-pack, that would be close to $3,900. If that same person also smoked a pack of cigarettes every day for thirty years, the total amount spent would come to approximately $11,000. Now, if that person put the $9.50 per week for beer and cigarettes in a savings account in the bank each week, at 6 percent interest compounded quarterly, he would have approximately $38,000 after thirty years."

Another interesting point the calculator can help you illustrate relates to the present interest in exercising. For example, "When they say we can add five years onto our life by exercising one hour per day, we forget that one hour is one less hour we have to do other things. When you figure this out for fifty years of exercising, we will spend two years of our life just to add five years on. That appears to be a net gain of only three years, not five."

The calculator can assist you in discovering all kinds of interesting figures to use in your presentations. To pursue the use of numbers and statistics further, you can go to your library and examine *Facts on File*, *The Statistical Abstract of the United States*, and other similar source books.

People are also becoming more aware of the use of statistics to produce false "truths." Nine out of ten doctors may recommend Gag toothpaste, but they may also have recommended three or four other brands along with Gag. Statistics must be analyzed. To do this, use the following checkpoints:

Checkpoints

- Remember that listeners do not always trust figures.
- Check to see whether statistics are complete, or whether they are lifted out of context. ("Three out of four people said they like Grit soap." You are not told that these statements were extracted from people after they were given free boxes of Grit in a store.)
- Check for dated statistics.
- Round off numbers when the decimals are not necessary, for example, 98.56 percent becomes 99 percent.

FACTUAL EXAMPLES

The best factual examples are specific instances of an event, process, or incident that have been observed and documented by objective sources. Personal examples, though they may be factual, usually carry the bias of personal involvement or emotion. We suggest that the most potent factual examples are those which are recorded by noninvolved outside observers who do not add a personal bias to interpretation of the event. An innocent bystander who observes an accident is seen as an objective witness and is believed to be more factual than either of the two or more parties involved in the accident.

Materials we have described as helpful in illustrating can also be used in supporting (proving) a point. Specific instances, analogies, examples, and so on can be used in a persuasive manner and will give additional impact to your message.

To get a clear idea of what we mean by examples, look back over the pages you have read so far in this book. Look for the instances where we have said, "for example." These should give you an indication of what examples are and how to use them.

Checkpoints

- Examples should be explained vividly and specifically, rather than generally.
- To aid in persuasive speaking, the example has to be believable.

HYPOTHETICAL EXAMPLES

The speaker openly creates an example as fiction, to make a point. Usually the example is invented because a factual example is not readily available, the factual example is too complex to be explained in simple terms, or some of the details of the factual example are not suited to the purpose the speaker has in mind. As with other speaking materials, the hypothetical example can be used either to advance the clarity of comprehension or to convince the listener through emotional or logical means.

Checkpoints

- In persuasive speaking, keep hypothetical examples to a minimum, as the listener knows they are fiction.
- Keep the hypothetical example believable by avoiding exaggeration in description of numbers, amounts, size, frequency, et cetera.
- Add some further interest to the hypothetical example by giving names to people, places, and things in the example, then refer to the items by name as if they might easily be real.

PERSONAL EXPERIENCE

Relating an actual experience you have had can be one of the most powerful methods of illustrating or supporting a point in the message. If you include when it happened and where it happened along with what happened, the listener will "relive" the experience with you. Colorful words and concrete images will add to the interest.

This book is the result of a personal situation your authors experienced. The three of us were puffing our way around the Brigham Young University football practice field. Between gasps we were musing that it was too bad that talking was not as good an exercise as jogging. As speech-communication teachers (notorious at our respective universities for our long-windedness in the classroom), we would surely be in top physical condition. We speculated that we could then write a book titled *Pumping Words* (a take-off on Arnold Swartzenegger's movie *Pumping Iron*). After an attempted laugh from lungs that could not spare the air, we slowed to a walk and this book began to take shape (much faster, by the way, than our bodies did).

Checkpoints

- Describe the personal experience so your listeners can identify with you and what you did or thought.

- If your personal experience is long (three or four minutes in length), build to a climax at the end.

ANALOGY

When you draw a comparison between a point you are attempting to make and an activity or situation with which the audience can readily identify, you are using an analogy. Many management-motivation and religious speakers use analogies to make their ideas clearer and more interesting. The process, for example, of managing a business may be compared to coaching a football team. When we wrote about gathering material for your speech, we compared it to shooting film for a television commercial. We were using an analogy.

Checkpoints

- Listeners tend to judge analogies from the perspective of whether they appear to fit or make immediate sense in terms of the point at hand.

- Analogies used in persuasive speaking cannot "break down" too easily; in other words, the analogy has to appear to parallel the point being made in both detail and the perspective of the situation.

VISUAL AIDS CREATE IMPACT
IN SUPPORTING OR ILLUSTRATING

It has been estimated that more than 75 percent of the information we take in during the day or in any given situation comes in through our eyes. The film *Visual Aids*[1] states that we learn

3 percent through taste
3 percent through smell
6 percent through touch
13 percent through hearing
75 percent through sight

Examining the data from a different viewpoint, the Industrial Audio Visual Association[2] reports that we remember:

10 percent of what we read
20 percent of what we hear
30 percent of what we see
50 percent of what we see and hear
80 percent of what we say
90 percent of what we say as we act

It may be only recently that we have received scientific confirmation of these facts, but intuitively, we have known them for a long time. There is an ancient Chinese proverb that reads: "I hear and I forget. I see and I remember. I do and I understand."

Another study by R. Benschofter[3] reports the influence of using sound and sight, separately or combined, as a teaching tool:

| | Percent of Recall | |
Methods of Instruction	3 hours later	3 days later
Telling, when used alone	70%	10%
Showing, when used alone	72%	20%
Combination of telling and showing	85%	65%

Taking into account that the average speaker talks at 125 to 130 words per minute and that our brains can think four or five times that fast allows us to understand why listeners get bored and distracted. Now add to this that

[1]BNA Communications Inc., 5615 Fishers Lane, Rockville, MD 20852.
[2]P.O. Box 656 Downtown Station, Chicago, IL 60690.
[3]"In-Service Training Aids," *Proceedings of Nebraska's In-Service Training Conference.* Omaha, NB, 1974.

our language can be up to 60 percent redundant, and you have a clearer picture of why people tune out when presentations are totally verbal in content.

When speakers use visual aids, they "entertain" or focus the visual attention of the listeners on material related to the talk. Thus the speakers have more influence over the total information processing of the listeners. It is common knowledge in the fields of education and speech communication that visual aids are helpful in the comprehension and recall of information. Visual aids can add interest and impact. In this sense, visual aids add greatly to the effects of persuasive messages. Also, specific messages that can be supported by facts and figures are strengthened by visual materials that are consistent with the verbal aspects of the speech.

The old saying, "Use a visual aid when you need to make a complex idea clear" should in light of the evidence give way to a saying such as, "Use visual aids *whenever you want to enhance what you are saying.*"

Reinforcing a spoken message with a visual presentation not only helps entertain listeners but also enhances their ability to recall and understand the information.

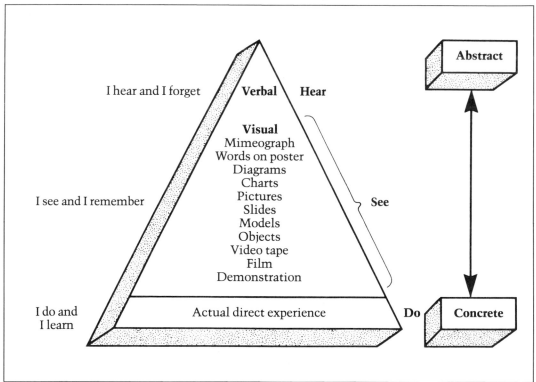

TYPES OF VISUAL AIDS AND VISUAL-AID EQUIPMENT

The following types of visual aids are ways of presenting information visually. They are listed in order from the most static materials to the most active.

1. Mimeographed, dittoed, or Xeroxed handouts (color coded or keyed for easy reference)
2. Samples of actual written materials
3. Lettered posters
4. Diagrams (bar graphs, pie charts, organizational diagrams)
5. Photographs (usually enlarged or projected on a screen)
6. Slides
7. Models (of objects, processes, et cetera)
8. Actual objects
9. Video tapes
10. Films
11. Demonstrations

There are also other frequently used pieces of equipment that aid speakers in presenting visual materials to the audience:

1. Boards: Magnetic board, flannel or felt board, hook and loop board (Velcro), metallic- or plastic-surfaced board, chalkboard
2. Flip chart
3. Overhead projector
4. Opaque projector
5. Slide projector
6. Video tape record and playback unit
7. Film: 16 mm, 8 mm

We will note some simple considerations for the use of each piece of equipment.

Boards   Stand to the side of a board as you write or display your materials. Write clearly and thickly with chalk or felt-tip marking pens (Magic Markers). Do not use thin-line "writing" felt-tip pens on visuals. Use key words only; do not put every single word down. Look at the audience after you write a word or phrase on the board. Also, after you look to see where you are pointing on a prepared visual, be sure to look at the audience as you talk. Do not get caught talking to the board or visual, rather than to the listeners. Try to talk while you are writing or pointing or putting up

Always stand to the side of the board as you discuss your materials.

material. Not saying anything while you manipulate parts of a board can create an awkward silence that can ruin the pacing of your presentation. Finally, do not keep turning your head and looking at the visual aid—look ahead at your audience.

Flip Chart   This may be prepared in advance so that as you flip the pages up and over the top of the easel, each page appears already complete. The same guidelines for writing and pointing when using a board apply to using a flip chart. With a flip chart though, you have to be careful that the felt-tip marker used for writing does not "bleed" through to the pages behind. It may be necessary to try out different marking pens until you find one that has ink that dries on contact.

Overhead Projector   This works on the principle that light passing through a clear or tinted plastic sheet on which there is printing or a picture will project the image on a screen or wall.

Special transparent marking pens are available for writing or drawing on the plastic sheets used with overhead projectors. It is important to use these specially designed pens, especially if you are going to prepare your

Flip charts may be prepared in advance of your presentation.

overhead visuals hours or days ahead of time. The ink from a regular felt-tip may go on the plastic properly, but it will evaporate over time. Many a speaker has used a felt-tip pen to draw overhead transparencies the night before the presentation only to wake up in the morning to find that half of the visuals have disappeared.

You should be careful as you talk not to stand in front of the light being projected to the screen. You also have to choose whether you are going to stand beside the overhead, and face the audience while you talk, or have someone run the overhead for you while you stand back by the screen with a pointer, again facing the audience.

Be sure to rehearse with the overhead. Learn how to turn it off and on without looking for the switch. Locate the side the fan is on, because the fan could blow your notes or transparencies onto the floor during your presentation. Learn how to focus the overhead quickly. Once it is focused, put a piece of tape or chalk marks on the floor so you can quickly roll the overhead to the exact spot and the focus will already be set. Always have an extra bulb for your overhead projector or a backup projector in case the light burns out.

Positioning the overhead and the angle of projection is important for the audience to be able to view the screen. If the screen is the permanent kind which requires the overhead to be in the middle front part of the audience, you will want to arrange the seating so that the listeners sit on the sides and not in the middle.

Overhead projection hints: Tilting the overhead screen (shown at the top) or placing it toward the corner of the room (shown below) reduces the possibility of the speaker and equipment blocking the vision of some viewers, as might be the case when the projector is located in front of the group (lower left).

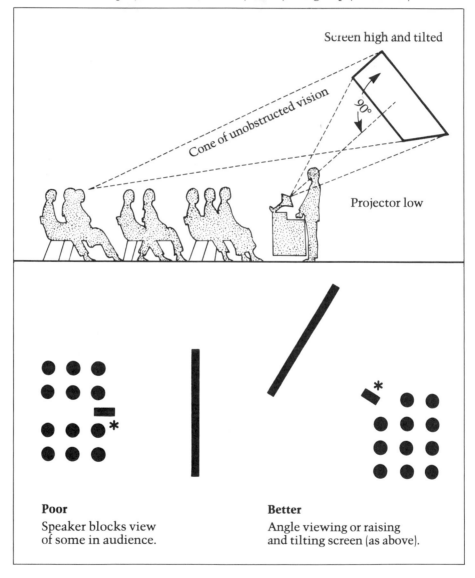

Poor
Speaker blocks view of some in audience.

Better
Angle viewing or raising and tilting screen (as above).

Opaque Projector   This projector projects the actual image of a page in a book, a letter, or a diagram that is no bigger than twelve by twelve inches. Light does not pass through the printed page as it does through overhead transparencies. Opaque projectors can enlarge and project original materials, but they are notoriously cumbersome and noisy machines to use and sometimes do not focus the complete picture at one time. It also is difficult to get the material into the machine straight and the right side up without considerable practice. Thin sheets have to be taped to cardboard to keep the fan from blowing them out of the machine. Also, because opaque projectors get very hot, materials covered with plastic coating will melt and wrinkle before your eyes. In some instances, highly combustible paper will start to smoke. However, opaque projectors allow you to show original material in full color and detail.

Slide Projector   The use of a slide projector requires that the order of points to be covered in the presentation be set firmly prior to the talk. Jumping back and forth between more than two adjacent slides is awkward to do. If there is an automatic advance cord for the projector and it will reach the screen while the slide is being projected, you can stand by the screen and face the audience. This will allow you to have eye contact with the listeners. Speaker-audience interaction is difficult if the speaker has to stand behind the slide projector and talk to the backs of the heads of the listeners.

Video Tape and Film   With video tape and film it is important to edit to the precise sections desired so that there is no need to run the machines ahead or back to pick up segments. There is nothing more frustrating for listeners than to sit and watch a speaker run a video tape back and forth for five minutes to find a piece that has been "lost" because the footage notations are off.

With film and video tape, you need to be careful that the segment to be shown is not so engrossing in itself that listeners lose the perspective of the point that is being made. You can avoid this problem by "setting listeners up" for the specific things you want them to observe or notice in the segment.

GUIDELINES TO VISUAL-AID DESIGN AND USE

The two key guidelines for designing and using all visual aids are not readily observed even in some professional speaking situations today. The reason is that speakers tend to design and use visual aids the way they see others doing them rather than thinking through how the visual can sequentially and systematically aid their presentation. The two guidelines are:

- visual aids must unfold with the speaking
- visual aids should exploit the visualness of the medium

It is not difficult to find a speaker who has designed the visual aid as it would appear in a magazine or book. The complete working and diagramming is totally exposed for the viewer to read or see ahead of, during, or after the actual speech. Since the audience members can read or see the points much faster than the speaker can talk, the listener tunes out what the speaker is saying and focuses on the visual, then tunes the speaker back in again. If the visual is confusing or complex, the listener may tune the speaker out and stay with the visual long after the speaker has finished referring to it.

For greatest impact and effectiveness, the words of the speaker and the words or pictures on the visual should be absolutely synchronized. *The visual must unfold in front of the listeners' eyes and in exact synchronization with what the speaker is saying.*

What this means is that visuals, such as posters, flip charts, boards, et cetera must utilize techniques that keep images covered or make images appear at the point of actual verbal reference. This is where creativity in covering and uncovering images and sticking images onto the board or poster will pay off.

This will take a different kind of thinking about the design and use of visual aids than you may be used to. For example, one of the authors attended a three-day banking conference. The closest thing to effective use of visual aids he observed was in a speaker who put a blank piece of paper across the bottom of an overhead transparency and moved the paper down to the next point every so often. Many times the sheet being used to mask the bottom lines of the visual was crooked on the screen. Our level of awareness regarding effective visual-aid design and use will not necessarily be enhanced by observing others. For some reason there is a distinct gap between our academic knowledge regarding visual support materials and actual practice by teachers and professionals alike.

The second guideline, that visuals should exploit the visual medium, is also not easily observed in educational settings. Too often the total content of the visual is words, words, words—so many words the speaker and listeners have to read them as they would a memo. A visual aid should be understandable and clear at a glance. This means words should not be the focus; images should be the focus. You often hear the phrase, "A picture is worth a thousand words." We don't believe many people really listen to that statement.

Graphs and charts that are designed for written reports are *not* usually

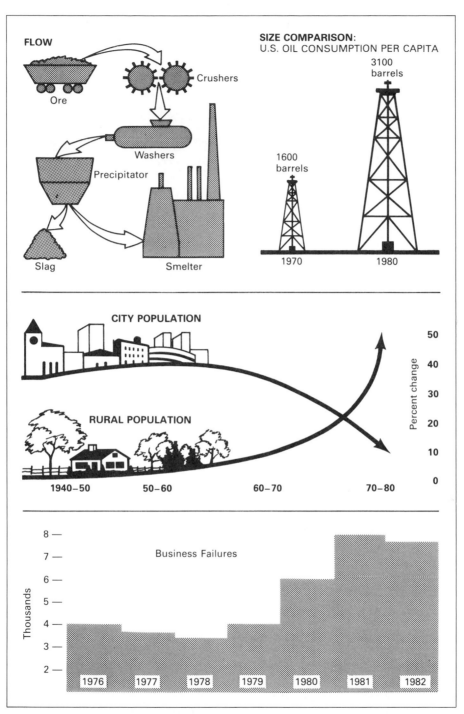

FLOW

Ore

Crushers

Washers

Precipitator

Slag

Smelter

SIZE COMPARISON:
U.S. OIL CONSUMPTION PER CAPITA

3100 barrels

1600 barrels

1970   1980

CITY POPULATION

RURAL POPULATION

Percent change

50
40
30
20
10
0

1940–50   50–60   60–70   70–80

Business Failures

Thousands

8
7
6
5
4
3
2

1976   1977   1978   1979   1980   1981   1982

Note how visuals above use the visual medium more completely than the simple bar graph below.

effective for oral presentations. For example, this table from a written report is *not* appropriate to use in speaking. Written reports can be studied and analyzed closely over time by the reader. This is not possible with visuals.

Economic Assumptions (Calendar Years: Dollar Amounts in Billions)

Item	Actual 1973	Actual 1974	Assumed for Purposes of Budget Estimates					
			1975	1976	1977	1978	1979	1980
Gross national product:								
Current dollars:								
Amount	$1,295	$1,397	$1,498	$1,686	$1,896	$2,123	$2,353	$2,606
Percent change	11.8	7.9	7.2	12.6	12.4	12.0	10.8	10.8
Constant (1958) dollars:								
Amount	$839	$821	$794	$832	$879	$936	$997	$1,061
Percent change	5.9	−2.2	−3.3	4.8	5.6	6.5	6.5	6.5
Incomes (current dollars):								
Personal income	$1,055	$1,150	$1,232	$1,365	$1,536	$1,717	$1,900	$2,102
Wages and salaries	$692	$751	$792	$884	$999	$1,117	$1,236	$1,367
Corporate profits	$123	$141	$115	$145	$163	$185	$208	$233
Prices (percent change):								
GNP deflator	5.6	10.2	10.8	7.5	6.5	5.1	4.1	4.0
Consumer Price Index	6.2	11.0	11.3	7.8	6.6	5.2	4.1	4.0
Unemployment rates (percent):								
Total	4.9	5.6	8.1	7.9	7.5	6.9	6.2	5.5
Insured[1]	2.8	3.8	7.5	6.9	6.4	5.1	4.4	3.6
Federal pay raise, October (percent):	4.77	5.52	5.00	8.75	7.25	6.50	5.75	5.25
Interest rate, 91-day Treasury bills (percent)[2]	7.0	7.9	6.4	6.4	6.4	6.0	5.0	5.0

[1]Insured unemployment as a percentage of covered employment: includes unemployed workers receiving extended benefits.
[2]Average rate on new issues within period; the rate shown for 1975 was the current market rate at the time the estimates were made.

DESIGN FEATURES OF VISUAL AIDS

Other important items in designing visuals are the figure/ground relationships, the colors, the size, the type of lettering, the simplicity, and the use of graphics and abbreviations.

1. **Figure/ground relationships.** A picture needs to have a central figure or focus for the eye. The remaining portion of the picture supporting the central part should complement the focal point.

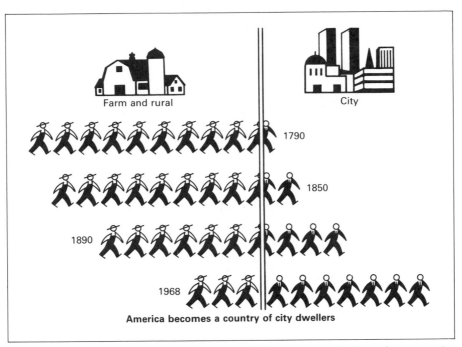

Farm and rural

City

1790

1850

1890

1968

America becomes a country of city dwellers

Note how few words are needed to convey the facts because of the multiple visual cues the listener is given.

2. **Colors.** When color for the lettering or graphics is being chosen, creativity should come second to sound color combinations for ease of viewing. It is wise to avoid too many colors in one visual. Pastel or bright-colored posters look good with black lettering or graphics. White lettering shows up well on dark posters. Remember to avoid using poster paper whose color is too close to the color of the graphics.

3. **Size.** The poster, flip chart, or overhead projection should be large enough to be easily read. Plenty of empty space around the words and design is needed so that the item does not appear crowded. Twenty-four by thirty-six inches is a good size to allow for graphics and empty space.

4. **Lettering.** The size of the lettering on the visual needs to be tested prior to the design of the visual. Trace a word from a stencil with a Magic Marker, and then put the paper up and step to the back of the room for a look. How well can you read the word? How well could you read a whole line of words that size? Lettering of less than an inch and a half is usually too small for an audience of more than fifteen people.

When choosing a lettering style from stencils, use Roman or the style that looks most like block printing. Script, slanted letters, and fancy Gothic lettering are too difficult to read. If you plan to write on your visuals during the talk—PRINT.

Graphics Should Be Well-Spaced and Easy to Read	GRAPHICS SHOULD BE WELL-SPACED AND EASY TO READ

5. **Simplicity.** Too many words, diagrams, or drawings are difficult for an audience to read. The listener should be able to catch the meaning of the visual at a glance. Limit yourself to key words, and use graphics to say what you want to say whenever possible.

6. **Graphics and Abbreviations.** Use arrows, silhouettes, lines, and accepted abbreviations for long words to save space and reading time.

Another aspect of the design of visual aids for presentations is whether the visual is completely prepared prior to the presentation, whether it is designed during the actual talk, or whether it is somewhere on a continuum between these two points:

1. The speaker completely prepares the visuals prior to the presentation. During the presentation, the speaker shows each visual and points to the appropriate part. Using various techniques, you can cover up sections of the visual so that the audience will not read ahead of your speaking.

2. The speaker underlines, circles, and/or checks off points on the visual with a marking pen. Or the speaker uses a partially com-

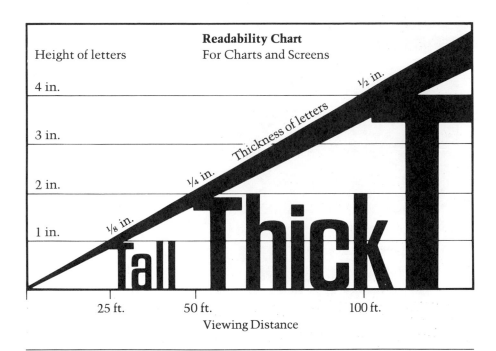

Readability chart for determining size and thickness of letters for nonprojected visuals. Size of lettering on projected visuals should be such that lettering is of adequate size when projected on screen. Make sure that thickness is proportional to height, that spacing between lines is about letter height, and that color aids readability, not fights it.

pleted visual with headings and roughed-in diagrams. During the talk the speaker fills in missing parts with marking pens or prepared stick-on pieces. Or the speaker can design overhead transparencies so that one visual overlays on another and a progressive picture can be shown.

3. The speaker completely develops the visuals during the presentation. (This does not mean preparation has not taken place.) This is the most difficult approach since visuals designed during the talk stand the greatest chance of being messy and incomplete. (Recall how some of your teachers use the chalkboard to design their in-talk visuals.) When writing or drawing on flip charts or overhead transparencies, you must take care not to run the writing (printing) up or down hill. To prevent this, you can trace lightly with a pencil the outline of the words or figures prior to the presentation. During the talk, then, the light lines can be traced over with a marking pen.

THIS IS WHAT A GROUP OF YOUNGSTERS LOOKS LIKE WAITING FOR A SCHOOL BUS AT 5 A.M.

Double and triple sessions are as close to becoming realities in the Capistrano Unified School District as March 7.

On that day, you'll have the opportunity to vote YES on a school bond that will buy us six new schools, 70 badly needed portable classrooms and a number of long awaited district-wide improvements.

Or you can vote NO and start sending your children to school for 6 A.M. classes. Even the five-year-olds.

This kind of alternative isn't out of spite. It's out of desperation.

We've also got over-crowding, tent classrooms and extended days to look forward to.

Here's the situation. A combination of last year's bond defeat, current bursting-at-the-seams enrollment and a projected 1000 students more per year has driven California's fastest growing school district to its knees.

And with building costs increasing at the rate of 1% per month, things can only get worse.

We need your help. Desperately.

Please take the time to get out and vote YES March 7. And help keep our kids' education out of the dark ages.

VOTE YES ON SCHOOL BONDS

Paid for by Bond Election Support Team. For additional information, call (714) 768-6978 or (714) 496-1215, between 8:00 A.M. and 4:30 P.M.

In some instances words cannot convey the message, whereas a visual can convey it immediately and with impact (left).

Sometimes a simple blend of an image and words has impact (below; facing page).

At 55 mph this is what happens to a common honey bee when it hits your windshield.

Survivors wear seatbelts.

The Pepsi Generation grew up and switched to coke.

It seems cocaine is in a class by itself. The upper middle class.

And in the Twin Cities you might be surprised to find out who's got the sweet tooth for nose candy.

Tonight on the *10 PM Report*, WCCO-TV's Mike Walcher investigates the local use of cocaine in a five part series entitled "The Rich Man's Drug." (It's a good title. A couple ounces of this stuff is worth a new car.)

Mike uncovers some startling facts. Like people snorting in Edina. North Oaks. Wayzata. All over suburbia. People who are local business leaders. Sound citizens.

How do these people get their cocaine? How much does it cost them? What are the physical and psychological side effects? What happens when it's mixed with other drugs? And how do the cops feel about these unconventional criminals?

Find out this week when the *10 PM Report* sticks its nose into cocaine.

Cocaine: The Rich Man's Drug
10 PM Report May 7-11

Work your off.

Michael Salerno Exercise for Men & Women, 840 S. Robertson Blvd., 659-4061. By Appointment.

This visual depicts a unique way of using some words for content and using other words only as graphics for visual impact. The words of the heading are to be read; the list of congress members is not meant to be read. The circle around Anderson's name at the end of the list is a graphic technique using words as image, not content.

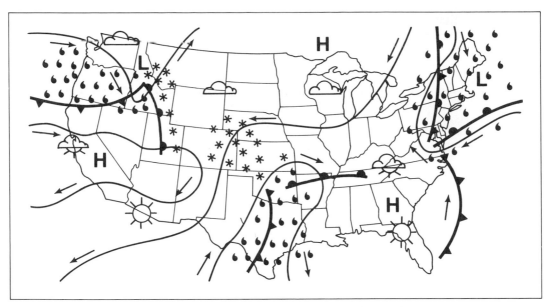

Perhaps the ultimate example of the design and use of a visual aid to convey a complex message in a simple manner can be seen daily on your television weather broadcast. Without the map and the graphics of the sun, clouds, rain drops, snowflakes, and high and low pressure lines, the average viewer would not be able to grasp the national weather. Can you imagine the weather person on your local television station standing erect, looking at the camera, and with no visual aid, attempting to verbally describe the national weather scene?

PRACTICE WITH YOUR VISUALS
PRIOR TO YOUR PRESENTATION

As in rehearsals for the presentation of a play, you should "try out" the parts of your presentation that involve visual aids. Many times speakers just rehearse the verbal part of the speech. Practice when, how, and where you will use the aids. Pay attention to where you will place the visuals once you have referred to them. Become so familiar with the visual aids that you can point to a section accurately with just a brief glance at the visual.

Your rehearsal(s) should include practice in operating the equipment, locating backup bulbs, testing the electrical outlets, measuring the length of cord needed, and testing viewing angles. Know how the drapes close, and where the light switch is.

Before a play is performed for the public, there is a dress rehearsal. You, too, must have a dress rehearsal to put everything together. We have seen that in classroom speaking, the complete rehearsal makes the difference between a B presentation and an A presentation. The dress rehearsal adds the polish that is necessary for excellence.

Word of Caution The visual is an *aid*. It should never become more important than the speaker it is aiding.

WHAT TO KNOW

Illustrative and supportive materials are used in speeches to give substance to the general points the speaker is making, forming what is called the basic message unit. Both illustrative and supportive materials can be used in combination in an informative speech or in a persuasive speech. However, heavy use of illustrative materials is more appropriate to an informative speech, whereas substantial use of supporting materials fits the needs of a persuasive speech better. Locating information on your chosen topic can be as creative as interviewing, surveying, observing, and experimenting, and as traditional as library research.

Visual aids are used in informative and persuasive speeches to enhance the points being made. Visual aid must unfold in synchronization with the speaking. Visual aids should exploit the visual medium. The type of visuals used will depend on the time, resources, and equipment available to the speaker. Visuals should be designed with use of figure/ground relationship, color, size, bold lettering, and simplicity in mind. The effective use of visuals comes with practice.

WHAT TO DO

TV versus Radio Commercials Tape-record five radio commercials for national products and five TV commercials for the same or similar national products. Analyze the commercials along the following lines:

1. Is there a difference between the use of illustrative versus supportive materials in the total group of commercials?
2. Examine the number of illustrative and supportive materials in radio versus TV commercials. Are there more, less, or about the same in the two mediums?
3. In the TV commercials, does the use of visuals meet the criteria given in this chapter?

Use of Supportive and Illustrative Materials in the Classroom Observe the instructors' lectures in your various classes. When your instructor is attempting to prove a point or illuminate the advantages of a particular viewpoint, does he or she use more supportive or more illustrative materials? When your instructor is lecturing on a noncontroversial topic, are more illustrative or supportive materials used?

Visuals in Magazine Advertisements Examine several magazine advertisements for their use of visuals.

1. Can you find definite figure/ground relationships?
2. Note the use of color, size, lettering, and spacing in the ads.
3. If there are people or activities in the ad, how is the product pointed out?

Making a Point The next time you have difficulty giving instructions, directions, procedures, or explaining a complex point, sketch the main points in words on a diagram on a piece of paper for the listener. Also, draw a diagram of circles or boxes that includes all the factors you should take into consideration in studying for an examination. If you haven't thought about this before, your diagram may prove useful in the future.

WHERE TO LEARN MORE

Applebaum, Ronald L., and Karl W. E. Anatol. *Effective Oral Communication for Business and Professions.* Palo Alto, CA: Science Research Associates, 1982. Chapter 9.

Eisenberg, Abné M., and Teri Kwal Gamble. *Painless Public Speaking.* New York: Macmillan, 1982. Chapter 7.

Kinikow, Robert B., and Frank E. McElroy. *Communications for the Safety Professional.* Chicago: National Safety Council, 1975. Chapters 19–25.

Phillips, Gerald M., and J. Jerome Zolten. *Structuring Speech: A How-to-Do-It Book about Public Speaking.* Indianapolis. Bobbs-Merrill, 1976. Chapter 6.

Rodman, George R. *Public Speaking: An Introduction Message Preparation.* New York: Holt, 1978. Chapter 5.

Samovar, Larry A., and Jack Mills. *Oral Communication: Message and Response.* 4th ed. Dubuque, IA: Wm. C. Brown, 1980. Chapter 5.

Walter, Otis M., and Robert L. Scott. *Thinking and Speaking.* New York: Macmillan, 1979. Chapter 3.

White, Eugene E. *Practical Public Speaking.* New York: Macmillan, 1982. Chapter 7.

Zannes, Estelle, and Gerald Goldhaber. *Stand Up, Speak Out.* Reading, MA: Addison-Wesley, 1978. Chapter 5.

ORGANIZING YOUR SPEECH INFORMATION

5

PROPER ORGANIZATION LEADS TO BETTER UNDERSTANDING

Everyone likes speakers who start well, continue on schedule, and quit on time. Also, speakers gain confidence when they know where they are going and how they are going to get there. A well-organized speech is easier for a speaker to give and for an audience to understand. In fact, the main purpose of organizing our ideas is to increase the possibility of having our information comprehended and retained by listeners.

He must adapt his speeches to occasions and persons: His openings must be tactful, his statement of facts clear, his proof cogent, his rebuttals trenchant, and his perorations vehement.

CICERO

Considerable research in theories and techniques of public speaking warns us, however, to be careful of how much emphasis we place on organizing a speech. Several studies indicate that the exact order of presenting main ideas has little relation to audience comprehension and attitude change. Other research shows that "well-structured" messages improve comprehension, and that the addition of repetition and transitions further increases the amount of material comprehended and retained. The conclusion is that some organization of materials is superior to poor or no organization of the message. Our suggestion then is to organize, but to organize simply. For, according to Gerald Kennedy, a Methodist preacher:

First, too many of us do not work on our preaching hard enough or long enough. The more gifted a man is, the more he is tempted to neglect his preparation. You listen to a man and he brings out an interesting point here or there, but there is no sense of solid structure. He makes too much of one point and too little of another. He milks an illustration dry, and what would have been effective if kept short and sharp loses its cutting edge and gets wearisome. Such a man circles back to something already dealt with and there is no sense of the inevitable, forward march of the thought.

Secondly, too many preachers fail to organize their material so that it is at once plain and clear. The people leave with a vague sense of something religious having been said, but the points which give a subject directness

"I would've left, too, but I'm the next speaker."

THE SATURDAY EVENING POST

are either hopelessly smudged and muddled or they were never there in the first place. I have lectured on this, written about it, and discussed it at every opportunity, but it has done little good. So many preachers will not believe that their first responsibility is to be understood. I still have church members come up after the sermon and say, with a kind of wonderment, "I understood you." To organize your material does not take special gifts and it does not demand any great intelligence. But it does demand the assumption that an involved and obscure style is not so much a sign of profundity of thought as of confusion of mind.[1]

Once you gain skill in ordering your ideas and settle on a method that works effectively for you, that same approach can be applied to writing articles and giving lessons, as well as to presenting speeches. Organizing ability is an extraordinarily valuable asset in effectively communicating your ideas to someone else.

[1] From *While I'm on My Feet* by Gerald Kennedy, copyright © 1963 by Abingdon Press. Used by permission.

TYPES OF ORGANIZATION

CONVERSATIONAL ORGANIZATION

The simplest form of organization is used in everyday conversation. We make a point and give an illustration or we give an illustration and make a point. For instance, someone dashes up to us and excitedly exclaims, "I'm the happiest person alive!" (That's the point.) "I lost fifteen pounds, John gave me this engagement ring, and we have set our wedding date!" (That's the illustration.) Or the sequence is reversed, with the illustration or example being given first, and the point being made immediately afterward. Diagrammatically, it looks like this:

I. I'm the happiest person alive
   A. I lost fifteen pounds
   B. I received an engagement ring
   C. We set our wedding date

Or, if reversed:

   A. I lost fifteen pounds
   B. I received an engagement ring
   C. We set our wedding date
I. I'm the happiest person alive

This conversational pattern is the basis for every approach to organizing a speech. Let's expand and vary it to see what happens.

ONE-POINT ORGANIZATION

If we start a conversation or speech with a story, a quotation, or some statistics that have a moral or a point, and then we state the point and follow with other research, illustrations, and examples that support the point; and if we conclude with a rephrasing or eloquent statement of the point, we have organized our talk into a pattern popularized by a speech teacher named Alan H. Monroe. In outline form it looks like this:

   A. Illustration or proof
I. Main idea
   B. Examples, quotations, research, stories, et cetera
I. Restatement of main idea

This is a rather simple organizational plan that can be used for presenting a short speech that has just one main idea. Many writers cast brief newspaper and magazine articles into this pattern of organization.

HO HUM! ORGANIZATION

So far we have followed a rational pattern for presenting a single main idea. Let's now examine the psychological aspects of organizing our ideas, so that we *feel* the "forward motion of thought" as well as think it.

Another noted speech teacher and author, Richard Borden, felt that too often students were organizing speeches for themselves and not for the audience. He designed a speech plan that looks like this:

1. Ho hum!
2. Why bring that up?
3. For example . . .
4. So what?

Ho Hum!   The Borden plan can be used properly when the prospective speaker imagines that as he or she stands up to speak, the audience will collectively sigh in boredom "Ho hum!" The speaker must plan something to capture their attention:

- Ask a series of questions that will stimulate thinking.
- Quote an impressive statistic.
- Tell a humorous story.
- Make a provocative statement.

THE SATURDAY EVENING POST

Why bring that up? If the speaker starts well and gains the interest of the audience, he or she then imagines the audience asking, "Why are you bringing that up?" The successful speaker must say something that gives the audience a desire or reward for listening. All of us are a bit selfish, and before we do anything, we want to know: What's in it for me? and Why is this important to me?

- Use illustrations to demonstrate the negative effects of not knowing more about the subject.
- Suggest benefits to be gained by understanding your subject.

For example . . . If the speaker gains the attention of the listeners and successfully stimulates them to seek the rewards of continued listening, then they will invite him or her to go on, "For example?" "What?" "Get on with it." The organized speaker will then unfold the main ideas:

- Give the main points and then three or four supporting points.
- Explain, illustrate, prove, or demonstrate each supporting point.
- Keep relating your ideas back to the main point and the importance of your subject.

So what? As the speaker nears the end of the presentation, everyone will want to know: "So what?" The audience is really saying, "Okay, you caught my attention, got me involved in your ideas, and explained everything in an interesting way, but so what? What specifically do you want me to understand or do when I leave here?" The speaker will then point out the main idea and give the audience a suggestion for using the information in some beneficial way:

- Present a challenge.
- Give a small inducement.
- State your own personal intention.
- Summarize by using a final illustration.

Remember, earlier we suggested that once you gain some skill in introducing, ordering, and concluding your ideas, you can use that skill in writing, speaking, and teaching.

Can you see a similar plan of organization in the presentation on page 111?

We can use conversational organization for very brief presentations, one-point organization for concise development of a single idea, and ho hum! organization to respond to the subtle requests that most audiences make to speakers.

Why do I love Wella Balsam Conditioner? Because beautiful hair doesn't just happen.*

—Cheryl Ladd

I love the outdoors. But wind, sun and water can really damage my hair. So I take extra-special care of it with Wella Balsam Conditioner, the original balsam conditioner.

I love Wella Balsam because it leaves your hair soft, manageable and full-bodied. Gives you back the smooth, supple texture and healthy-looking highlights you love.

You see, Wella Balsam has a special formula which actually unites with the hair shaft to help prevent damage and protect delicate hair strands. And Wella Balsam is pH-balanced and non-oily. To keep your hair feeling strong, silky and easy-to-comb between shampoos.

Do something beautiful for your hair today. Try Wella Balsam Conditioner. It's the original and, as far as I'm concerned, still the greatest. You'll love your hair.

*Trademark The Wella Corp. © 1977

In this advertisement, the first two paragraphs get our attention, entice us to listen, and give us the main subject. The third paragraph develops the subject with two main points. The final paragraph answers the "so what?" question and presents us with a challenge as well as a personal endorsement.

A Creative Résumé Helped Wilson Land a Better Job

It takes an all-out effort to find a good job, unless you have two or three years to spend in the process.

I knew an all-out effort was needed in 1975 when I wanted to make a switch from the health care field back to a communication position with business and industry.

I knew what kind of job I wanted, and I knew I wanted to stay in southern California, but I had two basic uncertainties: (1) how to uncover job openings (most of which are not advertised) and (2) how to impress the person with hiring power enough to at least get the interview.

Having been in the hiring situation myself, faced with 300 look-alike résumés, I decided a different approach was called for. With the help of some friends, my résumé was turned into a four-fold brochure with photos. My experience and education were outlined briefly, with emphasis on contributions I could make to a company or organization.

Many people think employers are turned off by the "cute" résumés, but it was successful in opening a lot of doors for me. I decided not to copy what others do, but to creatively devise something around my own personality and experience.

The second strategic decision was to mail the brochure to the president or chief executive officer of target companies. Why these top people? For several reasons. In my experience, these executives are more impressed with creativity than some may think. How often have you received a booklet from the head of the company with a note reading, "This is a good example of . . . "?

The president is also a good target because (a) if he or she sends the résumé to a subordinate with a positive note, the underling *must* follow up, and (b) the top dog may know of an opening that is about to occur or even create one if sufficiently impressed.

It took a lot of homework. I spent hours at the library with the Southern California Business Directory published by the Chamber of Commerce. From it, I selected some eighty companies based on size, industry, number of employees.

The brochure went out with a short personal note to the CEO or president.

The response was tremendous. Almost all wrote back. It turned up six job possibilities. And at least one that was just right for me.

SOURCE: Reprinted from *IABC Journal of Organizational Communication.*

INTRODUCTION, BODY, AND CONCLUSION ORGANIZATION (IBC)

Most experts in the speech profession agree that an important idea should be introduced, developed, and concluded. Plato suggested that in order for a speech to come alive it must have a head, body, and tail. As you develop a plan for organizing your ideas, keep in mind this checklist:

1. Does my introduction get attention, help the listeners feel the importance of my ideas, and lead them to the main subject of my speech?
2. Does the body of my speech present about three main points and clearly illustrate or prove each one in an interesting manner?
3. Does the conclusion review the main ideas, tie everything back to the main subject, and motivate my listeners to accept and use my ideas?

For an organizational plan capable of handling a main theme and several supporting points as well as following the psychological needs of a listening audience, we recommend the following:

INTRODUCTION   **Attention** Your "attention getter" goes here.

Importance The importance of your subject to the audience comes next. "Why should we listen?"

Theme or Purpose What specifically are you going to explain or suggest that the listeners do?

BODY   **First main point**
Illustrative or supportive materials

Second main point
Illustrative or supportive materials

Third main point
Illustrative or supportive materials

CONCLUSION   State what you want the audience to understand or do and end with a final summary, illustration, or application of your main theme.

Check whether the "attention" and "importance" ideas lead directly to a specific main theme. Then examine each main point to determine whether it directly supports the main theme. Finally, determine whether the conclusion creates a strong final impact on the audience and actually concludes the main theme. If your answer is yes to each of these questions, you probably have a well-organized speech.

THE BODY OF THE SPEECH

Usually, in preparing and organizing a speech, the speaker selects the main topic and develops the body of the speech first. Deciding how to begin and end the speech is generally left until later in the preparation process.

> *If art is a power reaching its end by a definite path, that is, by ordered methods, no one can doubt that there is such a method and order in good speaking.*
>
> QUINTILIAN

The body of the speech must have valuable and interesting information. That information must be organized in such a way that it moves the speech along and at the same time makes sense. Most speech authorities agree that there are four basic ways of organizing the main ideas presented in the body of the speech: chronological or time sequence, space or geographical sequence, topical sequence, and logical sequence.

CHRONOLOGICAL OR TIME SEQUENCE

This pattern of organizing the main points in the body of the speech means that what you say moves forward or backward in time from a specific point in time. In other words, you organize according to the time when the events occurred. This sequence works well when you are talking about a person's development, a scientific process, or how to do something, or reporting an experience of some sort. For example, a talk on hypnosis might be arranged into a discussion of its origin, present use, and future expectations. A report on how to prepare a speech might include: (1) selecting a subject, (2) gathering material, (3) organizing ideas, and (4) preparing the delivery. Presenting a talk on your trip around England could move chronologically from: "Our first impressions . . . later on we saw . . . And, finally, we discovered . . . "

SPACE OR GEOGRAPHICAL SEQUENCE

The subject matter of your speech may divide more naturally into a spatial pattern. If, for example, you were describing the present state of education in the United States, you could talk about education in the northern, southern, eastern, and western states. You might talk about a university in terms of the peripheral, central, and core buildings. In using a space sequence, you compare one area of something with another area so that the audience moves systematically through the subject matter.

TOPICAL SEQUENCE

When the preceding patterns seem unsuitable for organizing the main ideas to be presented in the body of your speech, you could determine whether the main ideas fall into a "natural" sequence. For example, talking about university personnel might include a discussion of the administration, faculty, and student body; or you might talk about the effects of pornography on men, women, and children. If your speech seems to consist of three or four similar or related main ideas, the topical pattern is probably the best way to organize.

It is usually preferable to move from a less interesting idea to a more interesting one. If, however, your "topics" or main ideas are unequal in their strength for stimulating audience interest, you may want to put a stronger idea first, a strong idea second, and the strongest idea last. In this way, you avoid a presentation that concludes on an anticlimactic note. Consider, also, that if the subject matter is complex, it will be best to move from simpler ideas to more difficult ones, as when explaining a highly complicated skill or process.

LOGICAL SEQUENCE

The logical pattern for arranging ideas involves moving from a cause to an effect, or from a problem to a solution. As a speaker you may wish to inform an audience of the effects of raising income taxes, or you may wish to inform your listeners how a certain problem was solved. In either case, you are informing your audience. The logical sequencing of ideas is more often and more easily used in persuasive speeches, when you take sides on an issue and present arguments in support of your position. "Yale locks are the best in the world because (1) they are made of U.S. steel, (2) they are burglarproof, and (3) they are easily installed." Following a logical order simply means to move from one point to another so that a position is defended with evidence and reasoning. Or an explanation is presented to describe how a position was defended, a problem was solved, or an effect followed a cause.

Whenever possible, use one of these patterns of organization because it will serve as a memory device to assist you and the audience in remembering the ideas presented in the speech. Our minds have already been programmed to think chronologically, spacially, topically, and logically. When we are well organized, it becomes easier for us to remember the order of ideas presented, and a minimum of notes are needed. If we then organize the ideas in the minds of the listeners they also will have a better chance of remembering our main points.

Having devoted time to the body of the speech, we now need to consider more carefully the introduction and conclusion. Every good speech, whether long or short, must have a strong beginning and end. Many speakers devote so much time to their main ideas that they do not plan how to open and close a speech effectively. An effective speaker, as we have shown in our former examples of speech plans, gains attention quickly at the outset of the talk and wisely uses the conclusion to create a strong impact on the audience.

THE BORN LOSER　　　　　　　　　　　　　　　　　**By Art Sansom**

THE INTRODUCTION

Good introductions get audience attention, demonstrate the importance of the subject, and lead into the main idea of the presentation. We will now take a look at some popular ways to start a speech.

REFERENCE TO THE AUDIENCE, OCCASION, OR PURPOSE OF THE GATHERING

This approach tends to quickly unite speaker and audience. Even though the speaker is a stranger, he or she may soon become a friend by referring to something that is familiar to the audience. A certain informality and relaxation is present when the speaker associates with the mood of the audience and the nature of the occasion that brings them together. An excellent example is provided by Nikolai A. Bulganin, Premier of Soviet Russia and second successor to Stalin, when he opened the Geneva Conference of July 18, 1955:

> On behalf of the Soviet government, I am happy to greet Mr. Dwight Eisenhower, the President of the United States, M. Edgar Faure, the Prime Minister of France, and Sir Anthony Eden, the Prime Minister of Great Britain, and also the members of their delegations and to express a sincere wish that the work of our conference be a fruitful one. . . .

> We were glad to hear President Eisenhower's statement, namely: The American people want to be friends with the Soviet peoples.

> There are no natural differences between our peoples or our nations. There are no territorial conflicts or commercial rivalries.

> Historically, our two countries have always been at peace. Further, Mr. President pointed out the need to lift artificial barriers between the two peoples.

> We are in complete agreement with that since the lifting of the said barriers would meet both the national interests of the Soviet and American peoples and the interests of universal peace.

> The principal purpose of our conference is to find ways to achieve the necessary understanding on the problems to be settled. The delegation of the Soviet Union has come to this conference with the desire to find, through joint efforts by all the participants, solutions for the outstanding issues and for its part, is prepared to give careful consideration to the proposals advanced by the other participants.[2]

---

[2]In Lewis Copeland, ed., *The World's Great Speeches*, 2nd ed. New York: Dover, 1958, p. 631.

Identifying with the audience by including yourself among them in terms of general interests, common problems, and similar backgrounds is one of the most popular ways to begin a speech. Referring to the occasion or purpose for which the audience has gathered also generates a common bond of interest between the speaker and the audience.

DIRECT REFERENCE TO THE TOPIC

Probably the most common method of beginning a speech when time cannot be wasted is direct reference to the topic, if the subject matter is not abrasive to the audience. Examples of the direct-reference approach sound like this:

> Today I would like to examine some of the results of poor public-speaking techniques and make three suggestions for correcting the situation.

> Every day we engage in the decision-making process without knowing how to check our efficiency for making good decisions. I would like to explain an assessment instrument designed by Organizational Associates to measure our decision-making effectiveness.

> Religion is not the opium of a capitalistic society used to keep the poor from rebelling against the rich, and I will prove it!

The direct-reference approach assumes that the audience is ready to listen and does not need much "attention getting" stimulation. Consequently, the introduction is brief and uses few words.

RHETORICAL QUESTIONS

A speech may begin with a series of questions that the audience is not expected to answer. The questions serve to stimulate the listeners' interest and lead them to the main topic of the speech. Jawaharlal Nehru, former prime minister of India, began a speech at the Asian Conference in 1947 in the following manner:

> Friends and fellow Asians, what has brought you here, men and women of Asia? Why have you come from the various countries of this mother continent of ours and gathered together in the ancient city of Delhi? Some of us, greatly daring, sent you invitations for this Conference and you gave a warm welcome to that invitation. And yet it was not merely the call from us, but some deeper urge that brought you here.[3]

[3] In Lewis Copeland, ed. *The World's Great Speeches*, 2nd ed. New York: Dover, 1958, p. 617.

In a more provocative question approach, you might ask your audience, "What would you do if you had just been informed of your wife's death?" or, "What if you had just inherited $10,000; how would you invest it?"

HUMOR, STORIES, AND QUOTATIONS

Using humor and/or beginning with stories and quotations are also helpful ways to win audience attention. But be sure, in each instance, that the humor, story, or quotation is connected to the main topic of your speech. To fail in this respect will only mislead the audience and label your introduction "gimmicky" instead of sincere. Notice the following use of humor in an introduction:

> You are right about teachers. If everything else fails, you become a teacher. Look at me. I came to this university ten years ago and applied for the job of elevator operator but was quickly fired because I couldn't learn the route!

In this case, the punch line might be funny but where does it direct us? Are we to conclude that university faculty members indeed are fired from previous positions and that they are intolerably stupid? Humorous beginnings are effective if they are not misused.

The type of introduction you select must be brief, relevant, and attractive. For every minute of introduction, you should have about three or four minutes of body or development and at least a half minute for the conclusion. The introduction must clearly lead to the theme or topic of the speech. And, of course, any beginning needs to stimulate the listeners and put them in a "willingness to listen" frame of mind.

Examine the introductions of speeches by a university president, a lecturer, a speech professor, and a U.S. president that follow on pages 120–122.

THE CONCLUSION

In our final efforts to keep our ideas organized and leave a good impression on the audience, we must consider how to conclude our speech. Your authors heard a former president of the United States end a magnificent speech so abruptly that the startled audience sat quietly until a senator rose to his feet and started applauding.

A Private University Looks at Government Regulation: The First Amendment and the School

Dalin H. Oaks, President, Brigham Young University

Delivered before the National Association of College and University Attorneys, Dallas, Texas, June 18, 1976

I think it was Will Rogers who tried to give comfort about high taxes by reminding us that "We're just lucky we're not gettin' all the government we're payin' for." Since Will Rogers' time taxes have soared, but government has rocketed. I contend that our tax dollar is now buying too much government, and we ought to hold out for less.

Twenty-five years ago, higher education was generally free from government direction and anxious to defend that freedom. In 1952 the Commission on Financing Higher Education declared that the strength of higher education was "founded upon its freedom," which "must be protected at all costs." The Commission predicted that dependence on federal financing would bring government controls that would destroy cherished originality and diversity and "would in the end produce uniformity, mediocrity, and compliance."

That prediction has been realized.

In the Heads of the Listeners: Principles of Communication

Waldo W. Braden, Boyd Professor of Speech, Louisiana State University

Delivered before the Louisiana Trial Lawyers Association, New Orleans, Louisiana, September 9, 1977

When I looked over your program I felt very much alone. Among your speakers are the mayor of New Orleans, a former governor of Arkansas, a dean of a law school, the speaker of the Louisiana House of Representatives, a law professor, and a psychiatrist. I noted that the other speakers are speaking upon highly technical subjects connected with the practice of the law. What is a speech professor doing in this company?

As I studied the program I was reminded of a story that Sol M. Linowitz, a prominent lawyer, told about William Howard Taft's great-granddaughter.

When she was asked to write her autobiography in the third grade, the young lady responded: "My great-grandfather was President of the United States, my grandfather was a United States Senator, my father is an ambassador, and I am a brownie."

On this morning at this elegant hotel here in the French Quarter in this distinguished company, I feel like a brownie.

Panama Canal Treaties: A New Sense of Trust among Neighbors

Jimmy Carter, President of the United States

Delivered to the American people from the White House, Washington, D.C., February 1, 1978

Good evening. Seventy-five years ago our nation signed a treaty which gave us rights to build a canal across Panama—to take the historic step of joining the Atlantic and Pacific Oceans. The results of the agreement have been of great benefit to ourselves and to other nations throughout the world who navigate the high seas. The building of the canal was one of the greatest engineering feats of history.

Although massive in concept and construction, it's relatively simple in design and has been reliable and efficient in operation. We Americans are justly and deeply proud of this great achievement.

The canal has also been a source of pride and benefit to the people of Panama, but a cause of some continuing discontent because we have controlled a 10-mile-wide strip of land across the heart of their country. And because they considered the original terms of the agreement to be unfair, the people of Panama have been dissatisfied with the treaty.

It was drafted here in our country and was not signed by any Panamanian. Our own Secretary of State, who did sign the original treaty, said it was vastly advantageous to the United States and not so advantageous to Panama.

In 1964, after consulting with former Presidents Truman and Eisenhower, President Johnson committed our nation to work toward a new treaty with the Republic of Panama. And last summer, after 14 years of negotiations under two Democratic Presidents and two Republican Presidents, we reached and signed an agreement that is fair and beneficial to both countries.

SOURCES: Vital Speeches 32:23 (Sept. 15, 1976): 722 (*left, facing page*). *Ibid*. 44:2 (Nov. 1, 1977): 42 (*right, facing page*). *Ibid*. 44:9 (Feb. 15, 1978): 258 (*above*).

The Little Platoon We Belong to in Society: Do We Dare to Have Children?

Russell Kirk, Author and Lecturer

Delivered at the Center for Constructive Alternatives, Hillsdale College, Hillsdale, Michigan, September 25, 1977

On the cover of a textbook used last year by my little daughters in their parish school, there was printed the legend, "The family does things together." Over this line appeared a picture of a family doing things together. What were they doing together? Why, they were sitting in a semicircle, watching the television set.

Were familial submission to the boob-tube the chief surviving common bond among members of the same household, then indeed society's fabric would be very nearly unravelled. For the family always has been the source and the center of community. In the phrase of Edmund Burke, the family is the origin of "the little platoon we belong to in society," and it is "the germ of public affections." The family is held together by the strongest of human bonds—by love, and by the demands of self-preservation. The family commences in *eros,* but grows into *agapo.* Its essential function is the rearing of children. Those societies of the past and the present which we call good societies have been strongly marked by powerful family ties. These have been societies possessed of a high degree of both order and freedom. Societies in which the family has been enfeebled have been disorderly and servile societies—lacking love, lacking security.

SOURCE: *Vital Speeches* 44:7 (Jan. 15, 1978): 200

Some ways to conclude a speech so that audiences leave with a favorable impression, remember the speech longer, and are more persuaded to think as you do are demonstrated in the following examples, which use restatement of main topic, quotations, and various personal appeals.

After You Get Where You're Going, Where Will You Be? Pucker Up and Let Her Go

Max D. Isaacson, Vice President, Macmillan Oil Company

Delivered to the Optimist Club, Des Moines, Iowa, November 9, 1977

Finally, the Optimist Creed tells us to "press on to greater achievements of the future" and I want to leave you with a beautiful thought by some unknown author . . . perhaps a teen-ager . . . who wrote:

God said "Build a better world" and I said "How? The world is such a cold dark place and so complicated now: And I so young and useless, there's nothing I can do." But God in all his wisdom said: "Just build a better you!"

SOURCE: *Vital Speeches* 44:7 (Jan. 15, 1978): 205.

A Universal Measurement Language: Why the Metric System?

Ernest L. Boyer, United States Commissioner of Education

Delivered at the National Metric Education Conference, Providence, Rhode Island, September 25, 1978

Change in the metric sense is moving not from bad to worse but from bad to good.

Ideally, this move should be made swiftly, not incrementally. Senator William Fullbright pointed up the disadvantage of a conservative approach in this way: When the Swedes decided to switch drivers from the left side of the road to the right side, they decided to first switch only the truck drivers to the right side. Six months later, they agreed, automobile drivers would convert.

Metric will not happen overnight, but it will happen. No country can survive in a world of measurement isolation.

SOURCE: *Vital Speeches* 45:7 (Jan. 15, 1979): 204.

Democratic Convention Keynote Address: Who Then Will Speak for the Common Good?

Barbara Jordan,
Congresswoman from Texas

Delivered to the Nation, July 12, 1976

Now, I began this speech by commenting to you on the uniqueness of a Barbara Jordan making the keynote address. Well I am going to close my speech by quoting a Republican President and I ask you that as you listen to these words of Abraham Lincoln, relate them to the concept of a national community in which every last one of us participates:

As I would not be a slave, so I would not be a master. This expresses my idea of Democracy. Whatever differs from this, to the extent of the difference is no Democracy.

SOURCE: *Vital Speeches* 32:21 (August 15, 1976): 646.

Former President of the United States, John F. Kennedy, gave one of the most eloquent and remembered conclusions to a speech when he ended his 1961 Inaugural Address:

> And so, my fellow Americans: ask not what your country can do for you—ask what you can do for your country. My fellow citizens of the world: ask not what America will do for you but what together we can do for the freedom of man. Finally, whether you are citizens of America or citizens of the world, ask of us here the same high standards of strength and sacrifice which we ask of you. With a good conscience our only sure reward, with history the final judge of our deeds, let us go forth to lead the land we love, asking His blessing and His help, but knowing that here on earth God's work must truly be our own.

And, of course, even elementary school children are acquainted with the patriotic conclusion used by Patrick Henry before the Virginia Convention of Delegates in 1775.

It is in vain, sir, to extenuate the matter. Gentlemen may cry peace, peace—but there is no peace. The war is actually begun! The next gale that sweeps from the north will bring to our ears the clash of resounding arms! Our brethren are already in the field! Why stand we here idle? What is it that gentlemen wish? What would they have? Is life so dear, or peace so sweet, as to be purchased at the price of chains and slavery? Forbid it, Almighty God! I know not what course other may take; but as for me, give me liberty, or give me death!

A speech conclusion presents a final opportunity for a speaker to have an impact on the audience. Such an opportunity must not be wasted by poor preparation. Succinctness, eloquence, and sincerity are the hallmarks of successful conclusions.

> *The sound rhetorical student cannot discard all rules. Eloquent speeches are not the result of momentary inspirations but the product of research, analysis, practice, and application.*
>
> QUINTILIAN

If you haven't already noticed the organization of this textbook, take a careful look at the first chapter, the table of contents, and the concluding chapter and see whether the authors have followed the principles of effectively introducing, developing, and concluding their ideas! Look at each chapter and decide whether it has an "attention" step, stresses the importance of the subject, develops a main idea successfully, and summarizes and applies the main idea in the conclusion.

BRINGING IT ALL TOGETHER

Most speakers, after spending time gathering and organizing ideas, make the mistake of assuming that they have a well-organized presentation ready for delivery. They omit a final opportunity to "bring it all together." We have developed the following procedure as a guide to good organization. Try it when you think you have a speech ready to present.

In brief sentences write:

1. The main theme or purpose of your speech.
2. Three points that support and develop the main point.

3. a. One thought that gets attention
   b. One thought that shows the importance of listening to your subject.
   c. One thought that would make a great conclusion.
4. Now arrange these sentences so that they follow this sequence:
   a. Attention
   b. Importance
   c. Theme or purpose
   d. Three supporting points
   e. Concluding idea
5. See whether you have an illustration, some evidence, or an example to support each of your three points.
6. Run through in your mind the whole sequence of ideas, and answer these questions:
   a. Do the attention and importance steps lead directly to the thesis idea?
   b. Do the three points specifically support the thesis idea?
   c. Does the conclusion directly relate to the thesis and specific purpose of the speech?

FINAL CHECK

- Does every point direct my audience to the response I want?
- Does every point lead to the next one?
- Do I make easy transitions, repeat my thesis several times, and summarize so everyone knows where we are at all times?
- Am I apologetic, too long, or irrelevant?
- Are my ideas exciting and rewarding to my listeners and myself?

WHAT TO KNOW

A public speech requires some kind of organization, though the exact steps should be a product of the speaker, the speaker's material, and the audience. There is no standard structure for organizing all speeches, but definite organization is necessary. The basic message unit (point → illustration/proof or proof/illustration → point) is the beginning of organization even in conversing. This chapter focuses on other organizational patterns such as Borden's Ho Hum structure and your authors' variation of the traditional introduction, body, and conclusion format.

Within the speech, the main body also needs its own structure. Four basic ways of sequencing main ideas in the body are: chronological-time, space/geographical, topical, and logical.

Attention should also be given to introducing and concluding your speech. Your introduction should get audience attention, demonstrate the importance of the subject, and lead into the main idea of the presentation. Your conclusion should tie the whole speech together. A restatement of the main theme, a summary of the points covered, an appropriate quotation, a personal appeal, or a statement of challenge, among others, can be used to effectively conclude your speech on a high note.

WHAT TO DO

Reader's Digest Examine the various articles in an issue of *Reader's Digest*. What purpose does the brief summary statement directly above or below the article's title serve? Skim some of the articles, focusing on topic headings and the first sentence in paragraphs. Note the organizational structure of the content of the articles. Now concentrate on reading just the opening few paragraphs and the closing paragraphs of the articles. What introductory and concluding methods appear to be used the most frequently?

Having looked at the articles in *Reader's Digest*, why do you think more "stolen" or plagiarized student speeches have come from *Reader's Digest* than from any other magazine?

(*Note:* Most speech-communication teachers subscribe to *Reader's Digest* nowadays.)

Vital Speeches Read or listen to two or three speeches from *Vital Speeches*. Analyze the overall organizational structure. Evaluate how well you like the introductions and conclusions.

WHERE TO LEARN MORE

Bormann, Ernest G., and Nancy C. Bormann. *Speech Communication: A Comprehensive Approach.* 3rd ed. New York: Harper & Row, 1981.

Ehninger, Douglas, Alan H. Monroe, and Bruce E. Gronbeck. *Principles and Types of Speech Communication.* 8th ed. Glenview, IL: Scott, Foresman, 1978. Chapters 9–12.

Minnick, Wayne, C. *Public Speaking.* 2d ed. Boston: Houghton Mifflin, 1983. Chapter 4.

Samovar, Larry A., and Jack Mills. *Oral Communication: Message and Response.* 5th ed. Dubuque, IA: Wm. C. Brown, 1982.

DELIVERING YOUR IDEAS

6

EFFECTIVE DELIVERY IS IMPORTANT

One of the most fascinating observations of changes in human behavior can be observed in the classroom. The class members are all sitting in a circle in the room. The instructor directs a question to the whole class: "Let's discuss what the aspects of good delivery are. Does anyone want to start by mentioning a factor you think is related to a good delivery? Be sure to give an example in your comments."

Most of the students are looking at the instructor or at other members of the class. A few students offer their remarks. After four or five students have commented, the instructor says: "Now let's shift gears a minute. Will those of you who haven't said anything yet think about what you'll say when I call on you. Describe a factor that you feel is related to good delivery and give a specific example also."

There is now a noticeable shifting and straightening of posture by those left to speak. Eye contact with the instructor diminishes as the students appear to be thinking. As these next four or five students give their comments as requested, it is obvious that the talkers are more nervous. They tighten up when called on and appear to sigh in relief when their "talk" is over. There are more "ahs" and "uhms" between their words.

The next time the instructor speaks, she says: "For those of you who have not had the opportunity to comment, I would like you to take two minutes to write down on a piece of paper a few key words related to what you want to say. And oh, yes, would you please stand when I call for your comments."

Those class members who have not spoken go into a frenzy of shifting around. They take out a piece of paper but little writing takes place. Some look at the clock as if they are hoping the hands of the clock would get to the end of the hour before they have to speak. Some have a "why me?" look on their faces. The students who have already spoken glance at each other with a look of relief on their faces. As the remaining students stand and attempt to make their comments, it is obvious that they are very nervous—they stare at the floor, twist the paper in their hands, and shift from one foot to the other.

What has gone on here? In one respect, very little is different in the three situations. The request for personal comments has remained the same. The second group were given a few minutes to think about their remarks, and were instructed to speak rather than to volunteer comments. The last group were told to write a few words on a piece of paper and speak from a position about two feet higher than the previous speakers. On the other hand, something quite significant has gone on in the last two groups' minds. They have reacted with increased stage fright the closer the request came to their mental picture of "giving a speech." A similar reaction can also be witnessed when someone is on the way to the dentist, or is going to get an injection from the doctor. Our mental picture of what is going to happen is sometimes more difficult to deal with than the event itself.

Much of the beginning speaker's problem is learning to deal with nervousness or anticipation of speaking. The beginner will eventually learn that there will always be nervousness on an important occasion, but that this nervousness can be used to advantage.

> *What you are stands over you the while, and thunders so that I cannot hear what you say to the contrary.*
>
> RALPH WALDO EMERSON

How we say something is as important as what we say. Let's move ahead to some items related to the delivery of a presentation that will help channel nervous energy to more constructive use.

"Seems a bit nervous."

THE SATURDAY EVENING POST

FOUR TYPES OF DELIVERY

There are four basic types of delivery—manuscript, memorized, impromptu, and extemporaneous—each with its respective advantages and disadvantages. We will look at each and take the position that extemporaneous delivery is the best type for most general speaking situations.

MANUSCRIPT DELIVERY

Manuscript delivery refers to a presentation that is completely written out in advance. The speech is then read to the audience.

Reasons for Reading from Manuscript

1. The speech is a major policy statement by an official.
2. Technical or legal material is being presented and will be quoted or covered in the news media.
3. A careful choosing of words is crucial to the success of the presentation.

Disadvantages of Reading from Manuscript

1. The sentences may look good on paper but may not sound adequate when read; the speech may sound mechanical.
2. Any spontaneous directness with the audience is lost. The audience feels it is being "talked at."
3. Speaker's eye contact with audience is reduced.
4. Speaker flexibility is reduced. Speaker cannot adapt to changed conditions—cannot lengthen or shorten the speech.
5. Preparation time is longer than that of the extemporaneous speech.

MEMORIZED DELIVERY

Memorized presentation means the speech is written out, as in the manuscript approach, but rather than being read, it is committed to memory. People who have difficulty "thinking on their feet," and who do not want to read to their audience often attempt to memorize their talks.

Reasons for Memorizing

1. The speaker can present a very precisely worded speech and yet have the freedom to move about and use materials.

2. The speech may contain colorful language or quotations that can be delivered with more impact and expression because the speaker is able, with eye contact and gestures, to direct attention to the audience.

Disadvantages of Memorizing

1. The speaker can forget.
2. Unless there has been considerable rehearsal and practice with vocal variety, the presentation will sound mechanical. (The speech will sound memorized.)
3. The speaker cannot adapt to special conditions prior to or during the talk.
4. If the speaker does deviate any time during the talk to elaborate or make additional comments that were not part of the memorized speech, the audience will be able to notice the difference in delivery.
5. The audience senses that it is being "talked at."

IMPROMPTU DELIVERY

An impromptu presentation is a speech given with little if any advance preparation. The speaker relies on personal knowledge and speaking skills to get through the situation. The content of the talk depends on what the speaker can think of and express on the spot.

Reasons for Impromptu Speaking

1. A person is called on unexpectedly to speak, as in a meeting.
2. The speaker wishes to appear spontaneous, and talk "to" the group rather than "at" them.
3. The speaker can be extremely flexible in adapting to the listeners and the situation, including questions and comments.

Disadvantages of Impromptu Speaking

1. The speaker can ramble or be repetitive.
2. The speaker may make inappropriate or immature judgments.
3. The speaker may have nonfluent delivery.

EXTEMPORANEOUS DELIVERY

An extemporaneous presentation is one in which the speaker has planned the talk thoroughly but has not planned which words will be used to express each point. The desired points and their order are known, but their final form is uncertain. Thus the extemporaneous speech combines the best of the manuscript and impromptu approaches.

Reasons for Extemporaneous Speaking

1. Direct communication with the audience is encouraged.
2. The artificial manner of the manuscript and memorization presentations is avoided because the speaker must consider the final form when speaking.
3. The speaker can adjust the length of the talk by skipping a subpoint or adding an example or two.
4. The speaker can adjust to the feedback and apparent response from the audience by going into more or less detail.

Disadvantages of Extemporaneous Speaking

1. The speaker may have poor language choice.
2. The speaker can deviate too far from the speech's outline by developing a point further than was intended in the original outline.
3. If the presentation must be repeated, it will vary each time it is given.

Unless the situation demands otherwise, extemporaneous delivery is the best bet for presenting your ideas in a style that your audience will consider direct, spontaneous, and not distracting.

A good style of delivery is like a well-dressed woman or man. The clothes should help to complete the image but should not be so noticeable as to draw attention away from the person wearing them. Whenever the listeners begin to notice how the person is speaking, the delivery is getting in the way of the message. The characteristics of poor delivery are rather obvious to the sensitive listener. Aspects of delivery often considered annoying include:

- Avoidance or lack of eye contact with members of the audience
- Nervous movement and fidgeting
- Monotone voice quality
- Too many "ahs," "uhms," and "ers"
- Frequent looking at notecards
- Holding and rattling notes
- Failing to smoothly operate equipment and visual aids
- Pacing back and forth

One of your authors conducted a survey of four hundred university students to see what speaking characteristics were associated with "good" college lecturers versus what speaking characteristics were associated with "bad" college lecturers. The results indicated clearly that aspects of the teacher's delivery were by far the most important characteristics associated with "good" and "bad" lecturers. The characteristics of the "good" teacher's delivery appeared in the following rank order:

1. Vocal variety
2. Dynamic, enthusiastic; uses gestures and facial expressions
3. Clear voice and articulation
4. Moderate rate of speaking (not slow but not too rapid-fire)
5. Strong, loud voice
6. Eye contact
7. Language and terminology easily understood
8. Neat appearance and good grooming, whether casual or dressed up
9. Conversational delivery
10. Calm and relaxed
11. Smiles

The characteristics of the "bad" teacher's delivery appeared in the following rank order:

1. Monotone voice
2. Speech rate too fast for note taking
3. Lack of expression or enthusiasm in voice
4. Lack of movement; stays behind a podium
5. Reads directly from notes
6. Poor voice quality (harsh, rasping, et cetera)
7. Poor eye contact with class (looks at wall, ceiling, or out the window)
8. Uses "big" words, technical terms
9. Uses a lot of "ahs," "uhms," and "dahs"
10. Not loud enough
11. Nervous behaviors with hands and body
12. Sloppy appearance
13. Paces back and forth too much

The results of this study were used in a series of teacher-improvement seminars. Several of the teachers looked at the study and commented that although they did not feel they had those problems, they knew some colleagues who did show the symptoms of the "bad"-delivery teacher.

VOICE

If you have ever heard your voice on a tape recorder, you have experienced the enlightened act of hearing yourself as others hear you. We normally hear ourselves talk through a combination of the air compressions our talking makes on our eardrums and the vibrations of the bones of our head caused by the sounds in the oral and nasal cavities, called bone conduction. As a result of this dual type of hearing, we can never hear ourselves as we sound to others, unless we use a tape recorder. Just as we are unaware of how we sound to others, we may be unaware of the particular voice qualities, defects, or habits we have. Others may recognize them, but we don't. Speech pathologists consistently show that people reported to have minor speech defects (lisps, slurs, sound substitutions, and so on) do not hear these defects in their own speech.

A fascinating example of this was seen when one of your authors recorded a mock job interview with an older student who grew up in Spain. His "accent" was still noticeable although he was easily understood. After the mock interview, the student was to critique his recording. After about five minutes in the adjoining room, he returned complaining that something must have gone wrong with the taping because the person on the tape had some kind of Mexican accent, and he couldn't locate on the tape where his interview started. Had his American wife not been in the audience to help add support to our allegation that that *was* his tape—he *did* sound that way—he may never have been convinced.

If the voice is important in delivery, and delivery is sometimes a more important message cue than the words spoken, we have good cause to examine the key characteristics of voice. What can we do to go beyond simply "living with the way we talk now"? In examining voice, we will include: articulation, pronunciation, voice qualities, vocal qualifiers, use of pauses and timing, and distracting vocalizations.

THE BORN LOSER   **By Art Sansom**

The Beauty Asset You Never Knew You Could Have

■ Do people often ask you, "What did you say?" Do you fade out, especially at the end of phrases? Too soft is as hard on listeners as too loud. I find this often in women who have been programmed from childhood not to put themselves forward. They don't like to speak out and it takes steady practice to overcome the habit. People may constantly ask you to repeat yourself or, worse, may pretend they've heard but tune you out.

■ Do you try for extra-deep tones in an effort to sound breathily sexy? Or, does your voice seem tight, as if it were produced by a pressure cooker? Does your throat feel constricted, frequently sore? Do you sound harsh and angry even if you don't actually feel that way? Talk to a mirror to see if the veins on your neck stand out. All these are signs that you are beating up your vocal cords, possibly because you think they are the source of power. They are not. We speak through them, not with them.

■ Does your voice have a little-girl quality? A boy's voice drops about an octave during puberty. Normally, a girl's pitch also descends several notes. If yours didn't, probably no one worried; after all, it didn't matter much in a girl, or so people thought. But today, a childlike intonation seems to contradict firm statements. No one waits long enough to discover the brains and talent beneath the babyish voice.

■ Our nasality has been called "The American Sound," although each area of the country seems to have a different explanation for it. Ralph Waldo Emerson wondered whether the New England twang came about because people feared opening their mouths to let in the cold. Someone else suggested that the vowels of the Midwest flattened to match the Great Plains. Whatever the reason, this unpleasing trait is no cause for pride. Actual "talking through the nose" is rare—the metallic sound we call nasal comes from tones trapped in a constricted throat. The vowels have a whining sound: "man" becomes "maan," "dance" becomes "deeunce."

■ Then there are monotonous voices. Flat and colorless tone and inflection turn people off. The human voice has unrealized flexibility to stretch both up and down.

■ Talking with runaway speed strains the attention just as inaudible speech does: "The ????? Company, Mr. ????? office. Please leave ????? number ?????." You hang up frustrated.

■ Jagged speech rhythms agitate the very air where many of us live. The pace of the sentences we hear is abrupt, stop-and-go. As our ears sop up the tense beat, we seem to infect each other. It's not easy to close off these jerky sounds, but an attractive speaking voice should have a smooth, flowing rhythm—the speaking equivalent of *legato* in music, which means "without abrupt break in movement and in a manner smooth and connected."

Each of these faulty patterns inter-feres in some way with your body. To change, you must become sensitized to how the parts of your body feel when they're working properly. Then you will be able to *feel* the tension in your throat, the shallowness of your breathing or the locked-up nasality of your tone. And you master a good speaking voice as you would any other physical activity—through exercise. You don't attack voice production aggressively—the way you would your tennis forehand, for example. It's more like the relaxed, flowing coordination essential to playing a good game.

There are three indispensable components to the proper use of your body that will change the way you sound: (1) releasing the necessary muscles; (2) improving breathing; and (3) learning to use the body's built-in resonators.

To relax muscle tension: First show yourself the worst that muscle tension can do: Tighten your hands at the back of your neck, bunch your tongue toward the back of your throat, fill up your chest with air—and try to count out loud to ten. I dare you.

What concerns us specifically is tension in the head, neck, shoulders, chest—the areas closely related to voice production. By getting rid of unnecessary strains there, you permit the muscles of your voice box the freedom to function the way they were meant to.

Do these exercises on a straight-back chair facing a mirror. Sit tall, legs comfortably apart and parallel, feet flat, hands folded palm-up in your lap. First, rotate your head gently on your neck. "Cut a pie eight ways" by moving your head up and down with graceful, unjerky nods as you rotate. Tilt your head to one side as if you were asleep on an imaginary pillow for the count of ten; repeat on other side, front, back. Next, rotate your head slowly in a small circle, keeping eye contact in the mirror.

Now give your face a light massage. Slide your hands from your hairline

down your cheeks until your jaw sags with an idiotic expression. Stick your tongue out, flopping on your lower lip. With a hand on each side of your chin, move your jaw from side to side and up and down. With your fingers under your chin, swallow, feeling the small muscles you use to do so. Soothe and soften them with small circular motions of both hands.

These exercises should leave the muscles of your face, neck, and shoulders relaxed and calm. A dividend: You should see a face without grimaces, quiet cheeks, a calm mouth, and a supple throat. This is an important image to remember. Our faces are frequently far too active—exaggerated gestures of mouth, eyes, eyebrows. Once you become aware of how these muscles feel when they are quiet, you will also begin to sense when they are not, and correct that.

Next we'll deal with the breathing that is essential to a full-bodied voice. We require less air than you probably think. Women tend to breathe too high—what I call "brassiere breathing." As well as making you look insecure, it's a bosomy rise and fall that is incompatible with solid tone (proper breathing is almost invisible).

The best way to feel the breathing you *should* be using is to lie stretched in a swimming position on a rug, flat on your stomach, one arm on the floor above your head, the other at your side with you head turned toward it. Place a small cushion under your head and another between your navel and pelvis. Sink into the floor with a feeling of letting go. Sigh long breaths over and over again, silently inhaling and exhaling, feeling your muscles *expand and contract* against the pillow on the floor. That's where it's at—the muscle girdle of support for speaking and singing. There should be no feeling of ballooning, just a gentle swell of air deep within the body. Now make your sighs audible, to connect that relaxed breathing with sound. Make low, almost moaning sighs from an open, relaxed throat.

To get this same feeling in a more normal speaking position, try this: Sitting on a chair, place hands just under your lower ribs at your sides; feel your breath moving into your fingers. The front of your stomach will be flat. If you feel air ballooning into this or any other part of the chest or stomach area, you are overbreathing (this may happen in the beginning, but with practice it will ebb). The motion against your fingertips should be gentle; it may help to think of it as "side" breathing.

These brief exercises will also help you get a sense of the muscles you use when breathing properly: (1) Suck in air deeply several times as if sipping through a straw. You will feel a low tug below the waist. (2) With a loose jaw, exhale very slowly as if steaming a glass for cleaning. Then continue breathing in and out, without pushing. (3) Exhale. Then, airless, count down aloud 5–4–3–2–1. At "one," is the reaction below your waist more like an ache? Relieve it by feeding a little air back in, then breathe in and out evenly. If your chest and shoulders do not stay quiet, try placing your hands firmly (not rigidly) beneath the chair seat and then breathe.

These essential routines will help you to build strength, so that you can speak without forcing, and you'll stop fading mid-sentence. Believe me, there is no personality change so telling as a voice that can at last be comfortably, rather than barely, heard.

Resonance is the third component of a good voice. It reinforces the voice like added speakers in a stereo. Taking an easy breath, begin with humming, tongue resting behind lower teeth, jaw relaxed, sustaining the sound of "mmmmm" at a comfortable pitch. Feel the vibration with your fingers on your lips and cheeks. Hum in your speaking rather than your singing voice. Important: Focus the hum up front on the roof of the mouth (the hard palate) for the clearest possible sound. Once you get a solid feeling of this forward placement, fix it securely in your sense memory—this is where your tones should always be placed.

Imitate a siren, humming in circles of sound. Gradually hum louder, rolling your head to keep loose. Dropping your head and shoulders toward your lap will produce a richer, deeper sound. Put your hand on your forehead and upper chest to feel them vibrate.

Block your ears with your hands and hum up and down the scale—again with your speaking rather than singing voice. Stop at the note that reverberates loudest inside your head. Then change the hum to the word "so," saying "so" up and down the spoken scale until you reach that same tonal area. Say a whole sentence there: "So! This sounds pretty good to me." This register is probably the best for your speaking voice—in most women, approximately three notes lower than the one habitually used.

In public, if you feel your voice sliding up to its former high, little-girl pitch, or becoming shrill or out of control, stop, breathe out quietly, release your shoulders, and feel yourself literally moving a load off your chest. As a psychological aid, finger a button or necklace as though you were holding down your pitch.

Now, how do you put the proper relaxation, breathing, and resonance together? The best way is by reading aloud, using a cassette recorder. First, tune the instrument: Make sure the proper muscles are relaxed, do a breathing exercise, do a humming exercise, ending with a sentence in the proper register. Then read aloud into your recorder. Pick pieces with varying pace and theme, a mixture of prose and poetry. As you read, speak out as strongly as you can, but avoid pressure. Don't be afraid of overdoing— underdoing is usually the problem.

Reading aloud, playing back, reading again is a necessary, regular routine. It eases the way to a smooth, vital speaking voice. It helps you imprint the right breathing and relaxed muscles and resonating sound, to *know* how your voice is beginning to sound, and to carry over this improved voice more naturally to your everyday speaking. After all, that is what you are ultimately after—raising the performing level of the voice you take with you everywhere in your life.

SOURCE: Reprinted by permission of Curtis Brown Ltd. Copyright © 1977 by Conde Nast Publications Inc.

ARTICULATION

Articulation technically refers to the distinctness of the formation of the speech sounds. The lips, tongue, and jaw are the main components brought into play when vocal sounds are formed. A habit of lazy lips, a sluggish tongue, or a stiff jaw, if not the result of a physical or neurological problem, can be "unlearned" and replaced with new, more acceptable, speech habits. "hooow nooow brooown cooow" is an articulation exercise.

A fool's mouth is his destruction.

PROVERBS 18:7

PRONUNCIATION

Pronunciation is the production of the specific sounds of words in a correct and acceptable manner, as judged by the local or regional speech community. How many times has the "accent" of a person or the way certain words are pronounced given you immediate cues regarding where the person lives or has lived, or how educated that person may be? The following are some examples of accent placements that cue the listener: *genu-iné, dé-vice, ré-fer,* and *ráp-port* instead of the more acceptable *geń-uine, dvicé, re-feŕ,* and *rap-poŕt.* Deleting sounds results in *li-berry* for *library, guh-mnt* for *government, fur* in place of *for, git* for *get.* Adding additional sounds, such as *ath-a-lete* instead of *athlete,* are common also.

What may be acceptable in social conversation may well be considered objectionable in public speaking. Sloppy articulation and poor pronunciation can produce negative audience judgments.

VOICE QUALITIES

Voice qualities distinguish one speaker from another. These are the main cues we pick up when we recognize a voice before we actually see a person. It is from these cues that we "get a feeling" about an individual's age, background, social class, and so on. Four specific voice qualities are:

Pitch Range   The wide or narrow band of vocal sound

Resonance   The rich and full or thin and wispy depth in the sound produced as it "echoes" in the oral and nasal cavities

Rate   The speed of sound production

Control   How smooth, precise, and rhythmic the sound is

In paralanguage, several types of voice quality are distinguished: (A) pitch range, (B) resonance, (C) rate, and (D) control, which includes lip control, articulation control, and rhythm control. (Randall P. Harrison, Beyond Words, © 1974, pp. 106–107. Reprinted by permission of Prentice-Hall, Inc., Englewood Cliffs, New Jersey.)

VOCAL QUALIFIERS

Vocal qualifiers are the more temporary characteristics the voice takes on to accomplish momentary expression of feelings. Specific qualifiers are:

Intensity   The loudness or softness of the sound

Pitch   The height or depth of the sound as in the musical scale, "do, re, mi, fa, so la, ti, do"

Extent   Drawing out or clipping the sound before it is completed

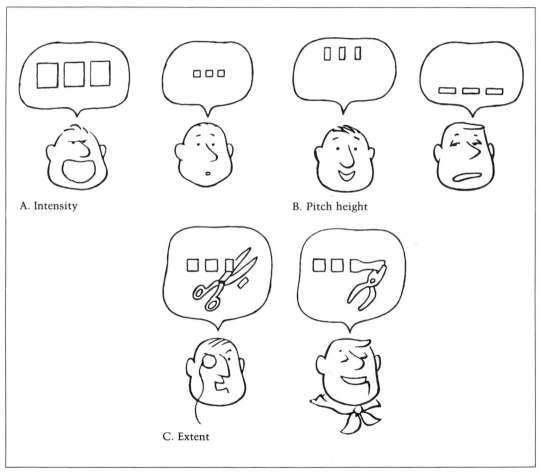

Vocal qualifiers include (A) intensity, such as overloud or oversoft; (B) pitch height, such as overhigh or overlow; (C) extent, such as clipping or drawing. (Randall P. Harrison, Beyond Words, © *1974, pp. 106–107. Reprinted by permission of Prentice-Hall, Inc., Englewood Cliffs, New Jersey.)*

PAUSES AND TIMING

Pauses (silence between spoken words) can be an effective means of emphasis, especially if the rate of speaking is rapid-fire. A well-placed moment of silence will draw the listener's attention because it is such a contrast. For example: "There is only one way we can solve this problem. And that one way is . . . [pause] . . . to go directly to the president's office and talk to her personally." The pause builds a few seconds of suspense about what is going to be said.

Timing is changing the tempo (rate) of speaking in conjunction with the use of pauses to produce maximum effects. Johnny Carson is a master of timing in his monologues in the sense that he can lead up to a punch line with a rapid-fire description of the "news event of the day," take a long pause, and then deliver the punch line in a slow tempo that appears nonchalant rather than eager. In order to get a feeling of the acceptable length for a pause and how changing the pacing of the spoken words will sound, you will have to tape-record yourself several times and listen to the playback. Don't expect to use pauses and timing perfectly the first time.

DISTRACTING VOCALIZATIONS

Distracting vocalizations are the sounds and words people use to fill the awkward silences between thoughts or phrases of the speech. Examples include "ah," "uhm," "and ah," "so ah," "ya know," and the like.

LANGUAGE

One of the main points a speech-communication teacher must convey in the classroom is that the best language for speaking is the simplest language, short of using slang and clichés. These teachers are fighting a long history of reinforcement that supports the learning and use of "big" words. An adult gives attention to children when they use big words. Sometimes term papers and public speeches that are full of abstract terminology receive misguided praise.

One way to examine the idea of using small instead of big words does not deal with the number of letters in the word, rather it looks at how *concrete* versus how *abstract* the word is. Abstract words or phrasing are those which refer to theoretical ideas that cannot be directly experienced or observed through our senses. *Democracy, justice, capitalism, economy, freedom,* and *evaluation* are abstract. These terms do not create clear mental pictures. Concrete words or phrasing refer to actual objects,

events, or experiences in reality. Concrete is the opposite of abstract. We can see, touch, smell, taste, or feel that which is concrete. We can see a "flashing red light," "smell a barbequed steak," "cash a ten-dollar check," and get anxious over "a ten-point quiz."

A second way to look at the idea of big and small words is to examine *specific* versus *general* words. Specific words are those which have a limited meaning. General words refer to a large group or category of things. The term *politician* refers to a large group of people. "Ted Kennedy, senator from Massachusetts," is more specific. "Speech teachers" is general. "Larry Kraft, the instructor in my speech-communication class" is specific. Language is an inexact tool by which we communicate. Words refer to meanings that are in people and that vary with people. Therefore the more abstract we get, the more we can expect to be misunderstood by our listeners.

In summary, it is not the magnitude or the banality of the symbol that is significant. Rather it is the specificity of its referent category. (It is not the size or commonness of the word that is important, rather it is how specific and concrete its meaning is.)

THE DIFFERENCE BETWEEN CONVERSING AND PUBLIC SPEAKING

Have you ever noticed that national newscasters such as Dan Rather, Tom Brokaw, and Jane Pauley do not have regional accents? They speak what is called the general American dialect, which is the nationally accepted pronunciation for speech. Local or regional television and radio people who are attempting to break into the big time spend hours taking courses or private training to rid themselves of accents that pinpoint their formative years.

We have become so accustomed to hearing general American dialect that even people from the South, New England, or other notorious accent-stereotyped areas do not hear anything "different" when they listen to

national newscasters. We have grown to accept two speech standards—our own style and that of the general American dialect. So what does this have to do with language? There is a parallel.

In conversations among close friends, clichés, slang, jargon, poor grammar, habit phrases ("ya know," "right," "see"), vocal fillers ("uhm," "ah") and even obscenity can be acceptable language forms. However, in public speaking, such language forms are not acceptable. Just as we have learned to speak or at least "hear" general American dialect as appropriate speaking in certain situations, we have also learned to expect "proper" language in public presentations or business conversations.

Cliché   When a phrase or saying is labeled a cliché, it is considered worn out. Phrases such as *burned out, happy as a lark, that's for sure, you better believe it, you think that's bad . . . , big deal!, I'm sick and tired of . . .* , were once uniquely fresh as expressions because they were different. Once a statement is overused, it loses the special meaning it may have had at one time. Clichés used in public-spreaking situations are a cue that the speaker lacks originality in thinking and expression and must rely on worn-out phrases.

Slang   Slang terms may ultimately become a part of standard word usage, such as *mob, plane, fresh air,* and *bus,* but until they do, they are considered substandard forms of expression in public-speaking situations. *Ripped off, up tight,* and *wired* are presently considered slang words. Slang words pick up their meaning from the informal atmosphere and situations in which they originated. To frequently transfer this wording to a more formal situation is not considered appropriate.

Jargon   Doctors, teachers, businesspeople, sports fans, military personnel, law officers, computer specialists, lawyers, truckers, and others use jargon in their communication. Jargon is a semi-private vocabulary used by a specialized group to communicate something the group feels they have in common. Children (and adults) go through stages where jargon becomes very important to their sense of identity. When the general population begins to pick up the use of this jargon, the jargon loses its meaning for those who originally used it. A good example of this can be "heard" in the standardization of truckers' CB jargon. Not only have terms such as *handle, ten-four, smokey, on the side,* and *"10–36"* become popularized among nontruckers, they are being used in everyday conversation. The final blow has been the publication of dictionaries that translate truckers' jargon into standard English.

You may momentarily impress audience members by using jargon they do not regularly use, but you may also alienate them.[2]

Other Problems Poor grammar such as *hadn't outta, ain't gonna,* and *they is;* habit phrases such as *ya know* and *ah;* vocal fillers such as *uhm* and *ah;* and obscenities are considered weak and sometimes offensive substitutes for specific and concrete language.

USING TRANSITIONS

Many times when a presentation is difficult to follow or appears to be unorganized, a lack of transitions is the culprit. Transitions tie separate ideas together. They show the listener how one idea is connected or related to another. For example: "And now that I have explained the problem, I would like to outline what I think is a feasible solution that we can all use."

Transitions help the listener see and feel the progression of the speech from beginning to end. The speaker knows how the ideas are arranged in a certain way, but listeners may not be so quick to follow this progression without the aid of transitions.

Transitions can be complex in that they can summarize the points covered before providing the link to the points still ahead. For example:

> To this point I have described the advantages and primary disadvantages of adopting the new system. The advantages appear to outweigh the disadvantages at this point. But before we go any further without thinking, one question that we have failed to examine is, Will our people agree to change to a new system with the Christmas rush coming on? I did some checking around and here's what I found . . . .

Or transitions can be very simple. For example, "and the second point is . . ." "Another advantage is . . ." "To wrap this up, I would like to suggest . . . ."

---

[2]One of the authors has considerable experience in coaching physician's, dentists, and lawyers in their use of simple terminology, rather than jargon, when being interviewed by the news media or addressing a public meeting. These professionals realize that jargon is not appropriate when they have to communicate to the general public.

The Way People Talk Reveals Their Personality

The way people speak reveals their personality—especially if they use certain familiar types of words or phrases, says noted psychologist Dr. Robert K. Alsofrom.

Dr. Alsofrom finds there are a number of distinct types of conversationalists, including:

1. The Evaders. "These people try to get out of making any uncomfortable admission," says Dr. Alsofrom, of West Palm Beach, Fla. "For example, if a friend or mate asks, 'Are you ready?' this type will answer, 'Not really'—which means no.

"This type is not very affirmative or aggressive, tends to want the other person to be the decision maker. A man using these phrases is one with a rather childish personality, unwilling to accept responsibility."

2. The Walking Dictionaries. "These are the people who use long words, French phrases and even Latin quotations—unnecessarily. They are often trying to call attention to themselves, to sound superior, or to conceal their ignorance behind a lot of syllables."

3. The Name Droppers. "Some people drop names constantly because they are in that social circle; others do it to attract attention. Name droppers generally are ambitious, desire to impress others, are outgoing and likely to be sociable."

4. The Challengers. "The Challenger often asks others, 'What do you mean by that?' or 'How do you know that?' He often backs up his own statements with a string of facts and figures. This type tends to be critical, questing, searching, sometimes inventive, with soundly based views."

5. The Gossipers. " 'Have you heard about . . .' or 'Just between you and me . . .' are hallmark phrases of the Gossipers. They're gregarious, cheerful, outgoing people who love parties and tend to be snoops."

6. The Cliché Experts. "People who use stock phrases like, 'Drop dead,' 'I couldn't care less,' and so on, tend to be followers, loyal to their own group, not adventurous, and find it hard to make decisions."

7. The Salesmen. "These people are trying to persuade you to try something—a new diet, a shop, a philosophy. They'll load you with literature and phone you to find out if you tried it. They're usually sincere."

SOURCE: *The National Enquirer,* May 2, 1978, p. 60.

NONVERBAL ASPECTS OF DELIVERY

Our nonverbal behavior cues the listener how we feel about:

- Ourself
- The message
- The audience or listener
- The situation
- The anticipated outcome of the talk or exchange

Our words represent the ideas we wish to express, but our facial expressions, tone of voice, gestures, posture, appearance, and so on express how we feel. Words help us express the **content level** of communication: our thoughts, ideas, and reasoning. Nonverbal behavior helps us express the **relationship level** of communication: our feelings and attitudes and how intense they are.

THE IMPORTANCE OF NONVERBAL COMMUNICATION

Research in the last decade indicates that nonverbal cues may represent from 65 percent to more than 90 percent of the total impact of a message. Specific research by Albert Mehrabian[3] has shown that in social, emotional, and first-impression situations, the impact of verbal and nonverbal cues breaks down in this manner:

Percentage of Total Impact of Verbal and Nonverbal Cues

Verbal	Nonverbal	
	Face	Voice
7 percent	55 percent	38 percent

Many people are surprised to learn that the voice is considered a nonverbal attribute. It is true that words cannot be separated from how they are vocalized but, nevertheless, voice quality is a prime nonverbal attribute than can be manipulated to increase message impact.

"Born speakers" or "natural speakers" did not inherit the ability to hold an audience. These people are not gifted with something the rest of us do not have. They have simply learned on their own that nonverbal

[3]Albert Mehrabian, *Silent Messages* (Belmont, CA: Wadsworth, 1971), p. 44.

behaviors an audience responds to readily, and how to combine and manipulate these nonverbal behaviors in the most effective pattern.

Understanding how the brain processes verbal and nonverbal cues is fascinating in itself. The right side (hemisphere) of the brain is responsible for processing nonverbal—nonword—cues. A high percentage of this processing goes on below conscious awareness. The left side (hemisphere) of the brain functions best with words, reasoning, judgments, the sequencing of events, and drawing relationships among thoughts. Often the left side "thinks" about an event while the right side subconsciously experiences the event. When information from the right and left hemispheres conflict, the left makes a judgement based on information from both hemispheres. For example, you may have been in a situation where the "vibes" you picked up from a person were "good" or "bad" even though the words were not particularly appealing or distasteful. What you picked up may have been primarily nonverbal cues that you processed at a below-conscious level, while the conscious decision or judgment was rendered by the left hemisphere as it used that information. (See Robert E. Ornstein's *The Psychology of Consciousness*, New York: Viking, 1972, for a further discussion of how we process verbal and nonverbal data.)

Perhaps you have heard a person intently questioning a companion as to why he did not like a specific person he had just been introduced to:

"Why didn't you like him."

"I don't know, I just didn't care for him."

"Is it something he said?"

"Naw . . ."

"Well, what's wrong with him?"

"Oh, he's just not my type, I guess."

"What is your type?"

"Forget it . . . don't make a federal case out of it."

THE DIFFICULTY IN STUDYING NONVERBAL COMMUNICATION

The difficulties in examining nonverbal communication for purposes of increased understanding and better self-control are numerous. The following remarks highlight some of these difficulties.

Nonverbal behavior cannot be separated from verbal behavior in real life. In everyday interactions hundreds of nonverbal and verbal behaviors blend in complex patterns of message exchanges that are almost beyond analysis. For the lay person to understand and express this complexity would be akin to trying to describe how several hundred separate drops of different colored dyes disperse and combine in a bucket of water already a mixture of colors from previous dilutions.

Each person's nonverbal behavior is unique and represents different meaning or intent. If you will, each person has a separate body language. In order to "read" that person's body language accurately, you have to study it in many situations and somehow verify what it represents. Noticing differences in a person's behaviors in specific situations does not mean you know what the behavior represents. What you think the behavior stands for may be wrong. In order to be sure, you have to find some way to compare what you think the behavior means with what is actually going on in the head of the other person. Sometimes you can subtly test your guess by asking the person, "Are you feeling a bit upset?"

As soon as we begin to stereotype a person's nonverbal behavior, we are in for trouble. Folding arms across the chest, stepping back, looking away, wringing the hands, and so on can mean different things for people from different backgrounds. We always need to check out the behavior with the individual to be sure our interpretation is accurate.

Also, it is better to observe a cluster of nonverbal behaviors in interpreting nonverbal communication than to look at one single behavior. Look for consistencies or inconsistencies among several nonverbal behaviors. When many nonverbal cues appear to be consistent in the pattern they form, you are in a better position to infer their meaning. But if inconsistencies appear between, let us say, facial expressions and tension shown by the hands, be careful about drawing conclusions. However, a general observation related to inconsistent cues (when two or more nonverbal cues conflict or when verbal and nonverbal cues conflict) is that the receiver will tend to believe the cue he or she feels is *under least conscious control* by the speaker.

When a person becomes emotionally involved in a situation or interaction, he or she usually has a heightened awareness of particular nonverbal cues, and ignores other nonverbal cues completely. Research also indicates that though there is heightened awareness of some nonverbal cues, the accuracy of their interpreation may be less.

Each individual is capable of an infinite number of combinations of verbal and nonverbal behaviors which are singularly unique to that person. Even though in language there are only so many separate words, and in the nonverbal language system there may be a limited number of separate nonverbal cues, when these behaviors are mixed together, completely unique and never before executed combinations are possible.

MANAGING AND MONITORING OUR NONVERBAL COMMUNICATION AS A SPEAKER

Our goal is to assist you in raising your nonverbal processing from the below-conscious level to the conscious level. In this way you will be in greater control of the nonverbal cues you display to others, and be better able to interpret the feedback from your listeners (which can be completely nonverbal in many talks). In this examination we will look at the following nonverbal elements important to the speaker: the face, gestures, posture, body movement, use of space, appearance, and use of time.

The Face   The face is one of the richest areas of nonverbal cues. It is capable of more complex cue combinations (for example, by the eyes, mouth, forehead, eyebrows, and so on) than any other area of the body. Though the face has more potential cues, it is also an area people are good at controlling. Facial expressions supply important cues to the audience about how to interpret what the speaker is saying.

The eyes are the primary means for speaker and listeners to establish and maintain interpersonal rapport. The speaker's eye contact can personalize the message to individual listeners in a way that words cannot. The most effective type of eye contact to establish with your listeners is one-to-one. Focus in on an individual in the audience for a few seconds and then move to another individual in the group and so on, randomly having direct eye contact with various listeners.

Gestures   Gestures are the punctuation marks of nonverbal communication (much as commas, question marks, colons, and so on are the punctuation marks of written communication). The accompanying

movements of the hands and arms often supplement in a consistent manner what is being said verbally. To be effective, gestures should be full and varied rather than partial and repetitious. Some people make abbreviated gestures during a talk, with their hands making tiny movements at waist-level. Full gestures require that the arms be raised to chest height so the hands and arms are in full view. The bigger the audience, the more sweeping or large your gestures need to be so the people in the back can pick them up. Some speakers have hand and arm movements that they repeat over and over, no matter what point they are making. For example, some teachers gesture only with their right or left hand and seldom use both; consequently their hand gestures become repetitious and boring.

Posture Body posture is usually what listeners mean when they describe a poised speaker. Standing straight, not rigidly, with your weight equally distributed on both feet at once is an appropriate speaking stance. Shifting your weight from one foot to the other, leaning on a desk or podium, or crossing and uncrossing your legs in some weird balancing act is not appropriate for public speeches. A common saying among speech-communication professionals is that if you want your ideas to stand up, you have to stand up (and stand up appropriately).

Body Movement The speaker's body movement that is not included under gestures and posture has to do with movement from one location to another. Such body movement is possible if the speaker is not tied to notes on the podium or lectern. For example, notecards held in the hand make it feasible for the speaker to move periodically, to add variety and life to the delivery. However, listeners, particularly students, do not like it when speakers pace back and forth in a steady pattern. Poise is the effective use of posture and body movement with gestures and facial expressions. When posture, body movement, gestures, and facial expressions are synchronized with the wording of the speech, the whole delivery is improved dramatically.

Use of Space Speakers can put more or less physical space between themselves and the audience depending on where they place themselves when delivering the speech. The closer you stand to your listeners the more personal you appear to be. Standing behind podiums or desks can add psychological distance between the speaker and the listeners. The use of a microphone, when it is not necessary for hearing, also adds psychological distance. When you observe a speaker handling questions or comments from the audience, notice whether he or she moves closer when the

listener's response is positive or genuinely inquisitive. Notice, as well, whether the speaker takes a couple of steps backward before responding to a negative or critical remark. The speaker's use of space definitely gives many cues about how the speaker feels toward the audience, the situation, and the reception of the message.

Appearance   Dressing for a presentation can be important, especially for the speaker who is not known by the listeners. "Dress appropriately" is a better guideline than "Dress up for your speech." Of course, the more formal the speaking situation the more formal the dress, no matter what the audience wears. But it is also possible to overdress for a presentation. Wearing a three-piece suit or an evening dress may be acceptable for an awards banquet, but is hardly appropriate for speaking at a professional meeting. Speech-communication teachers usually shake their heads when a student speaking about the survival of our planet stands up in cutoffs, sneakers, and sweat shirt with the sleeves torn off. There is something a little less than believable about the speaker's appearance. The student speaker has forgotten that words are only part of the message.

What Does the Clothes Line Say?

Dan Danbom, ABC

Here it is. A homespun guide to what your clothes say about you by an author whose clothes say a lot about him.
The human mind does not resist making quick judgments, so what many people perceive us to be is a result of what we wear. To paraphrase Mark Twain, one only needs to examine the recent history of the world to see that naked people have very little influence.

Everyone knows that. What many of us overlook is the direct application of how to make clothes achieve a desired effect.

John Malloy, the country's first "wardrobe engineer" and author of the best-selling *Dress for Success,* can tell you how to dress to succeed in business, attract the opposite sex or lead people to believe you are a total buffoon, merely by the clothes you wear.

As a communicator, I found *Dress for Success* a fascinating book. But as a person in the habit of wearing clothes, I found it depressing. My wardrobe, I learned after reading the book, would lead a person to believe that I was a salesman of rubber sex aids.

First off, the colors of my clothes were not colors found in nature, definitely connotative of the "lower class," according to Malloy. Two of my suits were in violation of the city's new sign code prohibiting "gaudy public displays." People make tourniquets out of ties nicer than mine, and my shoes had "hick" written all over them.

Even my college ring, which I have treasured because my name was correctly spelled on it, was not what was needed to dress for success.

The lessons to be learned from Malloy are important: He neither haws nor hems, and his research is anything but off the cuff. Rather than have you run out to drop your hard-earned bucks on the book, however, I have provided you with the list below to help you see the wisdom of Malloy's way. It is based not only on Malloy's tenets, but also on my experience of being laughed at by bus drivers.

Your Clothes . . . What They Say About You

Dark blue pin-stripe suit, white shirt, maroon tie, black wing tip shoes.

I am conservative and responsible. I have good table manners. I never use incense, but I always use "interface, dichotomy and low profile."

Grey wool dress, mid-calf length, not low cut, black high heel shoes

I might be interested in being a mother, but only after the fiscal year ends.

Red blazer, white pants, shirt, shoes, socks and belt

Where is the pizza parlor ground-breaking?

Corduroy sports coat, contrasting corduroy pants, negative heel shoes, patterned shirt open at the collar

I am into Zen and eating elm bark. I like all things cosmic. In my spare time, I make sand candles.

Red mini-skirt, fish net stockings, knee-high white boots, halter top, chewing gum

I like conventions. With proper guidance, I can do elementary typing.

Tan sports coat, light blue oxford cloth shirt, navy blue slacks, "rep" tie, cordovan loafers

I still remember my fraternity handshake. Let's go TP the Sig Eps.

Electric blue leisure suit, patterned light blue shirt, yellow tie, white belt, white shoes, green socks

I aspire to the cultural heights achieved by Billy Carter and used car salesmen. I can chew gum and a toothpick at the same time.

Full-length dark brown dress with sequins and lace cuffs, brown high heels

I'm leaving after work for my opera/wedding/night club audition.

Seal skin sports coat, alligator shoes, leopard skin pants, tie depicting last carrier pigeon being shot

Marlin Perkins is looking to give me a fat lip.

SOURCE: Reprinted with permission of International Association of Business Communications, *Journal of Organizational Communication.*

Use of Time   Starting and ending a presentation on time indicates a professional speaker. This shows respect for the audience and its span of attention. If you haven't made your point with the listeners after the first eight or ten minutes, your listeners will not be around mentally when you do get to your point.

Why Rehearse?   Not rehearsing for a speech situation is like your college football or basketball team learning all the basics, training, diagramming all the plays and moves, but never practicing before the first game. Speakers get nervous enough before presentations without having the added tension of "hoping" everything will go well. A rehearsal is the speaker's way of planning ahead to *insure* that everything will work out as planned. You may rehearse small parts at a time just to try them out. At some point, however, see the whole presentation in your mind. See it flow from beginning to end in a mental rehearsal. If you are not comfortable imagining the speech presentation, then rehearse it aloud.

The purpose of rehearsing is not to make the speech more and more "canned" so that by the time it is presented to the audience it is all but mechanical. The purpose of rehearsing is to "try out" the speech to see how it will flow together naturally.

WHAT TO KNOW

Much of the stagefright about delivering a speech is uncontrolled mental anxiety caused by the anticipation of speaking. Of the four main types of delivery (manuscript, memorized, impromptu, and extemporaneous), extemporaneous is the most preferred.

The voice as a mechanism for transmitting spoken language can be examined in relation to articulation, pronunciation, voice qualities, vocal qualifiers, pauses and timing, and distracting vocalizations. Becoming aware of your present voice qualities and speaking characteristics is the first step in improving your overall use of voice in speech delivery.

Language for speaking follows the general principle of KISS (keep it simple student). Language should be concrete rather than abstract, specific rather than general. The use of transitions and unique wording can add interest to a speech.

An awareness of the nonverbal aspects of delivery can aid the speaker in managing nonverbal cues and in interpreting feedback from the listeners.

WHAT TO DO

Audio Taping   Audio tape the next speech you give in or outside of class. Listen to your delivery. Pay particular attention to your voice control and the following:

- Articulation
- Vocal qualities (range, resonance, tempo)
- Vocal qualifiers (intensity and pitch)
- Use of pauses
- Use of "ahs," "uhms," "ya knows"

After analyzing your delivery, use a new tape or cassette to record your speech again; this time practice corrective techniques. Now listen to both the first speech and your second attempt.

Johnny Carson   Tune in the Carson show on TV and turn the sound off during Johnny's monologue. Record on a sheet of paper all the nonverbal behaviors you observe him using.

Tune in the Carson show on a second evening and turn the picture black with the brightness knob and listen to Carson's delivery. Record on paper all the aspects of delivery you recognize. What type of delivery is he using during the monologue? What kind of delivery does he use when he is interviewing a guest?

Vocal Impersonators   Obtain a recording of a show-business person who does impersonations, such as Rich Little. Listen to the vocal qualities and qualifiers used to accomplish the impersonation. What aspects of the vocal delivery does the impersonator exaggerate to achieve the imitation effects?

WHERE TO LEARN MORE

Bradley, Patricia H., and John Baird, Jr. *Communication for Business and the Professions.* 2d ed. Dubuque, IA: Wm. C. Brown, 1983, Chapter 13.

Burgoon, Judee K., and Thomas Saine. *The Unspoken Dialogue: An Introduction to Nonverbal Communication.* Boston: Houghton-Mifflin, 1978.

Ehninger, Douglas, Alan H. Monroe, and Bruce E. Gronbeck. *Principles and Types of Speech Communication.* 8th ed. Glenview, IL: Scott, Foresman, 1978. Chapters 13–16.

Knapp, Mark L. *The Essentials of Nonverbal Communication.* New York: Holt, 1980.

Knapp, Mark L. *Nonverbal Communication in Human Interaction.* 2d ed. New York: Holt, 1978.

Ornstein, Robert E. *The Psychology of Consciousness.* New York: Viking, 1972.

Ross, Raymond S. *Speech Communication Fundamentals and Practice* 5th ed. Englewood Cliffs, NJ: Prentice-Hall, 1980.

PART THREE

SPEAKING
WITH
A PURPOSE

Every speech ought to be put together like a living creature, with a body of its own, so as to be neither without head or without feet, but to have both a middle and extremities, described proportionately to each other and to the whole.

PLATO

INFORMATIVE SPEAKING

7

ACCURATELY INFORMING OTHERS IS A CHALLENGE

The scene is a speech-communication instructor's office. A student is attempting to clarify her class assignment, which is to prepare and present an informative speech.

STUDENT: I think I see what the difference between an informative speech and a persuasive speech is. The persuasive speech attempts to influence the listener's beliefs, attitudes, feelings, and/or behavior. The informative speech simply furthers the listener's understanding of a topic without attempting to convince.

INSTRUCTOR: Yes, that is generally correct, Karen.

STUDENT: What I am having difficulty doing is finding an interesting topic on which to speak. In my high-school speech class I remember how bored I would get trying to listen to speeches; I don't think I heard one new idea. I don't want that to happen with my speech.

INSTRUCTOR: You have just identified a critical element in the informative speech. If the material does not clarify or give new knowledge to the listener, it is not an informative speech. To inform means to make known, to enlighten, to amplify, to make one aware of something. If the material you were hearing was not new to you, you were not being informed. Maybe someone else in your high-school class was being informed, but you were not.

STUDENT: Are you saying my speech has to be on a topic that our class knows nothing about, in order for the speech to be informative?

INSTRUCTOR: Not necessarily. You could clarify or go into depth on a topic with which the class is already familiar. You can extend the listener's understanding of the topic by relating it to other ideas or to their lives in ways that have not been done before.

STUDENT: So I could talk about safety pins if I could approach the topic in a unique and different way?

INSTRUCTOR: Yes, I suppose you could, although I was hoping for something with a bit more significance.

STUDENT: Now wait a minute, do you mean you know all that is useful to know about safety pins?

INSTRUCTOR: You caught me there. I think I'm about to hear something new about safety pins next Monday at ten. Am I right?

STUDENT: If I can get to the library and pin down some information . . .

INSTRUCTOR: Ouch! Watch the puns.

THE INFORMATIVE SPEECH

The exchange between teacher and student just presented points out the defining aspects of the informative presentation. The key to understanding the purpose of the informative speech lies in the dictionary definition of *inform*. In one way or another the material must be unknown previously to the listener in order to be considered information. From this perspective it is possible that an extensive amount of material you hear day in and day out is not informative to you—commercials you have heard before, excuses you have heared before, explanations you have heard before, lectures that repeat the reading assignment verbatim, and so on.

The diagram[1] shown here depicts informative and persuasive speaking as falling on a continuum. Up to this point you may have thought that certain topics are informative and certain topics are persuasive in nature. This is an inaccurate conclusion. It is not the topic that makes the mate-

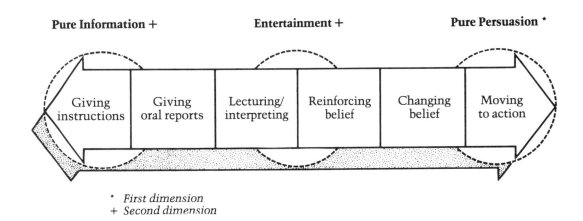

Pure Information +   Entertainment +   Pure Persuasion *

| Giving instructions | Giving oral reports | Lecturing/ interpreting | Reinforcing belief | Changing belief | Moving to action |

* *First dimension*
\+ *Second dimension*

[1]Adapted from a diagram by Paula Michael, Zannes, and Goldhaber: *Stand Up, Speak Out*, Addison-Wesley, Reading, MA, 1978, p. 65. Reprinted by permission.

rial informative or persuasive, it is the treatment of the material by the speaker and the resulting perception of the intent of the speaker by the listener that determines the informativeness or persuasiveness of the talk. All speeches are informative to the degree that they present new information. However, not all speeches are persuasive unless you view the art of speaking in its broadest sense: When we interact with others, we are attempting to influence others' perceptions of ourselves even if in the smallest way.

A specific question may have entered your mind by now. "If it is not so much the topic but the treatment of the material that makes a speech informative, how can I give an informative talk on a controversial topic such as test-tube conception?" For the material to be presented in such a way that the listeners do not believe that the speaker is putting forth a biased position, the information must be:

1. Objective and accurate—the speaker's opinion should not enter into the content either verbally or through nonverbal cues

2. Balanced and complete—both pros and cons of the material must be given

Today Americans are suffering from "information overload." We are bombarded from our youth through our waning years with messages, few of which are objectively presented. The messages come to us from the media, friends, community, and state, and from national and international groups and organizations. These messages attempt to influence our hygiene habits, our purchasing preferences, our religious values, our political affiliations, our financial support of nonprofit agencies, our living standards, our recreation preferences, our personal goals, and even our preparations for leaving all these messages behind (death). Undoubtedly the most controversial aspect of this constant message manipulation is the speculation by communicologists and psychologists that these messages ultimately affect the development and maintenance of our self-concept. We are constantly reminded that our image is related to our possessions—cars, clothes, homes, deodorants, jewelry, degrees, soft drinks, and on and on.

It seems that we hear and see persuasive messages everywhere that claim they have the way, the product, the service, or the answer. (Often the terminology of a persuasive message is subtly deceptive in that it implies the intent of the message is to inform. For example, "Did you *know* Sniff deodorant is more effective than . . ." "We simply want you to *understand* the difference between Pounds Off diet aids and other diet supplements." "Are you *aware* that Grub jeans last 50 percent longer?") To counterbalance the scales we need to teach people how to be critical listeners and we also need to teach people the value of presenting material in an informative, balanced manner. From these alternatives people can make their own decisions. We are not saying that persuasive messages are bad. We are saying that there is an admirable skill to presenting information in an open and objective manner.

HOW TO INFORM

Whenever you choose to give an informative speech, your major purpose is to gain audience understanding. Your specific purpose is to teach, instruct, clarify, and impart "new" information about something. The effective informative speech encourages the "I didn't know that!" response from listeners.

An informative speech is necessarily characterized by: (1) accuracy—derived from careful reading, research, and study; (2) completeness—sufficient information to allow understanding of the subject; (3) intelligibility—clarity and organization of ideas which leads to interest and understanding; and (4) usefulness—related to the audience's needs.

If you speak about how an IBM personal computer functions, the audience expects your presentation to be truthful, accurate, objective, interesting, well-organized, clear, complete, and useful. It would be important for you to see the IBM personal computer demonstrated, read the sales brochures and specifications, listen to a salesperson, compare IBM personal computers with other personal computers, check an eletronics consumer guide, look at journals dealing with personal computers, talk to someone who owns an IBM personal computer, and attempt to become an expert yourself before trying to present an effective informative speech on the topic.

IN ORGANIZATIONS

In organizational settings and at work, your informative speaking may deal with these topics:

- new employees orientation
- explaining a new promotion
- giving on-the-job instructions
- correcting a procedure that has gone awry
- describing departmental responsiblities to a group of employees
- reporting on the success of a recent effort to improve productivity
- implementing a new set of productions, training materials, or reporting procedures

OUTSIDE OF ORGANIZATIONS

You may also find yourself giving informative speeches to college students, club members, friends, family, and church and civic groups. Topics will range from "How to Buy a House" to the "Zen of Running." Included here is a list of possible informative-speech topics in case you do not want to tell us about your hobby or the "best way to succeed at anything you do."

- the history of acupuncture
- how to instruct a computer
- dressing for success
- why are there so many kinds of diets?
- what are natural foods?
- ways to find inner peace
- the evolution of hang gliders
- where are the best jobs in America
- what is the purpose of the national debt?
- can anyone become "physically fit for life?"
- Lazer technology in medicine
- the good and bad side of "drugs."

All of us are curious yet relatively uninformed about important and exciting things going on around us. Informative speaking gives us the opportunity to increase and enhance understanding, thus closing the gap between the unknown and known for the listeners.

Because the achievement of audience understanding is so important, if at all possible use visual aids like models, pictures, diagrams, and demonstration devices, and follow your informative speech with a question-answer period.

THREE STEPS FOR PREPARING AN INFORMATIVE SPEECH

Before you plunge into the detailed development of your informative presentation, you should acquire some background information on your audience, the speaking situation, topic, and desired response. Then organize the speech so that it is at once interesting and useful. Finally you must master the presentation so that you are able to speak directly and spontaneously to the audience.

STEP 1: GATHERING ESSENTIAL INFORMATION

Begin your preparation by analyzing your listeners, situation, topic, and desired response. Use the following guide:

1. **Analyze your listeners.**
   a. What do they already known about the topic and how often are they exposed to information on the topic?
   b. How interested or disinterested are they in the topic?
   c. What are their attitudes or feelings toward the topic?
   d. What are they likely to know or feel about you as a speaker?
      (1) How much credibility will you have prior to the presentation?
      (2) How much effort will have to be made to build your credibility during the presentation?
      (3) Given your credibility, what balance between your personal thoughts and outside source material will be most effective with this group?
   e. How can you build "thought bridges" between what the audience's experiences and attitudes are and the materials of your speech?

2. **Consider the situation.**
   a. How large is the room?
   b. How will the seating and speaker's stand be arranged?
   c. Any chalkboards, projection screens, microphones?
   d. How many people will attend?
   e. What is the purpose of the meeting.
   f. How many speakers will speak?
   g. Will there be any noise or visual distractions?

3. **Research the topic.**
   a. Examine your own knowledge and experience
   b. Ask friends and experts.
   c. Use direct observation if possible.

d. Read printed materials.

e. Check the library.

f. Consult newspapers and magazines.

g. Conduct surveys and interviews.

h. Examine research materials.

i. Allow time to think, incubate, and create.

4. **Determine the desired response.**

a. Decide on the central idea.

b. Decide on the specific response desired.

(1) Understand what about the topic?

(2) Remember what?

(3) See how to use what?

(4) Accept what?

(5) Reject what?

STEP 2: ORGANIZING THE INFORMATIVE SPEECH

Now that you have analyzed your listeners, considered the speaking situation, researched the topic, and decided on the purpose or desired response, you are ready to organize your presentation. The basic purpose behind speech organization is deciding what chunks of information to include and in what order to include them. When we take all the many separate points and lump them into categories, it is easier for us to remember what we want to say and it is easier for the audience to process the information.

Professional speakers have traditionally limited themsleves to three or four ideas in their speaking. Science and tradition are in agreement that if a speaker is going to be effective, the number of points covered in any one period of time should be limited. If a speaker has more than four separate pieces of information to cover (say, ten points), then those points will have to be organized into parts that do not exceed three or four.

Select the most important points by going back to the central idea of specific response desired and deciding what main points are needed in order to explain the central idea. Then select enough supportive material like facts, statistics, illustrations, quotations, expert testimony, comparisons, visual aids, logical reasoning, and definitions to prove, clarify, and add interest to each main point.

The following outline may be useful in organizing your informative speech.

Informative-Speaking Outline

	Potential Use of Visual Aids
INTRODUCTION	
I. Attention	Visual?
II. Purpose or Importance	
III. Forecast of Main Points	Visual?

BODY	
I. Main Idea	Visual?
A. Illustrative/Supportive Material	
B. Illustrative/Supportive Material	
II. Main Idea	Visual?
A. Illustrative/Supportive Material	
B. Illustrative/Supportive Material	
III. Main Idea	Visual?
A. Illustrative/Supportive Material	
B. Illustrative/Supportive Material	
IV. Main Idea	Visual?
A. Illustrative/Supportive Material	
B. Illustrative/Supportive Material	

CONCLUSION	
I. Summarize highlights and tie back to introduction	Visual?

When a speaker gets down to the level of simply making a general point and then illustrating that point with a specific example, statistic, personal experience, or whatever, he or she is using the basic message unit for all speaking. If a general point is made and then followed by specific illustrative material, it is called the **deductive** basic message unit. If specific examples are given and followed by a general concluding statement, it is called the **inductive** basic message unit.

The organization of the material in the main body of the speech should fit the topic and purpose of the speech. The following table shows a variety of appropriate ways of structuring the information in the main body of the presentation.

Topic	Information Structure
History of the State of Alaska	Chronological
Staying in College Once You're Accepted	Enumerating the points
How to Study	What, where, when, how, why,
The Difference between Credit Unions and Commercial Banks	Comparison/contrast
Our Food-Producing Regions	Spacial sequence
The Cause of Legionnaire's Disease	Causel-effect sequence
Test-Tube Conception	Pros/cons

Let us take a number of ideas about how to recognize a good diamond to purchase, and organize those ideas into a speech outline for giving an informative speech.

Recognizing a Good Diamond to Purchase

- Buying diamonds can be hazardous to your health.
- With a little luck and careful examination you can find a diamond for the right price.
- Carat, the first C, is the weight of the diamond.
- Today we are going to look at the four C's of carat, clarity, color, and cutting.
- Before buying a diamond, examine the four C's of carat, clarity, color, and cutting.
- Color, the third C, is the tint of the diamond.
- A 1-carat stone will cost about $3,000.
- A blue tint is most highly prized.
- Clarity, the second C, is the degree of blemish of the diamond.
- A 1/2-carat stone will cost about $600.
- Yellow or brown tints lower the value.
- Cutting, the final C, is the shaping of the diamond.
- Virtually no diamond is free of all blemishes.
- Poor cutting is the biggest factor in reducing the value of a diamond per carat.
- High-priced diamonds reveal only minor blemishes.
- Proper sawing, faceting, proportioning, and shaping make a diamond more valuable.

Organizing these ideas into a meaningful sequence for giving an informative speech is easily done by following the Informative-Speaking Outline.

TITLE: Recognizing a Good Diamond to Purchase

INTRODUCTION

I. Buying diamonds can be hazardous to your health!

II. With a little luck and careful examination you can find the right diamond for the right price.

III. Today we are going to look at the four C's of carat, clarity, color, and cutting

BODY

I. Carat, the first C, is the weight of the diamond.
   A. A 1-carat stone will cost about $3,000.
   B. A 1/2-carat stone is worth about $600.

II. Clarity, the second C, is the degree of blemish of the diamond.
   A. Virtually no diamond is free of all blemishes.
   B. High-priced diamonds reveal only minor blemishes.

III. Color, the third C, is the tint of the diamond.
   A. A blue tint is most highly prized.
   B. Yellow or brown tints lower the value.

IV. Cutting, the final C, is the shaping of the diamond.
   A. Poor cutting is the biggest factor in reducing the value of the diamond per carat.
   B. Proper sawing, faceting, proportioning, and shaping make a diamond more valuable.

CONCLUSION

Before buying a diamond, examine the four C's of carat, clarity, color, and cutting.

If you gather good information, outline it according to the sample outline, and prepare a few visual aids to further clarify your main points, You are ready to mentally practice and "walk through" your presentation.

STEP 3: MASTERING YOUR PRESENTATION

Audiences often become interested and respond appropriately when a speech is delivered well. Think about what you would like to say to introduce your main points. Then visualize the order in which you will talk about the main points, and the ideas you will use to support them. Finally, imagine how you will conclude your speech on a high note.

If possible, practice using your visual aids. Go to the place where you are to present your speech and walk up to the speaker's spot and look around. How does it feel? Can you imagine giving an enthusiastic presentation?

Above all, think about being very direct with the audience. Be so well prepared that you can look into anyone's eyes without fear. Remember, you know more about the subject than anyone else, so wind up, be spontaneous, and let her rip!

TYPES OF INFORMATIVE SPEAKING

Informative speaking takes many forms. Listeners can be exposed to informative presentations of processes, instructions, and directions. Informative talks can involve demonstrations and descriptions of objects. Informative speeches can also define a term, concept, or value and can offer objective explanations of an idea, a theory, an issue, research, or an event.

The diverse types of informative speeches fall into two practical categories—those where the speaker is personally familiar with the process, procedure, object, and so on, and those where the speaker must use outside source materials to give depth to the speech.

As a speaker concerned about your credibility as a message source, you need to establish yourself as a competent and experienced source when presenting an informative speech. You also need to share the range of sources on which you have relied for your information.

GIVING INSTRUCTIONS

The key to giving effective instructions is to adapt the material to the learner's perspective (point of view, knowledge, experience, motivation, and so on). The following five steps represent a standard "how to" outline for giving instructions.

1. **The instructor prepares for the presentation:**
   a. Clearly identifies the various goals of the instruction (knowledge, attitude, and behavior).
   b. Determines the knowledge, attitudes, and skills of the learners.
   c. Breaks down the instruction into manageable steps or units.
   d. Arranges the environment where the instruction will take place (materials, equipment, visuals, seating, and so on).

2. **The instructor presents the information:**
   a. Explains the purpose of the instructions and how the learner will benefit. Warns of any difficult areas. (Creates a favorable atmosphere for learning.)
   b. Describes how the results will be measured.
   c. Tells in steps or units.
   d. Proceeds from known to unknown.
   e. Demonstrates.
   f. Reviews, stressing key points.

3. **The learners try out the information:**
   a. The learners participate as the steps are gone through again, or
   b. The learners practice under guidance, or
   c. One of the learners, as a group representative, tries out the instructions while the rest of the learners look on and assist the chosen representative.

4. **The learners practice independently:**
   a. The learners practice independently within an acceptable time frame (minutes, hours, days).
   b. The learners are encouraged to ask questions or ask for assistance (which will only be offered if requested or if the instructor sees a dangerous development or the reinforcing of a negative habit).

5. **Results are measured:**
   a. The learners will be required to demonstate their knowledge and skills with the following criteria set by the instructor:
      (1) Level of performance or knowledge required (how well).
      (2) Time allotted.
      (3) Conditions under which performance will be measured.

For briefer, more spontaneous instructions, the following format may prove helpful:

Get the Listeners' Attention. Tell:

- **What**
- **How**
- **Where**
- **When**
- **Why**

GIVING DEMONSTRATIONS

In the previously described speech, the listeners actually learned how to perform a skill or task themselves through participation. However, not all demonstrations are conducted for the purpose of having listeners learn the task. The objectives of demonstration speeches can also be to get listeners to appreciate, understand, accept, or become enthusiastic about a procedure, process, or piece of equipment. An example of an informative demonstration of this kind is a speech on home fire safety where the speaker actually demonstrates how certain kinds of fires get started. The listeners are not invited to participate by starting the fires. Speeches on

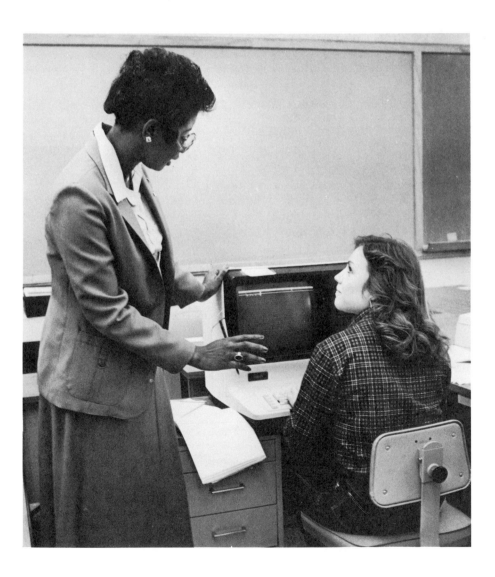

life-saving techniques such as CPR (cardiopulmonary resuscitation) can involve either participative or nonparticipative demonstrations. When listeners are observers rather than participants in the demonstration, steps need to be taken to involve and keep the listeners' attention.

1. **Everything hinges on the demonstration.** If it doesn't work, neither will the rest of the speech. Very thorough planning and pretesting needs to take place before the nonparticipative demonstration.

2. **Backup equipment is necessary.** In case a piece of equipment or material fails to perform as expected, you need equipment or materials in reserve. For example, if a speaker is demonstrating what happens to safety glass on impact, there should be a backup piece of glass in case the first piece doesn't react correctly.

3. **"Skip-ahead" technique can be used.** If the demonstration is a lengthy or complex process, you may want to have parts completed ahead of time so that you can skip the waiting period or lengthy (noninformative) process. You explain what will happen and then display the result already completed prior to the speech. A classic use of this skip-ahead technique is on TV cooking shows where the host or hostess demonstrates how to prepare the food but the audience does not have to wait for the actual cooking. The host or hostess uses a verbal transition and displays the end product, which was prepared before the show went on the air. The skip-ahead technique is valuable as a time-saver and also allows for better continuity in the presentation.

   If you need to demonstrate something that may fail, it is a good idea to have the skip-ahead technique as a backup to save the presentation from total disaster.

   When the skip-ahead technique is used, a demonstration that would normally take several minutes, hours, or days can be presented in a short informative speech.

4. **Reminding the listener of the purpose of the demonstration.** In the participative demonstration, the listener obviously becomes aware, through direct involvement, of the objective of the demonstration. In the nonparticipative demonstration, the speaker may have to remind the listener of the purpose of the demonstration, what the demonstration is supposed to prove or reveal. For example, in a demonstration dealing with the conditioning of mice in an experimental device, the listeners can get so engrossed in the behavior of the mice that they forget what the demonstration is proving or showing. The speaker will want to take a minute at the end of the demonstration to review the demonstration and relate it to the initial objective of the presentation.

DESCRIPTIVE SPEECHES

Descriptive speeches, like the other informative speeches discussed, must meet the principal test of presenting new information, and if the topic is controversial the information must be presented objectively. Descriptive speeches break down into speeches which describe objects and places; define terms, concepts, and values; or offer explanations of ideas, issues, and events.

> *Above all, the orator should be equipped with a rich store of examples both old and new; and he ought not merely to know those that are recorded in history or are transmitted by oral tradition or occur from day to day, but also fictitious examples invented by great poets.*
>
> QUINTILIAN

Describing Objects and Places When the purpose of your speech is to describe a city, a sports stadium, a modern recording studio, or the like, you will want to use a spatial organization pattern in presenting the material. Visual aids will be very important in allowing your listeners to "see" what you are talking about. Many slide presentations fall into this category. Aunt Bertha's slide show of her trip to Egypt also falls into this category. Talking in specific terms about location, size, weight, age, color, shape, and so on is important in this type of informative speech. The speaker's language must be especially vivid in word pictures to assist the listeners in sensing the smells, tastes, sounds, and atmosphere of the place or object described.

Defining Terms, Concepts, and Values The ability to define terms, concepts, and values clearly is important for the effective speaker. Although the principles of definition can be applied to any type of presentation, we are going to focus on the informative speech. It is rather difficult, but not impossible, to objectively define controversial or emotion-laden concepts such as birth control, abortion, religious cult, euthanasia, and communism. In a persuasive speech, the speaker may build the whole presentation around an attempt to get the audience to accept the speaker's definition of, let's say, "abortion as murder." The definition of the term in this case is definitely not objective, nor representative of all the various accepted meanings.

In an informative speech on definition, there are some methods for defining words (terms, concepts, and the like) that will improve the speaker's effectiveness.

1. **Give the historical derivation or development of the word.** The history of the term may add insight into its present meaning. If the word has a limited historical background, the speaker can connect the word to its original referent. Tems such as *jackass, brown nose, hot head, blabbermouth, slob, dummy,* and the like today have very general meanings whereas they once had singular, specific meanings.

2. **Classify or categorize a word in order to define it.** For example, over the last several years there has been a considerable attempt to classify alcoholism as a "disease."

3. **Use synonyms** (words that have nearly the same meaning) **and antonyms** (words that have the opposite meaning) **as another way to define.** This is the primary way the dictionary defines words. For example, *verbal* is defined in the dictionary as "spoken, oral, of words." The antonym given for *verbal* is *writing.*

4. **Break a term into its various parts as a way of defining it.** For example, a résumé is defined in the dictionary as "a summary" or a "summing up." For the college-placement director, a résumé is "a brief, clear, and neatly written summary of the key assets of the applicant with the information organized in order of descending importance." The speech on this topic would develop around explaining what is meant by the terms in the definition. What is "clear"? What is meant by "brief"?

Explaining Ideas, Issues, and Events   Some topics appear to be controversial simply by title. For example:

Pollution of our oceans	Smoking
School financing	Women's liberation
Advertising appeals	Nuclear power
Pesticides and wildlife	Defense spending

Other topics appear to be more informative by title:

The last Ice Age	Microwave ovens
Silent films	Gravity
The geology of the moon	Einstein's Theory of Relativity
The music of the Beatles	Weather repeats itself

As an informative speaker, our goal is to shed new light in an objective and representative manner whether the topic of our speech is controversial or noncontroversial. We are not trying to prove a harm, move others to take action, attempt to change attitudes, or stimulate others to renew a commitment to a practice they have become apathetic about. Our goal is to increase understanding. To *inform* an audience about, for example, nuclear power requires that the speaker include both the pros and cons. On the other hand, in an informative speech on alternate sources of power for the world, a speaker could cover nuclear power, solar power, wind power, and wave power *without* covering the pros and cons of each if the speaker's purpose is not to convince the listeners that one of these power sources is better than the others.

To be objective as a speaker you have to be objective in your analysis of the materials available on the topic and objective in the frame of mind you have while researching the topic. You should not begin your research with the thought, "What can I discover that shows that wind power (or solar power) would be our best alternate energy source for the future?" or "How can I make my audience see that venereal disease is a critical problem in the United States today?"

Material on some topics stands a greater chance of being new information to the listener than material on other topics that have been talked about frequently. However, it is not necessarily that the topic of the speech is uninteresting—*it is more likely that the listener's interest has not been aroused*. Presenting new material or a fresh perspective on an overworked topic can be a challenge—just ask ministers, schoolteachers, police officers, mothers and fathers, salespeople, industrial safety directors, and fund raisers how challenging it is to try to make an old point interesting in a new or unique way.

> *I seem to have been only like a boy playing on the seashore and diverting myself in now and then finding a smooth pebble or a prettier shell than ordinary, whilst the great ocean of truth lay all undiscovered before me.*
>
> ISAAC NEWTON

One of the keys to effective information speaking is research. The speaker must become thoroughly knowledgeable about all aspects of the topic. The speaker must become a "secondary" expert. During the speech, the speaker can build credibility on the topic by citing the sources of materials in the speech. In a term paper you use footnotes or end notes to reference materials and ideas that are not your own. In a speech you refer to your sources of materials as you are talking. In listening to presentations you may have heard oral footnotes such as:

The November 1978 issue of *Psychology Today* reports that research on eye contact is . . .

Deaths that occur in the home have gone up 23 percent in the last year. According to the National Safety Council's 1979 pamphlet *Accident Facts*, this increase is due to . . .

The latest Gallup poll reported in *Time* this week states that the American voter is . . .

I asked ten randomly chosen students on our campus to describe what this picture meant to them. Eight of the ten said essentially the same thing. The picture represented . . .

Finally, the speaker should be sensitive to the potential bias of the source material. The speaker needs to ask, "How objective or believable will my cited sources seem to my audience?"

FINAL TIPS FOR INFORMING OTHERS

These final suggestions for effective, informative speaking were developed by a student like yourself who had the chance to hear informative speeches, critique them, and suggest ways to improve our informational speaking.

1. **Supply new information.** The purpose of the informative speech includes providing the listeners with information they did not have before, adapting the information in such a way that it will seem important for the listeners to learn, and being clear and meaningful. A speech to inform seeks to analyze, explain, report, describe, or clarify some idea, object, event, or place.

2. **Establish the significance.** You have sat through enough speeches and discussions to know that sometimes the information the speaker is trying to give you does not sink in. If you do not feel that what is being said is of vital importance to you, you may feel it's not worth the effort to listen. As a speaker, you need to explain early in your talk that your information is of concern to your listeners—these particular listeners.

3. **Establish your authority.** Perhaps you have felt at times that the speaker was no better informed than you. Speakers should, of course, be more informed, and they should in some manner suggest that they are well-informed, through the use of pertinent data or even rhetorical questions or other devices. Often the use of a visual aid such as the object itself or a series of diagrams or pictures will help. Sometimes a map or a simple chart can be used not only to clarify a point but also to suggest that you have studied your topic in some detail. This can give you or any other speaker the necessary credibility with the audience.

4. **Explain new ideas through reference to familiar ones.** A speech to inform should relate new ideas to ideas already known. This applies

to sentences as well as to the total plan you use for your speech organization. For example, you probably remember a teacher comparing Italy's shape to a boot, or noting that Sicily looks like a football about to be kicked.

5. **Avoid unnecessary details.** How much detail you should use will depend on how much the listeners already know about the subject. The U.S. Air Force makes these suggestions to their personnel:

   a. Underline the key sentences in your message and then condense these by eliminating "deadhead" words, by making one sentence do the work of two or three, by discarding unneeded illustrations, and by making summaries of exact statistics.

   b. Avoid hasty conclusions, wordiness, repetition, loose expressions, and mental shortcuts.

6. **Direct yourself to the audience.** During your preparation, think of the people who will listen to your presentation. As you gather material, try to choose those items which will be most easily understood by them. You might try to find examples dealing with sports for one audience, but your examples on another occasion might relate to music or family.

   How many examples and illustrations you will need to use will depend on how easily you think it will be for your listeners to grasp the ideas. While speaking, you should watch the facial expressions of your listeners and you should be able to offer further elaboration of your topic whenever it seems necessary.

7. **Use special means to help the listeners remember.** Speakers generally want their audience to remember what they say, so they use key words, concrete examples, visual aids, and other devices they know will help. Sometimes speakers must rely on words to develop mental pictures and relationships in the listeners' minds; sometimes they use visible means such as charts, graphs, maps, and objects themselves.

   If you as a speaker can cause your listeners to see mental pictures of the ideas you are presenting just as you can cause them to relate your ideas with certain ones they already have, they are most likely to remember.

   One way to accomplish this is through **exaggeration.** The cartoonist often uses this procedure, especially with caricatures. The cartoonist seeks some prominent feature of the person, such as "Teddy" Roosevelt's broad smile and the big teeth of FDR's jutting jaw and his cigarette holder. Jimmie Durante built a character around his nose; we still hear John Barrymore spoken of as the "Great Profile."

WHAT TO KNOW

Speaking to inform requires that the speaker present information or material that is new to the listener. A unique approach to an old topic or issue can meet the requirement of being new information to the listener. In order for a speaker to inform listeners about a controversial topic, the information must be presented in a representative and unbiased manner with both pros and cons balances.

Organizing the informative speech in terms of separate points makes it easier for the speaker to cover the information and easier for the listener to process the information.

Speeches dealing with a process, directions, instructions, demonstrations, and descriptions of objects usually require the speaker to be personally familiar with the material. Speeches defining terms, concepts, or values and speeches explaining an idea, theory, issue, research, or event usually require the speaker to use additional reference material outside his or her personal area of experience or expertise.

Speaking to inform is not as easy a task as one might initially suspect. However, the goal of allowing listeners to draw their own conclusions is an admirable one in today's age of mass persuasion. And to increase understanding in a world of complexity and confusion is certainly a noble and eloquent use of speech.

WHAT TO DO

Find an Informative Presentation Go to *Vital Speeches* and *Reader's Digest* and locate a speech and an article that you think are informative. Apply the criteria of informative material as presented in the chapter. Do they meet the standards of informative presentation?

My Major Sometimes it is very difficult for a speaker to inform listeners about knowledge or material he or she (the speaker) is so familiar with that he or she takes it for granted.

Prepare a five-minute talk on your major. If you don't know that much about your major yet, maybe it's time you found out. The challenger here will be to meet the criteria of "newness" or "uniqueness" of material for your listeners. Remember, if your listeners don't learn anything new or don't have an increased understanding of your major, then you failed to inform them—*you simply talked to them.*

Unbiased News Media? To what degree do you believe the news-media presentation of the "news" is unbiased? Do you believe investigative reporting such as that which precipitated Watergate is objective or unbiased in its intent? Why or why not?

WHERE TO LEARN MORE

Brooks, William D. *Speech Communication.* 4th ed. Dubuque, IA: Wm. C. Brown, 1981.

Diekman, John R. *Get Your Message Across.* Englewood Cliffs, NJ: Prentice-Hall, Inc. 1979.

Frank, Allan D. *Communicating on the Job.* Glenview, IL: Scott, Foresman, 1982. Chapter 9.

Olbricht, Thomas S. *Informative Speaking.* Glenview, IL: Scott, Foresman, 1968.

PERSUASIVE SPEAKING

8

PERSUADING OTHERS IS A FORM OF COMMUNICATION

The student trying to persuade her teacher that she deserves an A, the schoolteacher trying to convince her class that math is important, the superintendent trying to get his men to work faster, the researcher trying to get her professional association to accept her research, the daughter trying to convince her father that she is old enough for a date, are all examples of people involved in the process of persuasive communication.

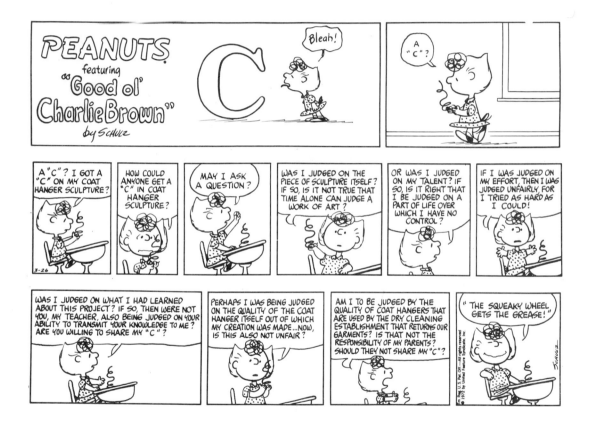

Persuading people is one of the most common types of communication in which you participate. Also, a good deal of your public speaking will involve your attempting to get people to change their behavior or to change their attitudes. A change of behavior and a change of attitude are the two major types of change we strive for in our speeches.

PERSUASIVE PURPOSE

The purpose of persuasive speaking is to cause others to believe, to feel, or act in a way that is predetermined by the speaker. According to Larry A. Samovar and Jack Mills,[1] there are three main purposes of persuasive speeches:

1. **To convince:** speeches whose immediate aim is to induce belief.
2. **To stimulate:** speeches aimed at reinforcing existing beliefs, attitudes, and emotions.
3. **To actuate:** speeches aimed at inducing action.

For the sake of our discussion about persuasive speaking, we shall call all of these purposes appropriate purposes for persuasive speeches.

PERSUASION AND THE AUDIENCE

We discussed audience analysis in chapter 3. But we now need to mention audience analysis as it relates to persuasive speaking. To bring about attitude change, the speaker must know, prior to the speech, the listeners' attitudes toward the topic that is to be presented. Speakers need to be concerned about the attitudes of the entire audience, not just a few individuals.

> *A man can get agreements from everything around him.*
>
> CARLOS CASTANEDA

The listeners' attitudes toward a subject can be learned in various ways. One method is to put yourself in their shoes. Try to reverse roles with them and see how you would feel about a certain matter. Another method is to sample your intended audience. Ask your listeners how they feel about a particular issue. Listen carefully to what they say and you will

[1] *Oral Communication: Message and Response* (Dubuque, IA: Wm. C. Brown, 1968), pp. 156–157.

quickly detect how they feel. The more familiar you become with the audience's attitudes, the better you can adjust your persuasive appeals and organizational pattern.

APPROACHES TO PERSUASION

When you have selected your persuasive purpose and you understand your audience, you must then become acquainted with approaches for persuading people. Samovar and Mills have this to say about modes or approaches to persuasion:

> Twenty-four centuries ago Aristotle in his *Rhetoric* observed that there are three instruments of persuasion: (a) ". . . persuasion is effected by the ARGUMENTS, when we demonstrate the truth, real or apparent, by such means as inhere in particular cases." (2) ". . . persuasion is effected through the audience, when they are brought by the speech into a state of EMOTION; for we give very different decisions under the sway of pain or joy, and liking or hatred." (3) "The CHARACTER of the speaker is a cause of persuasion when the speech is so uttered as to make him worthy of belief; for as a rule we trust men of probity more, and more quickly, about things in general, while on points outside the realm of exact knowledge, where opinion is divided, we trust them absolutely." The durability of Aristotle's classification may be seen by a cursory examination of rhetorical treatises from his day to the present. Perhaps different labels are affixed to the modes of persuasion, and perhaps some of the modes have been subdivided, but all are essentially Aristotelian in their origin.[2]

From Aristotle's early approach we shall briefly discuss arguments or logical appeals, emotions or psychological appeals, and character or personal credibility. Each of these is important for the effective persuasive speaker. Each shall be presented separately. However, in practice, they are inseparable. All the modes work together to effectively influence an audience.

Personality can open doors, but only character can keep them open.

ELMER LETERMAN

[2]Samovar and Mills, *Oral Communication*, pp. 160–161.

THE LOGICAL APPROACH

The major aspects of the logical approach are reasoning, testimony, statistics, and factual examples. Each of these was presented in detail in chapter 4 under forms of support. A brief review of chapter 4 should help you better understand the logical approach, which essentially is the rational approach for persuading others. Research seems to indicate it has a more lasting effect on audiences than the other two approaches.

> With you I want
> to be
> just like a blade of grass
> that moves as the
> air moves it—
> to talk
> just according to
> the impulse of the moment
> and I do.
>
> KAHIL GIBRAN

THE PSYCHOLOGICAL APPROACH

This approach is to persuade others to a point of view by making them feel part of the point of view. To be persuaded, the audience must feel a need to be persuaded. To be an effective persuader, then, you must have an understanding of at least some of the following human needs:

Self-preservation: the need to survive.

Self-esteem: the need to be "looked up to."

Personal enjoyment: the need for nicer things.

Altruism: the need to be unselfish.

Sex attraction: the need to be seen as sexually attractive.

If an audience has a need and you are aware of it, then you can play on the need to bring about persuasion.

THE CREDIBILITY APPROACH

What you are and how you are perceived are extremely important in persuasive speaking. Credibility is composed of a variety of factors. The three that seem most important to us are *trust, knowledge,* and *dyna-*

mism. Are you someone people can trust: Do you appear to be reliable? Do you really know what you are talking about? Do you come across as an enthusiastic, dynamic person? The composite use of these three aspects of credibility can make you a more or less effective persuader.

ORGANIZING THE PERSUASIVE SPEECH

There are a variety of approaches to organizing a persuasive speech. The problem-solution design, a foreshortening of educational philosopher John Dewey's reflective process, is an organizational structure that includes: a statement of the problem with its nature, extent, and causes; a list of all plausible solutions to the problem; a weighing and evaluating of each solution; the selection of the best solution; and the recommendation of action to implement the solution selected.[3]

The formula for successful advertising, AIDA, suggests the following organizational pattern: Attention, Interest, Desire, and Action.

Douglas Ehninger[4] advances a "motivated sequence," which blends the logical problem-solving approach with the psychological factors of attention, need, satisfaction, visualization, and action.

All these approaches have merit and are good methods for organizing the persuasive speech; however, the approach we shall present is called the **motivating process.**

THE MOTIVATING PROCESS

In 1926 John A. McGee wrote a book entitled *Minimum Essentials of Persuasive Speaking*. This work outlined an approach he called the motivating process is an organizational approach for developing a presentation that leads listeners through five steps of human problem-solving to motivate them to respond positively to the communicator's goal:

1. **Attention.** Attract favorable interest from listeners and direct their attention toward the main ideas in the presentation.

[3]See Brent D. Peterson, Gerald M. Goldhaber, and R. Wayne Pace. *Communication Probes* 2nd ed. (Chicago: Science Research Associates, 1977), p. 211.

[4]Ehninger, Douglas *et al. Principles and Types of Speech Communication,* 8th ed. Glenview, IL: Scott, Foresman, 1978.

2. **Need.** Develop a general problem and relate it to the desires of the audience. This is accomplished through the development of the following steps:

    a. State the need.
    b. Illustrate the need.
    c. Develop the need.
    d. Relate the need.

3. **Satisfaction.** Show how the belief or action proposed solves the problem. This is accomplished through development of the following steps:

    a. State the belief or action.
    b. Explain the proposed action.
    c. Show how the action theoretically solves the problem.
    d. Give actual examples showing that the proposed action has worked elsewhere.
    e. Overcome objections that might be raised.

4. **Visualization.** Intensify desire to see the proposed action adopted or carried out. This is accomplished by describing vividly how things will be in the future if the proposal is adopted.

5. **Action.** Translate the desire created into overt behavior. This is accomplished by using specific appeals to close the sale or secure the desired action.

These steps are helpful when developing a presentation designed to motivate listeners to accept and act on an idea. The technique provides a unified approach to developing a persuasive presentation.

When confronted with the necessity of making a decision, people tend to proceed through a fairly uniform sequence of responses. To solve the problem, they must first focus attention on the issues in order to reduce

distractions. Second, they must feel a need to change from the current situation, to sense that something about the situation is undesirable or at least could be made better. Third, they must be convinced of the soundness, desirability, and workability of the proposal. Fourth, they must be stimulated to want to act on the recommendation. And, last, they must be urged to actually move and do something about the proposal. The motivating process matches each of the steps in problem solving and leads listeners to accept the proposal.

A persuasive speech that uses the motivating process is organized in the following manner:

I.   **Attention.** Remember, the attention step is designed to gain the attention of the audience and to create goodwill and respect between the presenter and the audience. This can be accomplished

in several different ways, including opening the presentation with any of the following:

A. An example, illustration, or story with a point (the point should be made in a different manner in the need step).

B. A humorous anecdote that makes a point.

C. A quotation from an easily recognized personality or source that expresses a key point to be developed.

D. A striking statement involving some unusual information or unexpected way of phrasing a key point.

E. A rhetorical question that members of the audience can answer mentally and that gets them thinking about a key point of the presentation.

F. A personal greeting, a reference to the subject or occasion.

II. **Need.** This can be accomplished by following the procedure for developing the need step. Include each of the following forms of support in the order suggested:

A. A direct statement that describes an undesirable situation that could be improved or strengthened. For example, the statement might be phrased like this: "Just about everyone pays more taxes than they want to"; or, "Most homes have no fire-warning devices"; or, "Dishonesty has resulted in losses in the millions of dollars to average citizens."

B. An illustration that describes one or more detailed examples showing that the problem stated is actually a fact; tell, for example, about a home fire that killed several members of a family.

C. Further development that describes additional examples, instances, statistical data, and testimonies that show how serious and widespread the problem is.

D. A relationship that explains how the problem affects the members of the immediate audience.

III. **Satisfaction.** The objective of this step is to show how the problem can be alleviated. This can be accomplished by making:

A. A direct statement of the action proposed to meet the need established earlier. Having established the problem that most homes have no fire-warning devices, the statement of satisfaction might be "Although we may not be able to eliminate all fires, we can save lives by providing adequate warning to family members."

B. An explanation of the proposed action and what is involved in removing the problem by using the method suggested. This should be as clear and as complete an explanation as possible. The use of diagrams and other kinds of visuals should be considered.

C. A theoretical demonstration that explains how the proposed action should solve the problem. Explain that according to principles involved or the way things usually happen, the proposed action should alleviate the need in this way. Demonstrate that the proposed action is a logical and adequate solution to the problem.

D. A practical experience that provides support by giving real examples and instances in which such a proposal has solved the problem somewhere else. Add the testimony of experts, data, and the descriptions of real cases to support the proposal.

E. An effort to forestall objections by explaining how your proposed action solves the problem; try to answer any major objections you think members of the audience might have to your proposal.

The emotions that an orator wishes to evoke from his audience dare not be artificial. Nature has assigned special looks and tones to each emotion, and any artifice is quickly discovered.

CRASSUS
from *Cicero*

IV. **Visualization.** The function of this step is to intensify the desire of the audience to move ahead with the solution proposed. People are more inclined to adopt a new course of action when they are imaginatively carried into the future to visualize conditions as they would be when the action is carried out. This is accomplished by vividly describing members of the audience actually enjoying the security that comes from doing as you propose. Describe, for example, audience members in a situation in which their lives might be saved by an early fire warning.

V. **Action.** In this step you want to urge the audience to take the action you propose. The primary objective is to bring the presentation to a close with a sense of completeness that stirs the audience to action. Some of the most effective endings are these:

   A. Summary and challenge that make a short restatement of the main points or arguments and a direct request to take action.

   B. A quotation, poem, literary phrase, or saying that makes the point and implies the action to be taken.

   C. An example, incident, or story that contains the essence of the point and suggests the action to be taken.

   D. An inducement that makes an offer of some additional benefit for taking the action proposed. Salespeople use this approach when they give prizes or gifts for buying.

   E. Testimony that indicates you are committed to the action and are accepting the proposal yourself.

A one-paragraph persuasive speech that utilizes the motivating process might look like this:

1. Do you know how to organize a persuasive speech?

2. The inability to make a persuasive presentation results in the loss of thousands of dollars annually to many people.

3. Most of us can reverse that situation by becoming acquainted with the five-step motivating process.

4. Jerry Horkesheinier, a close friend of mine, tripled his salary last year by using the persuasive process to sell investment partnerships.

5. You have just read about the process in our text. Try it; it's easy. I intend to use it every chance I get.

THE MOTIVATING PROCESS APPLIED TO VARIOUS TYPES OF AUDIENCES

	(1) Favorable to Proposition	(2) Interested but Undecided	(3) Apathetic to Situation	(4) Opposed to Proposition

Attention	Intensify interest:
	1. Vivid illustrations.
	2. New aspects of situation.
	3. Challenge.
		Direct attention toward basic elements of the problem.
		1. Definition.
		2. Narrowing question.
		3. Historical data (Seek clarity; avoid dullness.)
			Overcome inertia:
			1. Startling statements.
			2. Hit vital spots.
			3. Vivid illustrations.
				Secure common ground:
				1. Emphasizing points of agreement.
				   a. Attitude.
				   b. Beliefs.
				   c. Experiences.

Problem (need)	Make problem more impressive:
	1. Vivid illustrations.
	2. Startling disclosures.
	3. Personalize; arousal of personal responsibility.
		Demonstrate basic causes of problem:
		1. Make certain that audience is aware problem exists.
		2. Why does the situation exist?
			Demonstrate existence of problem:
			1. Powerful evidence:
			   a. Facts.
			   b. Figures.
			   c. Testimony.
			2. Hook up with common experiences.
				Overcome opposition to change:
				1. Seek agreement on general principle; then apply principle to specific problem.
				2. Overpower objections:
				   a. Facts.
				   b. Testimony.

Solution (satisfaction)	State solution definitely: 1. Don't argue. 2. Be brief. 3. Command, if conditions warrant.	Demonstrate that your plan is best solution: 1. Explain the plan. 2. Offer proof that it removes causes of problem. 3. Expert testimony. 4. Examples of successful operation.	(Audience should now be interested but undecided. Follow technique in first column to the left.)	Demonstrate that your plan is the best solution: (Follow technique for solution step in column No. (2). In addition, relate the solution to the general principle agreed upon above.)
Visualization	Make results of solution more vivid: 1. Imagery. 2. Impelling motives. 3. Projection of the audience into the future. 4. Mild exaggeration.	Same as column No. (1). Beware of exaggeration.	Same as column No. (1). Beware of exaggeration.	Same as column No. (1). Beware of exaggeration.
Action	Request definite action: 1. Specific means by which individuals may help.	Request definite action: 1. Specific means by which individuals may help.	Request definite action: 1. Specific means by which individuals may help.	Request definite action: 1. Specific means by which individuals may help. 2. Appeal to habit.

The Motivating Process

John A. McGee

The motivating process Imagine yourself with twenty other people in a room on the third floor of a building. Some one smells smoke, and it is discovered that the building is on fire. Immediately, every one in the room is confronted with the very practical problem of finding a way to escape. A glance proves that the stairs are enveloped in flames. The way to the fire escape, also, is cut off. Three stories is quite a distance to jump. Somebody suggests that the only logical way to get out is by tying together a number of coats and using them for a rope. The solution appears to be the logical one, and the group, visualizing what will happen unless they take immediate action, proceed to carry out the plan.

This illustration discloses the essential steps through which the human mind goes in arriving at any conclusion and acting upon it. Since the object of persuasive speaking is to secure this sort of definite response from an audience, we may conclude that there are five steps which a speaker should use, under most circumstances, to gain his end. *First,* he must compel an audience to listen to him; *second,* he must make them feel a strong need for solving some problem; *third,* he must point out the logical solution; *fourth,* he must make the solution appear so attractive that a strong desire for it is aroused; *fifth,* he must invite definite action by pointing out practical ways of arriving at the solution. These are the five steps in organizing a speech. The entire series of steps is called the *motivating process.*

The good speaker gains his end by:

1. Securing attention;
2. Stating a problem [*need*];
3. Offering a solution [*satisfaction*];
4. Visualizing its desirability;
5. Inviting definite action.

Each of these steps is as indispensable to purposeful speaking as each ingredient is to the making of a good cake. Conditions may modify the various steps somewhat, or even dictate the omission of one or more of them, but most effective speakers under most circumstances secure their total effects by leading the audience through these fundamental steps.

A brief statement of the purpose of each step in the organization of a persuasive speech, and certain practical suggestions as to procedure in building each phase are in order at this point.

Attention step It is scarcely necessary to point out the fact that gaining and holding attention is the speaker's first and most vital problem. Attention may be defined as a state of readiness to respond, and the attention phase of a speech is that introductory part of your address that is calculated to focus all the faculties of your listeners upon the problem that you would discuss with them.

It must not be assumed that because we designate the first portion of a speech as the attention phase that the speaker is relieved of the responsibility of gripping his auditor's attention after he has disposed of his introductory remarks. *To dominate the attention of your listeners is your primary job during the entire course of time that you spend on the platform.* But, as the old saying goes, "First impressions are lasting ones"; and so we emphasize the gaining of attention at the outset of a speech by designating the opening as the attention step.

It is enough to notice that the attention step of a speech should lead the audience naturally into a consideration of the problem that the speaker wishes to present. This may be done in various ways. The speaker may tell a story or recite an incident or make a striking statement that leads up to or suggests the situation which he wishes to visualize for the group.

Below is printed an example of one method successfully employed to catch the attention of an audience and focus that attention upon a situation that demands a remedy:

A pale, thin moon looked down and grinned. The pert, young coupé stood lifeless, its hood stuck up like the broken wing of a bird. The girl bit her lips to keep from crying. The boy was stern, his shirt ruined—likewise his temper. And November didn't explain all of the frost in the atmosphere.

The boy said, "Never again!"
The coupé said, "Never again!"
The girl said, "Never again!"

The girl meant, "Never again will I go out with this man!" The girl was right. She never did. The coupé meant, "Never again will I be able to run!" The coupé was wrong. $80.00 worth of repairs and it did run again. The boy meant, "Never again will I be such a fool about my motor!" The boy was right, but a trifle late.

Use your own ingenuity and strive to secure unusual and vivid openings that will grip the attention of your listeners and compel them to listen to you. The first duty of the public speaker is to secure and hold the undivided attention of his audience.

Problem step (need) You will recall that in our illustration of the steps which the human mind takes in arriving at a conclusion, that occurrence which followed immediately upon the smelling of smoke was the realization that the group was confronted with the very practical problem of escaping from the burning building. In other words, a situation was revealed to them that alarmed them and impelled the conclusion that something must be done. Now it is precisely this thing that a speaker who wants to get a definite response from an audience must do after gaining attention. *A persuasive speech should give an audience some definite problem to solve.* Or, to put the matter in a different way, an address calculated to gain a definite response must make the audience visualize a condition of affairs that is completely unsatisfactory and about which something must be done. Abraham Lincoln, throughout the course of his famous debates with Judge Douglas, spent a large portion of his time arousing his listeners to a sense of dissatisfaction with prevailing conditions. He made them see the dangers that confronted the Union, half slave and half free. "A house divided against itself must fall." This was the burden of Lincoln's antislavery campaign.

In a general way, all human actions may be traced to one of two attitudes of mind: desire for a change; fear of a change. Either a man is dissatisfied with his social life, with political affairs in his community, and wishes to do something to change these conditions, or he eminently contented with these affairs and is afraid that some one will "throw a monkey wrench" into the wheels. His course of action with regard to his business life, or his social life, or is community life will be dictated by his satisfaction or dissatisfaction with affairs as he finds them. . . .

It is the duty of a speaker either to arouse a longing to change existing conditions or a desire to maintain those conditions in the face of impending change.

In the problem phase a situation is visualized—one that is quite alarming in its possible consequences to the audience. This problem is personalized. *It is this personalization of the problem phase that should be emphasized particularly.* We have endeavored to keep constantly in mind the necessity of the public speaker being objective—he must think in terms of the audience. And no place is this quite so necessary as in the problem phase. It is not enough for you to demonstrate that some alarming misfortune is about to overtake the human race in general, but it is imperative, if you want to get a response from a particular group, to show that group that they, themselves, are likely to suffer as a result of failure to act. . . .

When the speaker wishes to protest against an impending action, rather than urging a change, his procedure in the problem phase will differ somewhat from that described above. Suppose that you want your schoolmates to take action to prevent the resignation of an athletic coach. In such a situation, your job is to arouse contentment with conditions under the present coaching régime, and to alarm the group with the probable consequences of the impending action, at the same time making it apparent that the thing will happen unless they take steps to prevent it.

Two simple formulae will assist you in learning to develop the problem phase:

1. When you seek action to change conditions:
   a. Illustrate the situation; the more detailed the picture the better;
   b. Make that situation seem extremely undesirable to the particular audience before you.

2. When you seek action to prevent a change:
   a. Illustrate the present situation briefly;
   b. Make it appear desirable to the audience before you;
   c. Alarm them with the probable consequences of altering the situation;
   d. Demonstrate the imminent danger of such change occurring.

The problem phase, like the preceding one of attention, will be modified by the situation under which you speak. An audience of striking miners requires little persuasion on the part of a speaker to be aware of a deep feeling of dissatisfaction with existing conditions. A speaker may very easily develop this essential basis for action with such a group; yet, even here the step may not wisely be omitted. Sometimes a mere recital of grievances already felt is the quickest way to gain the response desired. . . .

Solution step (satisfaction) No very deep process of reasoning is required to conclude that the logical next step in the building of a persuasive speech is to offer some answer to the question which the problem phase brings before the audience. What shall be done? What is the best method of getting out of the unfortunate situation in which we find ourselves? *Very frequently, this is the* most important part of a persuasive speech, because while many persons may agree with a speaker that something should be done, there is frequently quite general disagreement as to what remedy should be tried out. After the group realizes that the building is on fire, they are keenly anxious to find the best and quickest means of escape. But not infrequently there is disagreement as to what constitutes the most desirable method. It is your job in the solution phase to prove to the group that the particular solution which you have to offer is the one for them to adopt. In other words, at this point, invite the particular response that you have had in mind from the first for the audience to perform. Having shown that political corruption is bankrupting the government and bringing untold hardship upon every man in the audience, propose the election of your candidate as the logical means of relief.

The necessity of this solution stage in the speech is so apparent that little space need be devoted to showing why it is used. The step is not, however, a simple or inconsequential one. Many good speakers have called it the most critical point in a speech: that time when you bring forward the new idol to replace the one torn down.

Without entering into a detailed discussion of the methods of developing this part of a speech under varying circumstances, it may be suggested that there are certain general questions about your proposition that it is well to answer for the audience. *Does your scheme supply a remedy for the major defects that you have alleged are prevalent in the present system?*

In addition to the question of the power of the proposed solution to remedy the defects of the existing system, *it is necessary to show that there are no vital objections to it.* Will it introduce new evils into the situation?

It will be apparent from the above discussion of the solution step that it is concerned in no small measure with logical demonstration. It seems to produce conviction in the minds of your auditors: to have them admit "this is what ought to be done."

An example of one sort of solution step is printed below. The difficulty of presenting a really adequate sample of this lesson is almost insurmountable, but the selection from an address by William Jennings Bryan, delivered in Chicago on September 13, 1899, will serve to illustrate the general method of building the solution step. Mr. Bryan had already portrayed in his majestic fashion the grip which corporations and trusts had on the American people. This portion of the speech in which the problem is developed is, obviously, omitted, as is also a part of the solution step, because space does not permit their inclusion.

Let me suggest one thing that I believe will be a step in the right direction. The great trouble has been that, while our platforms denounce corporations, corporations control the elections and place the men who are elected to enforce the law under obligations to them.

Let me propose a remedy—not a complete remedy, but a step in the right direction. Let the laws, state and national, make it a penal offense for any corporation to contribute to the campaign funds of any political party. Nebraska has such a law, passed two years ago. Such a measure was introduced in the state of New York, but so far it has not become a law.

You remember the testimony taken before a Senate committee a few years ago, when the head of the sugar trust testified that the sugar trust made it its business to contribute to the campaign funds, and when asked to which one it contributed replied that it depended upon the circumstances.

"To which fund do you contribute in Massachusetts?" was asked. "To the Republican fund." "To which fund in New

York?" "To the Democratic fund." "To which fund in New Jersey?" and the man replied, "Well, I will have to look at the books; that is a doubtful state."

If the people are in earnest, they can destroy monopoly, and you never can do anything in this country until the people are in earnest. When the American people understand what the monopoly question means, I believe there will be no power, political, financial, or otherwise, to prevent the people from taking possession of every branch of the government, from President to Supreme Court, and making the government responsive to the people's will.

Visualization step   The fourth step in a persuasive speech—that of arousing intense desire for the particular solution you offer to a problem—might be thought of as part of the solution step. *But this process that we term visualization is essentially one of emotional arousal.* It is a projecting of the audience into the future and portraying for them the successful realization of their desires as a result of adopting your proposal. The solution step, just discussed, is more concerned with logical demonstration. It seeks to produce intellectual conviction in the minds of your hearers. *But mere demonstration of a new and better plan of action than the one now used may not arouse an active desire to take the step.* Emotional arousal is an essential part of the process used to gain action. Picture for your audience how much more satisfactory conditions are likely to be if they will adopt your scheme; make them fear what may happen if they fail to act as you want them to.

As we shall see later, imagery of all kinds enters into this projection of the group into the future. We speak of it as visualization, but the process is not limited to the arousal of a visual image. It may be expedient to appeal to the sense of hearing, smell, and the like. But for the present, strive merely to paint a word picture of some sort showing your remedy in operation, meeting the demands of the audience. . . .

Action step   The final step in the securing of any action is that of summation and conclusion. *The importance of one final turn of the wheel cannot be overemphasized.* Notice the particularly effective conversationalist, when you have passed a pleasant evening with him. He does not say merely, "good night," and then retire. That would be distinctly a "let down" from the congenial plane upon which the evening has been spent. Instead, he tells one final anecdote more interesting, perhaps, than any he has yet related, thus leaving you with the impression that there are many more pleasant evenings in store for you in his company. The successful salesman, too, not infrequently saves his choicest bit until the decisive moment—that moment when his prospect is about to sign on the dotted line. Public speakers from Demosthenes to Beveridge have devoted no little attention to what we term the action phase of the speech. In the final moment of a talk, it is imperative that you make a good impression to leave in the minds of your audience.

Precisely how does one go about building this step of a speech? What should it contain? What methods are used to develop it? Only general directions will be indulged in at this point. . . .

In general, let your action phase sum up what has preceded, and invite definite action from the group. Notice the method employed by Senator James A. Reed in concluding a political speech at Sedalia, Missouri:

Let us demand the honest administration of government; the swift and sure punishment of all public plunderers, bribemongers, and other malefactors; the equalization of the burden of taxation; the repeal of all laws creating special privileges; the dismissal of an army of spies, snoopers, sneaks, and informers, the liberation of honest business from oppressive interference by governmental agents; the prosecution and punishment of those who, by trusts, combinations, and restraints of trade, make war on honest business and despoil the people.

Gaining attention, stating a problem [*need*], offering a solution [*satisfaction*],

making that solution appear highly desirable, and inviting specific action, then, are the five essential steps in the development of a persuasive speech. It is usually unwise to omit any of these steps.

SOURCE: Use by permission of Charles Scribners Sons from *Persuasive Speaking* by John A. McGee. Copyright 1929, Charles Scribner's Sons.

WHAT TO KNOW

A speaker attempting to persuade is trying to get listeners to believe, feel, or act in a manner she or he wishes. Four modes of persuasion are:

1. Persuasion through logical appeals that use evidence and reasoning.
2. Persuasion through information.
3. Persuasion through various psychological appeals.
4. Persuasion through personal credibility.

The organizational structure recommended for preparing and presenting the persuasive speech is an adaptation of John McGee's motivating process. This sequence contains an attention step, a need step, a sastisfaction step, and an action step. A detailed description is given as to how to accomplish these steps in the persuasive speech.

WHAT TO DO

How Credible Are You? Analyze the areas or topics on which you might be considered a credible speaker by your peers. In what areas that your peers do not consider you to be a credible speaker would you like to be considered credible? What can you do to enhance your credibility in these weak areas?

Reasoning in Advertising Review advertisements that appear in newspapers, magazines, radio, and television. Of the four kinds of reasoning, which is used most frequently?

Using the Motivating Process with Your Instructor Decide on something you and a few other classmates would like to persuade your instructor to do or allow you to do. (*Example:* You may want your instructor to change his or her mind about giving a final written test. Rather, you would like him or her to use your final speech as a method of evaluating your knowledge and skill in the course.)

Reason out your situation, gather facts and opinions, examine the appeals you could employ, analyze your credibility on this topic, analyze your instructor's probable position on the issue, and finally organize your material into the five-step process. Good luck!

WHERE TO LEARN MORE

Anderson, Kenneth E. *Persuasion. Theory and Practice.* 2nd ed. Boston: Allyn and Bacon, 1978.

Bettinghaus, Erwin P. *Persuasive Communication.* 3rd ed. New York: Holt, 1980.

Ehninger, Douglas *et al. Principles and Types of Speech Communication.* 8th ed. Glenview, IL: Scott, Foresman, 1978.

Peterson, Brent D. *et al. Communication Probes.* 2nd ed. Chicago: Science Research Associates, 1977, p. 211

Scheidel, Thomas. *Persuasive Speaking.* Glenview, IL: Scott, Foresman, 1967.

SPECIAL SPEAKING OCCASIONS

9

CEREMONY, PRECISENESS, AND TACT ARE ESSENTIAL

Most speeches are either informative, persuasive, or entertaining. However, occasionally you will find yourself in a situation where you must give a special kind of speech. These special speeches require ceremony, preciseness, and tact. For example, you may be asked to speak at a funeral. How do you approach this kind of speaking assignment? We know that you will need to be concerned for the bereaved and comfort them and that you will need to praise the deceased. There are many different special speaking occasions and each has its own demands. In this chapter we will consider six special speaking situations: introductions, presentations, acceptances, welcomes, tributes, and nominations. You will probably give several of these types of speeches in your lifetime. And, chances are good that you will find yourself giving one of these types of speeches when you least expect it.

INTRODUCTIONS

A noted authority in the field of communications was given a very interesting introduction before speaking to an audience of two thousand students who knew a great deal about him. The introducer began by announcing how great it was to have the foremost authority in mass communication in the United States to speak today. He then had to look at his notes to read the speaker's name! For the next fifteen minutes the

THE BORN LOSER　　　　　　　　　　　　**By Art Sansom**

introducer raved on about the speaker's accomplishments. Before sitting down, he announced that the speaker would be the greatest speaker the students would ever hear. The speaker moved to the podium and was a miserable failure. First, he could not regain the attention of the audience who had tuned out during the excessively long introduction, and second, he could not meet the expectations of being the greatest speaker the students would ever hear.

Introductory speeches are simple to make and to prepare. However, it is crucial that they be given appropriately.

THE PURPOSE

The introduction speech should help to create a friendly relationship between the speaker and the audience. The idea is to briefly teach the audience about the speaker and to reduce any concerns the audience may have about the speaker. As important as these speeches are, they are often mishandled. It is easy to fail if we do not adhere to a system for giving introductions. The following system can be beneficial.

THE SYSTEM

1. **You are not the main speaker.** Keep in mind that your function is nothing more or less than to *introduce* the speaker to the audience. You should do this in two to three minutes. Very rarely should an introduction be more than three minutes. If you exceed this time limit, you are no longer introducing, you are speaking. Subordinate yourself to the speaker when you make an introduction.

2. **Discuss the nature of the occasion.** Quickly review the reason for the meeting and why the audience is getting together. Present the purpose of the speech.

3. **Study the speaker and share this information with the audience.** Learn as much as you can about the speaker. Know how to pronounce names and titles correctly and make certain your information is accurate. There is a tendency to want to present everything you know about the person. This is dangerous. Select only information that is important and that can be presented within the appropriate time limit.

4. **Conclude.** The conclusion should include the name of the speaker and the name of the talk. Do not mess around! Hurry up and shut up.

SPECIAL CONCERNS

1. **Do not overpraise the speaker.** When too much good is said, the speaker has difficulty living up to the audience's expectations. Say enough to build the credibility of the speaker, but do not overdo it.

2. **Stay within time limits.** If you are not given time limits, do not exceed the three minutes previously mentioned.

3. **Know what you are going to say so you do not have to read it.** Reading the introduction of a speaker makes the speaker unimportant. If what he or she has done is not important enough to remember, then it probably would not be important enough to cause the audience to listen.

PRESENTATIONS

Oftentimes in our lives we may find ourselves presenting an award to someone. We may present an award for the best citizenship, the best athlete, the person with the biggest feet, the best employee of the month, the most outstanding parent, and on and on. There are many awards to be presented, and you will likely give this speech nearly as often as you give the speech of introduction.

THE PURPOSE

The purpose for giving a presentation speech is, obviously, to present a prize, gift, or award to someone. You should keep in mind that this speech is to emphasize the award and the person who is receiving it. Therefore you should be brief and to the point. Do not call attention to yourself but call attention to the award and to the recipient.

THE SYSTEM

1. **Discuss the award.** An effective speech will make the audience aware of the history and background of the award. If the award is, for example, a conference championship in football, then this should be brought out. The quality of the conference and its teams should be discussed so that the audience becomes aware of the significance of the award.

2. **Point out the accomplishments of the recipient or recipients of the award.** If the football team had a winning season or maybe an undefeated season, this should be brought out. If a player or players on the team received special recognition, this should also be included.

3. **Be as brief as you can.** Stand up and talk about the award as specifically as possible and then present the accomplishments of the recipient(s) and give the award. You need to know as much as possible about the award and the recipient(s) but you must be as brief in your presentation as you can be.

> *Each speech and its parts must be suited to the particular occasion; the same speech might not suit another man.*
>
> ISOCRATES

SPECIAL CONCERNS

1. **Make a proper presentation.** Be careful when presenting an award that you give it from your left hand to the recipient's left hand. This will allow your right hands to be free so that you can shake hands at the same time that the award is presented. If you are aware of this procedure it will reduce embarrassment and cause a smooth reception of the award.

2. **Do not go overboard.** Do not give more praise for the award and for the recipient than they deserve. This can instantly ruin a presentation speech.

ACCEPTANCES

Acceptances are necessary whenever you are given an award or honor. Those of you who have seen the academy awards have likely witnessed very effective acceptances and very bad acceptances. When you receive an award, you should accept it in a correct and polite manner.

THE PURPOSE

The purpose of this speech is to give an honest and brief thanks for an award.

THE SYSTEM

1. **Give brief thanks to those making the awards.** Thank all those involved in the presentation and creation of the award. Do not make too much of it.

2. **Thank those who helped you attain the award.** Again, this need be nothing more than a few words to give appreciation to those who helped you attain the award.

3. **Be brief.** This is extremely important. There is nothing that will make you appear to be less appreciative than to give a long acceptance speech and to linger on when you should be sitting down.

SPECIAL CONCERNS

Express your gratitude and then sit down.

WELCOMES

Welcome speeches are a very common type of occasional speech. For example, you may often find yourself introducing people to your class at school, or to your club, or to your team. Almost everyone at one time or another has had the opportunity to welcome people and introduce them to an audience or group of friends.

THE PURPOSE

This type of speech is a double speech of welcome. You should introduce the guests to your group and then the group to the guests. The purpose is to make everyone better acquainted.

THE SYSTEM

1. **Teach your guests about your group.** Familiarize the persons to be introduced with the group they will meet. Let them know as much as possible about the situation and the people.

2. **Get as much information as possible about the people to be introduced.** There is no excuse for presenting inaccurate information when you are making a welcome speech.

3. **Be organized.**
   a. Introduction—welcome the guests who are visiting and tell as much about them as you can.
   b. Body—introduce your guests to the group by telling them about the group and the situation.
   c. Conclusion—make a brief statement of your hope that the visit will be a profitable one for both the visitors and your group.

SPECIAL CONCERNS

1. **Be brief.** As in most of the speeches for special occasions, the welcoming speech should be as brief as possible.

2. **Be honest.** Be truthful about the people you are introducing and do not gush over them to the point of embarrassing them as well as yourself.

TRIBUTES

The tribute speech is used to pay tribute to a person's or group's qualities or achievements. At a funeral a speaker was eulogizing the deceased, a person who enjoyed the reputation of being a great talker, when the congregation began to laugh. The speaker pondered what had caused the audience to laugh in the middle of a serious funeral oration. Then it dawned on him that he had mentioned how great a talker the deceased had been. Almost everyone in the congregation had had experiences with this person's ability to talk unceasingly. Although a bit embarrassed that he had caused laughter at a funeral, the speaker continued his speech. Speeches of tribute should call attention to the qualities and achievements that a person attained. These kinds of speeches need not be without humor but they should seriously present the deceased's life.

THE PURPOSE

The purpose of a tribute speech is to praise someone's qualities and accomplishments. Tributes take place in a variety of diverse situations, such as funerals, birthday parties, retirement from a job or position, and so on. A special form of the tribute speech is called the eulogy. This is a speech of tribute that is given in memory of a deceased person.

THE SYSTEM

1. **Strive for sincerity.** When giving a tribute, do not overdo it. There is a tendency to say more than the person being praised deserves. When this happens, the audience often questions the sincerity of the speaker and the credibility of the person being spoken about.

2. **Collect as much detail as possible about the person being honored.** Audiences are primarily interested in information they have not heard. This is especially true when the information has to do with a person that the audience cares for. To give an effective tribute, you should collect as many specifics as possible about the person you are going to praise. Focus on laudable characteristics and be willing to mention and discuss special hardships that the person has overcome.

3. **Organize the speech around the subject's accomplishments.** If the subject is well known, you may wish to make the talk more general. If the person is not well known, then you may wish to focus on specific details. Whatever the situation, be certain to organize the speech around a series of the subject's accomplishments.

SPECIAL CONCERNS

1. **No one is perfect.** Even though a person is being praised, it is occasionally effective to bring out the person's negative characteristics. As in the funeral eulogy just mentioned, where the deceased had been a ceaseless talker and the speaker mentioned this, the humor will make the person seem more human.

2. **Be objective about the subject.** Tell the truth and say it with sincerity; do not overdo it. It is far better to underpraise than to overpraise.

> *Man excels above all other living things in the power to reason and speak.*
>
> QUINTILIAN

NOMINATIONS

Nominating speeches can be heard in small informal club elections and in the very formal nomination of a presidential candidate. This form of speaking is very similar to the speech of introduction and of tribute. It is very likely that at one time or another you will have the opportunity to nominate a friend for a position.

THE PURPOSE

The main purpose of a nomination speech is to review the accomplishments of your candidate. You must also cause the audience to move to accept the nomination of your candidate and to actively support the nomination.

THE SYSTEM

1. **Organize as a speech to persuade.** The speech to nominate is essentially a speech to persuade, to get the audience to accept your candidate. The organization for this speech should generally follow that of the speech to persuade.

2. **Get attention.** Create interest by pointing out the problems that must be met by a good nominee.

3. **Bring forth qualities of your candidate.** Tell how he or she can meet the problems that exist with the present system or office. Go into depth about the candidate's qualities. Don't go overboard but honestly and efficiently enumerate your candidate's qualifications.

4. **Conclude.** Formally place your candidate's name in nomination and ask for the support of the audience.

SPECIAL CONCERNS

1. **Be positive in your approach.** Do not be sarcastic or ridicule other nominees. Be positive and present your candidate in as positive a manner as you can.

The orator aims to instruct, move, and charm.

QUINTILIAN

2. **Use conviction and enthusiasm.** Be enthusiastic and speak with all the conviction you have. This will cause the audience to be more enthusiastic. It could have a very positive impact on your audience.

3. **Do not be too lengthy in your presentation.** As in all speaking situations, do not be too windy or take more time than is absolutely necessary to place your candidate's name in nomination.

SOME GENERAL CONSIDERATIONS

When giving any of these special-occasion speeches, be certain to be brief and to the point. But you should be prepared to be very formal if the occasion calls for it. The best motto for being prepared for these kinds of speaking assignments is to stay flexible and be willing to go with the rules and customs that the situation calls for. One last word of advice is to study the people involved and try to meet their expectations.

WHAT TO KNOW

Speeches of introduction, presentation or award, acceptance, welcome, tribute, and nomination are special kinds of speaking. They may be informative, persuasive, or entertaining. They require some "home-work" to be completed. The speaker needs to be familiar with the occasion or situation, the audience's expectations, and, in some instances, the person or persons being talked about. Because special-occasion speeches must be brief to be effective, they can be harder to develop than a more complete speech.

WHAT TO DO

Introducing a Fellow Class Member Choose someone in the class you do not know very well and interview him or her for the purpose of introducing him or her to the rest of the class. You may find that you will be able to incorporate into this speech ideas from more than one of the special-occasion speeches. For example, you may find ideas from the introductory, tribute, and nomination speeches usable here.

Tribute Prepare a five-minute speech paying tribute to a person, group, or organization that you personally consider worthy. This person or group may be one of national or international reputation or may simply be someone who has had a meaningful impact on your life.

WHERE TO LEARN MORE

Reid, Loren. *Speaking Well.* 4th ed. New York: McGraw-Hill, 1982.

Ross, Raymond S. *Speech Communication: Fundamentals and Practice.* 5th ed. Englewood Cliffs, NJ: Prentice-Hall, 1980.

Samovar, Larry A., and Jack Mills. *Oral Communication: Message and Response.* 5th ed. Dubuque, IA: Wm. C. Brown, 1982

Verderber, Rudolph F. *The Challenge of Effective Speaking.* 5th ed. Belmont, CA: Wadsworth, 1983.

SPEAKING IN
SMALL GROUPS
AND CONFERENCES

10

GROUPS ARE IMPORTANT IN OUR LIVES

In business and industry, schools and universities, churches and hospitals, homes and clubs—wherever people work and socialize together—individuals participate in groups. At your school you are often part of a class group of five to seven people organized to investigate and report on an assigned subject. At your place of employment you are often part of a work group that discusses work-related problems. At your home you are part of another group that meets frequently and discusses everything from the state of the economy to how to live together comfortably.

A group is defined as a collection of three or more individuals whose interaction is mutually satisfactory. Group satisfaction is usually derived from sharing values and building enjoyable social relations and/or cooperatively solving problems and completing various tasks. And participation in a group means *talking*—as a leader or as a group member. Either we participate as a contributor to reports or discussions or we act as a leader and attempt to organize, direct, and facilitate an effective discussion or conference. And, whenver a group or organization grows, institutes new programs, unifies members, and engages in decision making, the members of the organization find themselves in conferences and group meetings of all kinds. How we interact and participate affects our own productivity and happiness as well as the efficiency and contentment of other members of the group. And, of course, the primary vehicle for successful interaction is effective speaking and listening.

GROUP DISCUSSION VERSUS
GROUP PRESENTATION

Notice that when you participate in a small group or conference, either you make an individual presentation or report, usually hoping to persuade or provide special information, or you engage in group discussion with the hope of cooperatively pooling information and arriving at solutions to problems. If you are invited to a meeting or conference to make an individual presentation, we suggest that you carefully review the chapters on informative and persuasive speaking, and that you give special consideration to visual appeals and strong evidence.

Remember, there is a difference between an individual presentation to a group and ongoing participation in group discussions. Distinguishing which activity you are engaged in will help you determine the most effective speaking approach to use.

We are assuming here that you are not being invited to a group to make a once-only presentation, but that as a group leader or group member, you will be discussing ideas, questioning information, and making decisions.

Let us now examine the nature of groups, and some skills necessary to leading, participating in, and evaluating group discussions. We will also consider the best patterns to use in an information-sharing or problem-solving discussion. Finally, the phenomenon of "group think" and the place of "large group meetings" will be discussed.

THE NATURE OF GROUPS

GROUP ASSETS

Greater Sum Total Knowledge and Information[1]   There is more information in a group than in any of its members. Thus problems that require the utilization of knowledge should give groups an advantage over individuals. Even if one member of the group knows much more than anyone else, the limited unique knowledge of lesser-informed individuals could

[1]From Norman R. F. Maier, "Assets and Liabilities in Group Problem Solving: The Need for an Integrative Function," *Psychological Review* 74(1967): 239–249. Copyright 1967 by the American Psychological Association. Reprinted by permission.

serve to fill in some gaps in knowledge. For example, a skilled machinist might contribute to an engineer's problem solving, and an ordinary worker might supply information on how a new machine might be received by workers.

Greater Number of Approaches to a Problem   It has been shown that individuals get into ruts in their thinking. Many obstacles stand in the way of achieving a goal, and a solution must circumvent these. The individual is handicapped in that he or she tends to persist in an approach and thus fails to find another approach that might solve the problem in a simpler manner. Individuals in a group have the same failing, but their approaches may be different. For example, one researcher may try to prevent the spread of a disease by making humans immune to the germ, another by finding and destroying the carrier of the germ, and still another by altering the environment so as to kill the germ before it reaches us. There is no way of determining which approach will best achieve the desired goal, but undue persistence in any one will stifle new discoveries. Since group members do not have identical approaches, each can contribute by knocking others out of thinking ruts.

Participation in Problem Solving Increases Acceptance   Many problems require solutions that depend on the support of others to be effective. Insofar as group problem solving permits participation and influence, it follows that more individuals accept solutions when a group solves the problem than when one person solves it. When an individual solves a problem he or she still has the task of persuading others. It follows, therefore, that when groups solve such problems, a greater number of persons accept and feel responsible for making the solution work. A low-quality solution that has good acceptance can be more effective than a higher-quality solution that lacks acceptance.

Better Comprehension of the Decision   Decisions made by an individual, which are to be carried out by others, must be communicated from the decision-maker to the decision-executors. Thus individual problem solving often requires an additional stage—that of relaying the decision reached. Failure in this communication process detracts from the merits of the decision and can even cause its failure or create a problem of greater magnitude than the initial problem that was solved. Many organizational problems can be traced to inadequate communication of decisions made by superiors and transmitted to subordinates, who have the task of implementing the decision.

The chances of communication failures are greatly reduced when the individuals who must work together in executing the decision have participated in making it. They not only understand the solution because they saw it develop, but they are also aware of the several other alternatives that were considered and the reasons they were discarded. The common assumption that decisions supplied by superiors are arbitrarily reached therefore disappears. A full knowledge of goals, obstacles, alternatives, and factual information is essential to communication, and this communication is maximized when the total problem-solving process is shared.

GROUP SIZE

When groups become too large, some members tend to talk only to the leaders. Other members lose themselves in the group and hardly talk at all. The best size for a problem-solving group seems to be five to seven people. Members of small groups usually speak frequently to one another, and group interaction is quite high. Groups with fewer than five people seem to be too small, and groups that have more than seven members usually break down into smaller cliques.

GROUP ACCOMPLISHMENT AND ENJOYMENT

All groups must work and accomplish something. If the group is meeting to discuss a problem, members will want to get to the problem. If the group is holding a meeting, members will probably want to get to the agenda and start discusssing the items. However, when many people are trying to work together it is imperative that they feel good about their relationship to the group. In other words, members of a group must enjoy themselves as well as accomplish work. This means that the group members must have opportunities to joke a bit, to get acquainted with each other, to relax a little, and to pay attention to each other's needs. An atmosphere of fun and trust is vital to a group's being able to work hard on various tasks. When group members accomplish large amounts of work and at the same time feel a great sense of satisfaction, personal worth, and esprit de corps, the group is successful.

LEADING A DISCUSSION

Members of a group seem to work best when they feel best. A leader can help by paying attention to the seating arrangements, the heating and lighting, and the general "feel" of the meeting room. The best interaction occurs when members sit in a circle where everyone can visually interact. The temperature should be neither too hot nor too cold. The lighting should be easy on the eyes, and bright glares from sunlight should be avoided. The room's walls, floors, and ceiling should contribute to the kind of mood you desire for your particular group task.

HELP PREPARE THE PARTICIPANTS

The leader is responsible for making sure that group members know ahead of time what the meeting is about. The members need time to think about the subject to be discussed, so that they can arrive at the meeting prepared to contribute ideas. Putting together an agenda or list of items that need to be accomplished, and then giving the agenda to members before the meeting can help prepare the group. In regularly scheduled meetings, the agenda for the next gathering may be partially developed during the present meeting.

START THE DISCUSSION

When the time for the discussion arrives and the members of the group are seated, the leader should introduce any new members and then introduce the topic or objective of the meeting. You may, for example, make a few comments about the topic and its importance and then ask a question in order to start the group discussion. Questions like, "What is the specific problem we are trying to solve?" "What seems to be the main cause of the difficulty?" "What is the extent of the problem?" will usually set off a lively discussion. If, however, the questions fail to produce sufficient discussion, you may call on various members to respond.

DIRECT THE DISCUSSION

From start to finish, it is the leader's responsibility to keep the discussion close to the subject at hand. A leader should see to it that key ideas are adequately discussed but that the discussion moves toward a solution or closure. The leader's best tools are questions that move the discussion along and clarify information. For example, if the discussion seems to be drifting away from the topic at hand, you can ask, "Can we relate this to our problem?" Or, "How does this tie into our last point?"

When time seems to be running out, a leader can often create closure on a matter by asking, "Now, what have we decided?" Or, "How should we conclude this matter?" Or, "Who would like to implement that solution?"

Keep the participation balanced among the members. If someone talks too much, interject by saying, "Yes, we understand your point," and then call on someone who has been rather quiet. Ask participants to keep their contributions brief and to the point so that everyone has time to say something on the topic. Meetings usually gather momentum and become more efficient when individual contributions are brief.

If the discussion gets heated, call on more neutral members to contribute ideas, or suggest a short break, or get the focus back on information rather than feelings. For example, ask about the reasoning and evidence on which the disagreement is based. Most conflict can be reduced by retracing the steps leading to the interpretation of the facts. Urge a quick resolution of the disputed point or delay its consideration until a later time. Be aware, though, that constructive conflict and competition in a group can be good.

Be careful of time limits. You must keep things moving so that group members feel like they are making progress. And you must bring the discussion to a successful ending. Be conscious of obtaining closure or solving a problem. Try to encourage the group to make a decision, delegate an action, or arrive at a conclusion. Nothing is more discouraging than to discuss in circles, lose sight of the subject, and run out of time before reaching a mutually satisfying resolution of a matter.

PARTICIPATING IN A DISCUSSION

In any discussion, the participants must conscientiously prepare and contribute if the discussion is going to have real value. In fact, the more participants are involved, the less the leader has to lead. The best group member is usually one who tries to accomplish the same tasks in the discussion as the leader. A successful group member will:

1. Be aware of the feelings of other group members.

2. Talk briefly and to the point.

3. Help in solving conflicts by focusing on facts.

4. Work toward completing group tasks or agenda items.

5. And, perhaps most important, whenever possible, come to a group discussion with good information and a positive attitude, willing to listen to all ideas and then decide.

DISCUSSION PATTERNS

As you may know, discussion groups most often share information or make decisions. When a family sitting around the supper table talks about new automobile models, for example, it is having a learning, enlightening, information-sharing discussion. If, on the other hand, a group of students meet to decide how to reduce cheating in the classroom, they are having a problem-solving discussion.

Typical Information-Sharing Groups	Problem-Solving and Decision-Making Groups
Library study groups	Legislative committees
Hobby workshops	Executive board meetings
Scientific round tables	Governors' conferences
Pre-school conferences	Neighborhood action committees
Convention interest groups	Employee grievance committees
Sales briefing meetings	City councils
Management training groups	Work supervisors' meetings
Family socials	Family help sessions

In most cases, discussion will proceed more efficiently if it follows a specific pattern of organization. The idea is to reduce aimless conversation and yet not force everyone into idea slavery.

INFORMATION-SHARING PATTERNS

For typical information-sharing discussions, patterns used to organize the body of an informative speech can also be helpful for guiding a group discussion.

Time Pattern   Past, Present, Future

A group studying hypnosis, for example, might raise the following questions to stimulate and guide the discussion:

1. How, when, and where did hypnosis have its beginning?

2. What are the present uses of hypnosis?

3. What future development can we anticipate?

Spatial Pattern   North, South, East, West

A group trying to share information on the current state of employment could raise such questions as:

1. What jobs are available in northern states?

2. What kind of employment is needed in the southern states?

3. What kinds of jobs are most advertised in the eastern states?

4. What kind of employment is needed in the western states?

Topical Pattern   Questions drawn from the way a subject is naturally divided.

Students trying to become more informed about a university might ask:

1. What are the qualifications of the administrators?

2. What are the characteristics of the faculty?

3. What are the characteristics of the students?

4. What are the strengths and weaknesses of the curriculum?

Or, if a camera club was trying to better understand a Polaroid Land camera, it might discuss such questions as:

1. What are the special design features of the Polaroid?

2. How is the picture taken?

3. How does the film develop?

Other information-sharing patterns are cause-effect patterns, advantages-versus-disadvantages patterns, or the problem-solution pattern—how a problem *was* solved in the past.

PROBLEM-SOLVING PATTERNS

For problem-solving and decision-making discussions, the most popular patterns used for stimulating and giving direction to a group was popularized in the early 1900s by philosopher and educator John Dewey. Our version of Dewey's approach consists of five steps:

1. Examine the problem or difficulty. Consider the extent and causes of the difficulty. Ask what is happening and why.

2. Define the problem. Try to frame a *specific* statement of the problem. Avoid generalities. Distinguish between symptoms and causes of the problem.

3. Request all possible solutions to the problem. Good place to use "brainstorming techniques." Don't try to generate ideas and judge them at the same time.

4. Select the best solution or combination of solutions. Here is where you can develop criteria for picking the best solution (for example, money, time, and so on), or you can simply make intuitive judgments.

5. Implement the solution. Decide on a course of action, start the action, and plan to evaluate the results.

Sometimes groups get too cozy. Group loyalty and cohesion are so great that critical thinking is smothered. This leads to a condition called "group think," elucidated in 1972 by Janis. Read the following article and notice the precautions that are recommended to avoid "group think" and restore quality decision making.

Groupthink

Irving L. Janis

Irving L. Janis, professor of psychology at Yale, teaches courses in attitude change, decision-making, leadership and small-group behavior.

The idea of "groupthink" occurred to me while reading Arthur M. Schlesinger's chapters on the Bay of Pigs in *A Thousand Days*. At first I was puzzled: How could bright men like John F. Kennedy and his advisers be taken in by such a stupid, patchwork plan as the one presented to them by the C.I.A. representatives? I began wondering if some psychological contagion might have interfered with their mental alertness.

I kept thinking about this notion until one day I found myself talking about it in a seminar I was conducting at Yale on the psychology of small groups. I suggested that the poor decision-making performance of those high officials might be akin to the lapses in judgment of ordinary citizens who become more concerned with retaining the approval of the fellow members of their work group than with coming up with good solutions to the tasks at hand.

When I re-read Schlesinger's account I was struck by many further observations that fit into exactly the pattern of concurrence-seeking that has impressed me in my research on other face-to-face groups when a "we" feeling of solidarity is running high. I concluded that a group process was subtly at work in Kennedy's team which prevented the members from debating the real issues posed by the C.I.A.'s plan and from carefully appraising the serious risks.

By now I was sufficiently fascinated by what I called the "groupthink" hypothesis to start looking into similar historic fiascoes. I selected for intensive analysis three that were made during the administrations of three other American presidents: Franklin D. Roosevelt (failure to be prepared for Pearl Harbor), Harry S. Truman (the invasion of North Korea) and Lyndon B. Johnson (escalation of the Vietnam war). Each decision was a group product, issuing from a series of meetings held by a small and cohesive group of government officials and advisers. In each case I found the same kind of detrimental group process that was at work in the Bay of Pigs decision. In my earlier research with ordinary citizens I had been impressed by the effects—both unfavorable and favorable—of the social pressures that develop in cohesive groups: in infantry platoons, air crews, therapy groups, seminars and self-study or encounter groups. Members tend to evolve informal objectives to preserve friendly intra-group relations, and this becomes part of the hidden agenda at their meetings. . . .

The term "groupthink" is of the same order as the words in the "newspeak" vocabulary that George Orwell uses in *1984*—a vocabulary with terms such as "doublethink" and "crimethink." By putting "groupthink" with those Orwellian words, I realize that it takes on an invidious connotation. This is intentional: groupthink refers to a deterioration of mental efficiency, reality testing and moral judgment that results from in-group pressures.

When I investigated the Bay of Pigs invasion and other fiascoes, I found that there were at least six major defects in decision-making which contributed to failures to solve problems adequately.

First, the group's discussions were limited to a few alternatives (often only two) without a survey of the full range of alternatives. Second, the members failed to re-examine their initial decision from the standpoint of non-obvious drawbacks that had not been originally considered. Third, they neglected courses of action initially evaluated as unsatisfactory; they almost never discussed whether they had overlooked any non-obvious gains.

Fourth, members made little or no attempt to obtain information from experts who could supply sound estimates of losses and gains to be expected from alternative courses. Fifth, selective bias was shown in the way the members reacted to information and judgments from experts, the media and outside critics; they were only interested in facts and opinions that supported their preferred policy. Finally, they spent little time deliberating how the policy might be hindered by bureaucratic inertia, sabotaged by political opponents or derailed by the accidents that happen to the best of well-laid plans. Consequently, they failed to work out contingency plans to cope with foreseeable setbacks that could endanger their success.

I was surprised by the extent to which the group involved in these fiascoes adhered to group norms and pressures toward uniformity, even when their policy was working badly and had unintended consequences that disturbed the conscience of the members. Members consider loyalty to the group the highest form of morality. That loyalty requires each member to avoid raising controversial issues, questioning weak arguments or calling a halt to soft-headed thinking.

Paradoxically, soft-headed groups are likely to be extremely hard-hearted toward out-groups and enemies. In dealing with a rival nation, policy-makers constituting an amiable group find it relatively easy to authorize dehumanizing solutions such as large-scale bombings. An affable group of government officials is unlikely to pursue the difficult issues that arise when alternatives to a harsh military solution come up for discussion. . . .

The leader of a policy-forming group should, for example, assign the role of critical evaluator to each member, encouraging the group to give high priority to airing objections and doubts. He should also be impartial at the outset, instead of stating his own preferences and expectations. He should limit his briefings to unbiased statements about the scope of the problem and the limitations of available resources.

The organization should routinely establish several independent planning and evaluation groups to work on the same policy question, each carrying out its deliberations under a different leader.

One or more qualified colleagues within the organization that are not core members of the policy-making group should be invited to each meeting and encouraged to challenge the views of the core members.

At every meeting, at least one member should be assigned the role of devil's advocate, to function like a good lawyer in challenging the testimony of those who advocate the majority position.

Whenever the policy issue involves relations with a rival nation, a sizable block of time should be spent surveying all warning signals from the rivals and constructing alternative scenarios.

After reaching a   eliminary consensus the policy-making group should hold a "second chance" meeting at which all the members are expected to express their residual doubts and to rethink the entire issue. They might take as their model a statement made by Alfred P. Sloan, a former chairman of General Motors, at a meeting of policymakers:

"Gentlemen, I take it we are all in complete agreement on the decision here. Then I propose we postpone further discussion until our next meeting to give ourselves time to develop disagreement and perhaps gain some understanding of what the decision is all about."

It might not be a bad idea for the second-chance meeting to take place in a relaxed atmosphere far from the executive suite, perhaps over drinks. According to a report by Herodotus dating from about 450 B.C., whenever the ancient Persians made a decision following sober deliberations, they would always reconsider the matter under the influence of wine. Tacitus claimed that during Roman times the Germans also had a custom of arriving at each decision twice—once sober, once drunk.

Some institutionalized form of allowing second thoughts to be freely expressed might be remarkably effective for breaking down a false sense of unanimity and related illusions, without endangering anyone's reputation or liver.

SOURCE: Reprinted with permission from the January 1973 issue of the Yale Alumni Magazine; copyright by Yale Alumni Publications, Inc.

LARGE GROUP MEETINGS

The major emphasis in this chapter has been on small group meetings and discussions. There is, however, a place for large group meetings. In settings where it is necessary to convey information and receive reactions from several hundred people, a large group meeting seems to bridge the gap between group discussion and public speaking. The Boeing Aerospace Company's success with this type of audience participation is described in the following article. Perhaps Boeing has the answer to the perplexing problem of keeping massive numbers of people happy and informed through large meetings.

There's a Place for Large Group Meetings

James R. Douglas

James R. Douglas, ABC, is internal communication director for Boeing Aerospace Co., Seattle, Washington

Face-to-face communication—No. 1 on the totem pole of effective communication techniques—often is dismissed as impractical, time-consuming and too costly when trying to reach large numbers of people.

Before you reject face-to-face communications on these grounds, first explore all the possibilities. Boeing Aerospace did, and one division is giving it a lot of lip-service—literally—in group employee meetings.

Abraham M. S. Goo, vice president and manager of the Boeing Aerospace Company's B-1 Avionics Integration program, believes in keeping his people informed. And feedback from most of Goo's 800 people indicates his periodic all-employee group meetings are contributing to the program's success and to their performance as individual employees.

Following a recent series of meetings, Boeing Aerospace's internal communication staff conducted a survey of Goo's employees, seeking their evaluation of this type of communication. With an 81 percent response to a questionnaire, 76 percent of the employees said the briefings are definitely contributing to the programs success, 19 percent didn't know if they were contributing and 5 percent said no.

When asked if the meetings helped them do a better job, 72 percent said yes, 23 percent didn't know and 5 percent said no.

The meetings, which run 45 to 75 minutes, are given in three sections with 200 to 300 people at each. Meeting in a theater in the Boeing complex, employees may see a movie on the program, charts which relate progress and problems and similar business-oriented material. Goo tells them what's happening in their division, talks about the future, and encourages them to ask questions.

After each meeting, employees are asked to comment on the session. At the next meeting—if not before—Goo responds to any questions asked during the previous get-together. Most of the people in the B-1 Avionics program have commented, "This is the first time a program manager took the time to talk to us."

Meetings are run during working hours on the one-shift program. The three sections are offered on the same day, at about 9 A.M., 10:30 A.M. and 1:30 P.M.

The majority of employees in the Boeing B-1 Avionics program are professionally oriented, with only a small number of production workers.

Engineers, business administrative people and supervisors overwhelmingly supported the meetings, with up to 93 percent giving an affirmative answer to the above questions. Clerical employees and production employees were less definite in their support, with "don't know" responses runnng up to 33 percent.

In open-end questions seeking answers as to how the meetings helped the program, the majority of professional employees stressed the "cooperation promoted between functions" and a "coordinated effort to meet targets." As for individual performance, the majority of these employees commented on having "greater incentive to help the program" and a "better understanding of how their jobs tie into the program."

Most clerical and production employees stressed "teamwork" and "morale."

Management credibility for these meetings rated almost as pure as Ivory soap. In marking any one of six positive or six negative words regarding credibility, 98.4 percent selected words such as honest, straightforward, sincere. The remaining 1.6 percent selected words such as evasive or incomplete. No one chose dishonest, half-truths or lies.

In "open-end" questions asking for pertinent remarks about an employee's job, the program or the company, high praise was given to top management and the team spirit management had developed. Professional employees asked for more detailed information about the business plan and long-range goals. Clerical and hourly employees asked that the charts used in the briefiings be simplified.

Abe Goo has been conducting all-employee briefings for his people since taking over management of the B-1 Avionics program three years ago, holding meetings at least on a semi-annual basis. He discusses program performance, cost and schedule and problem areas needing special attention.

A comment on the success of the Boeing B-1 Avionics Integration program comes from the customers, who evidently think Goo and his people are on the right track. This is the only Air Force program ever to receive a 100 percent incentive award fee for its performance. And like a bowler rolling consecutive perfect games, Goo and his team have received back-to-back 100 percent incentive award fees.

SOURCE: Reprinted with permission of International Association of Business Communication's *Journal of Organizational Communication*, James R. Douglas.

EVALUATING GROUP DISCUSSIONS

Though you may not be called on to professionally evaluate a group discussion, we would like you to notice the following methods of analysis in order to further emphasize and clarify the principles of small group discussion contained in this chapter. If you do have an opportunity to evaluate your discussion group or your own leadership skills, then these tools of analysis should prove beneficial in giving you an opportunity to see whether everything is going well.

"I thought I made it clear that a discussion period would <u>follow</u>."

THE SATURDAY EVENING POST

Many tools have been developed for evaluating groups, individual participants, and leaders. The forms presented here[2] might even assist you in evaluating classroom group discussions. The first rating scale is for leadership evaluation. The group members as well as the leader can fill it out. The other questionnaires give the participants an opportunity to explain how they felt about the discussion they just completed.

[2] From Brilhart, John K., *Effective Group Discussion*, 2d ed., 1974, Wm. C. Brown Company, Dubuque, Iowa

LEADER RATING SCALE

Date _____ Leader _____

Time _____ Observer _____ _____

Instructions: Rate the leader on all items which are applicable; draw a line through all items which do not apply. Use the following scale to rate his or her overall performance as a group leader.

        5—superior
        4—above average
        3—average
        2—below average
        1—poor

Leadership Style and Personal Characteristics

To what degree:

_____ Was the leader poised, calm, and self-controlled?

_____ Could the leader be heard and understood easily?

_____ Did the leader show enthusiasm and interest in the group problem?

_____ Did the leader listen well to other participants?

_____ Did the leader show personal warmth and a sense of humor?

_____ Was the leader objective and open-minded to all sides?

_____ Was the leader resourceful and flexible in handling suggestions from members?

_____ Did the leader create a permissive atmosphere?

_____ Did the leader make it easy for all members to share in functional leadership?

_____ To what degree was the leader democratic and group oriented?

Preparation

To what degree:

_____ Were all physical arrangements cared for?

_____ Was the leader's preparation and grasp of the problem thorough?

_____ Were questions prepared to guide the discussion?

_____ Were members notified and given adequate guidance for preparing?

PROCEDURAL AND INTERPERSONAL LEADERSHIP TECHNIQUES

To what degree:

_____ Were members introduced and put at ease?

_____ Did the leader introduce the problem and supply necessary background?

_____ Did the leader guide the group to a thorough investigation and understanding of the problem?

_____ Did the leader suggest a suitable organization or pattern for group thinking?

_____ Were members encouraged to modify the leader's plan or agenda?

_____ Did the leader state questions clearly?

_____ Did the leader rebound questions to the group (especially requests for his or her opinion)?

_____ Did the leader make appropriate attempts to clarify communication?

_____ Did the leader keep the discussion on one point at a time, encouraging the group to complete an issue before going to another?

_____ Did the leader provide summaries needed to remind, clarify, and move the group forward?

_____ Was the group encouraged to evaluate critically all evidence and ideas?

_____ Were reticent members encouraged to speak without being coerced to do so?

_____ Did the leader stimulate imagination and creative thinking?

_____ Were aggressive members controlled with skill and tact?

_____ Were misunderstandings, conflicts, and arguments handled promptly and effectively?

_____ Did the leader determine group consensus before moving to each new phase of the discussion?

_____ Were important information, ideas, and agreements recorded accurately?

_____ Were plans made for follow-up and future meetings?

REACTION QUESTIONNAIRE

Instruction: Circle the number which best indicates your reactions to the following questions about the discussion in which you participated:

1. **Adequacy of communication:** To what extent do you feel members were understanding each others' statements and positions?

0	1	2	3	4	5	6	7	8	9	10

Much talking past each
other, misunderstanding

Communicated directly with
each other, understanding well

2. **Opportunity to speak:** To what extent did you feel free to speak?

0	1	2	3	4	5	6	7	8	9	10

Never had a
chance to speak

All the opportunity to
talk I wanted

3. **Climate of acceptance:** How well did members support each other, show acceptance of individuals?

0	1	2	3	4	5	6	7	8	9	10

Highly critical
and punishing

Supportive and
receptive

4. **Interpersonal relations:** How pleasant and concerned were interpersonal relations?

0	1	2	3	4	5	6	7	8	9	10

Quarrelsome, status
differences emphasized

Pleasant, empathic,
concerned with persons

5. **Leadership:** How adequate was the leader (or leadership) of the group?

0	1	2	3	4	5	6	7	8	9	10

To weak ( ) or
dominating ( )

Shared, group-centered,
and sufficient

continued

6. **Satisfaction with role:**   How satisfied are you with your personal participation in the discussion?

0	1	2	3	4	5	6	7	8	9	10

Very dissatisfied   Very satisfied

7. **Quality of product:**   How satisfied are you with the decisions, solutions, or learnings that came out of this discussion?

0	1	2	3	4	5	6	7	8	9	10

Very displeascd   Very satisfied

8. **Overall:**   How do rate the discussion as a whole apart from any specific aspect of it?

0	1	2	3	4	5	6	7	8	9	10

Awful, waste of time   Superb, time well spent

WHAT TO KNOW

This chapter deals with communicating (speaking and listening) in groups. To be productive, groups need to enjoy each other as well as to accomplish tasks. Leaders take direct responsibility for finding a meeting place, preparing participants, starting the discussion, and achieving satisfactory conclusions. Members come to a group discussion with information to contribute and in a mood of inquiry rather than with rigid opinions. By following a meeting agenda and either information-sharing or problem-solving discussion patterns, discussion will proceed efficiently. Checklists for evaluating leader and participant behaviors in groups are used to locate specific strengths and weaknesses so that group discussion and efficiency can be improved. "Group think" and the "large group meeting" are areas in which discussion could become less effective depending on whether you plan for quality decision making.

WHAT TO DO

Observation   Use the leader and group analysis rating scales in this chapter to evaluate the functioning of group meetings at school and in the community, such as student government, history club, city council, and faculty or staff meeting.

Your Speech-Communication Course Reflect back over the functioning of your class as a group. What parts of this chapter apply directly to the classroom? Examine socialization, cliques, group climate, leadership, and so on. In what ways does your class not fit the description of a functioning group? In what ways does it fit the description?

Life-Related Problem Solving   The next time you, your social group, your work group, or your family face the typical problem-solving situation of how, when, and where to get money for the next school term, or how to change the work schedule so it is fair to everyone, or how to choose a vacation plan the whole family will like, try using the five-step problem-solving approach (or a modification of it).

Have You Got a Problem?   To what degree is your chosen major going to provide you with the knowledge and skills to solve your present and future life- and work-related problems?

WHERE TO LEARN MORE

Applebaum, Ron L., *et al. The Process of Group Communication.* Palo Alto, CA: Science Research Associates, 1979.

Bormann, Ernest G. *Discussion and Group Methods.* 2d ed. New York: Harper & Row, 1975.

Bormann, Ernest G. and Nancy Bormann. *Effective Small Group Communication.* 3rd ed. Burgess, 1980.

Brilhart, John K. *Effective Group Discussion.* 4th ed. Dubuque, IA: Wm. C. Brown, 1982.

Doyle, Michael, and David Straus. *How to Make Meetings Work.* Chicago, IL: Playboy Press, 1977.

Gouran, Dennis S. *Making Decisions in Groups.* Glenview, IL: Scott, Foresman, 1983.

Patton, Bobby R., and Kim Griffin. *Decision Making Group Interaction.* 2d ed. New York: Harper & Row, 1978.

RESPONDING TO QUESTIONS AND COMMENTS

11

THE RESPONSE IS AS IMPORTANT AS THE SPEECH

In the beginning of the book we developed the point that speaking is a communicative activity that ranges from everyday conversing to formal public speaking. The basic elements of talking and listening (including nonverbal behaviors) are present in all speaking. The pattern or format of this give-and-take is altered to fit the informality or formality of the situation.

In everyday conversation, asking questions, making comments, and responding to others are the key ingredients to carrying on the transaction. As the speaking situation becomes more public in nature, the questioning and responding interchanges between speaker and listener become less spontaneous and more planned and controlled by the speaker. For example, in a problem-solving city-council meeting, the mayor can set the interchange rules; each council member may be allowed five uninterrupted minutes to state his or her position. A five-minute question-and-answer period may then follow where other members can probe the individual council member's position.

The speaker usually has the privilege of setting the constraints that will keep her or him in control of the talking and listening segments of the interchanges. You may know some people on whom you'd like to impose these constraints when conversing with them because they do all the talking. (Their idea of conversation is delivering an impromptu speech.)

CONTROLLING SPEAKER / LISTENER INTERCHANGES

Common sense seems to tell us that the more we can involve the listeners throughout our speaking by encouraging their questions and comments, the more effective we will be. This is not necessarily true. Too much direct audience participation during a speech can interrupt the progression or flow so that the rest of the listeners (and the speaker) lose the feeling for the main point of the presentation. Progressive development and timing are as important building blocks in speaking as in a play or movie. You can put a book down and come back and pick it up later. This is obviously not true with a speech.

One option the speaker has to control the interchanges with the listen-

ers is to set up the "game rules" before the presentation begins. For example, as the speaker, you may tell the listeners that you will:

1. Respond to questions and comments at any time.
2. Respond to comments or questions only at designated points.
3. Respond to comments and questions only after the prepared speech is concluded.

In summary, we are saying that making public speaking more like a conversation, by allowing or encouraging listener interchange during the speech, does not make for better speaking (although it may make for better teaching). Active speaker/listener interchanges have to be planned and controlled by the speaker.

PLANNING SPEAKER / LISTENER INTERCHANGES

In a one-to-many speaking situation, it may be difficult for you, as the speaker, to anticipate all the obstacles your message will encounter in the case of each individual listener. If you have done your homework on the audience, you have analyzed general characteristics and adapted your material to appeal to the majority or to the average listener. In reality, however, there is no real "average" listener—each listener is a unique individual with unique feelings, attitudes, and views of the world. This makes it difficult for any speaker to satisfactorily "reach" each and every individual in the audience.

Speaker/listener interchange periods allow the speaker an opportunity to take the basic message and further refine it to reach various individuals within the audience more successfully. In responding to individual comments or questions, the speaker can

1. Answer objections or concerns.
2. Clarify a misunderstood point.
3. Illustrate or support a general statement previously made.
4. Go into more depth with the material.

All of this assumes that you have been somewhat effective in communicating with your listeners in the prepared speech. If you have failed to establish yourself and your material during the monologue part of the speech, the audience interchange period will result in:

■ Silence.
■ A few polite questions or comments of a noncommittal nature.
■ A verbal assault on your credibility or your material.

Let's assume that you have been effective during the monologue section of your talk. There are several questioning techniques and specific guidelines that you should then follow in handling an interchange period:

REMEMBER—WHEN YOU STOP TALKING THE TRANSACTIONAL NATURE OF THE INTERCHANGE WILL CONTINUE.

GENERAL GUIDELINES FOR HANDLING QUESTION-AND-ANSWER PERIODS

1. **Plan ahead for the exchange.** Anticipate what questions or comments you may receive from the audience. If you find you have difficulty guessing what these will be, you have not done an adequate job of analyzing your audience. As you have prepared the content of your speaking, you can prepare your responses to potential questions and comments from the listeners.

2. **Understand the general types of questions and comments you are likely to receive, even though you may not know their specific content.** Audience members commonly respond with:

   a. **Agreement:** A statement or specific instance that essentially expresses approval or acceptance of what you have said in your speech.

   b. **Understanding:** A statement that indicates the listener comprehends or appreciates what you have said but doesn't indicate approval or disapproval.

   c. **Request for clarification:** A statement or question that asks for additional information or for another explanation of a particular point or idea.

   d. **Disagreement:** A statement or specific instance that essentially shows disapproval or nonacceptance of what you have said.

   e. **Request for your related opinions:** A statement or question that asks for your opinion on related points, topics, or issues that were not covered in the speech.

   f. **Checking material or sources:** A statement or question that requests additional description or substantiation of your material and the sources of that material.

   g. **Checking reasoning:** A statement or question that attempts to bring to light the logic or rationality of your reasoning in the speech.

3. **Respond to listener comments and questions by maintaining your poise and not overreacting to save face in front of the rest of the audience.** You do not have to know all the answers, or put every negative comment down, or match wit with wit. Your job is to keep your reasoning faculties about you and think before you respond. Some techniques for maintaining your poise are:

a. **Single out one person at a time to respond to if you have several questions or comments at once.**

b. **Repeat or paraphrase the question or comment.** This ensures that you have understood it correctly. If you have not understood the question, the listener will correct you and you save yourself the embarrassment of answering a question that was not intended. Repeating the question also "buys" you some time for preparing your answer. For example, "Are you asking me if I *personally* agree with the president's position?"

c. **Rephrase or simplify the question if you feel it is too wordy, too complex, or too technical for the rest of the audience.** You may show respect for the questioner by asking whether your simplification has distorted the intent of the question. If the answer is no, then you proceed to answer the question as you have rephrased it. If the answer is yes, ask for the question to be rephrased. For example, "Is your main question the apparent distortion in the listed MPG for American cars?"

d. **Postpone the question.** If you feel the question is irrelevant, is too personal, requires too much detailed information, or is not of general interest to the whole audience, you have the option of postponing your response to the end of the whole speaking situation. Thank the person for the question and indicate that you would like the time or freedom of a one-to-one discussion on this question. If he or she would hold the question until the speaking situation has drawn to a close, you will be happy to discuss it personally with him or her.

e. **Don't cover up.** If you don't know the answer or if you find yourself caught without an appropriate response, simply say so, and respectfully go on to the next question.

f. **Be sensitive to the time for wrapping up the interchange and officially ending the speaking situation.** You can watch the audience for waning attention and interest cues.

4. **Remember that while you are handling the question-and-answer period, the audience is still judging your credibility.** When you wrap up the question-and-answer interchange, the speech may be finished but the communicative transaction between you and the listeners continues until you leave the setting.

HANDLING UNPLANNED INTERRUPTIONS

The single worst problem speakers have in handling unplanned questions, comments, interruptions, and heckling from the audience can be seen in the speaker who responds to save face. We have learned to admire politicians, executives, and media people for their quick, cutting wit. We forget, though, that we do not have the experience they have—hundreds of speaking situations.

The best defense for an unplanned interruption is a good offense. Prior to speaking, indicate when and how you will entertain audience questions and comments. When interrupted, simply remind the person that you will be happy to deal with the comment in the allotted period. The important point is to remain poised. Do not become defensive or condescending in postponing the person's inquiry. How you handle yourself in these situations can be as important for your credibility as what you say.

As a speaker you may be subjected to several types of questions and comments. The following are samples:

- **Leading Questions:** The desired answer is directly implied in the question. For example, "The rest of the group believes the cost is too great, what do you think?"

- **Loaded Questions:** Agreement with the questioner is directly asked for though not expected by the questioner. This type of question usually has a contraction in it, such as *couldn't, don't,* or *shouldn't;* for example, "Don't you feel that would be too costly right now?" This is really a statement of disagreement or opinion in the disguise of a question.

- **Complex, Wordy, or Multiple Questions:** Sometimes a listener will string many questions together. For example, "I understand that your proposal will cost a lot of money . . . I wonder where this money will come from, who is going to administer the program even if we get the money . . . it doesn't seem as if the details have been worked out . . . uhm . . . are you sure this will work? . . . how can we afford it?"

- **Statement of Open Disagreement:** For example, "I don't buy what you are saying one bit."

- **Specific Contrary Example:** A member of the audience gives a specific example in which the point you are making does not hold true. For example, "But your solution is premised on the fact that the professional woman has worked out the balance between her career and her family. Not all professional women have done this. I know many professional women who can't decide if they want a family or not."

One of the best ways to prepare yourself to handle such unplanned interruptions is to practice. Practice your speaking with friends or classmates interrupting or at least asking difficult questions during the question-and-answer period. To practice speaking without practicing for the question-and-answer period would be like a basketball player practicing shooting and dribbling without anyone trying to disrupt his or her movement. In a real game such players would not be ready because their practice would not have helped them develop all the skills needed for the actual event.

There are specific responding techniques for handling interruptions or unplanned interchange periods. The following are some of the more commonly used techniques:

1. Label the questions that are leading, loaded, and multiple for what they are before you attempt to respond.

2. For the leading or loaded questions, you can sometimes respond with your own question, or request further information from the listener.

QUESTIONER: But don't you think that would be killing?

SPEAKER: I can see you think it would be; please tell me why you'd call it killing?

3. When asked a multiple question, you can ask which question of all those included the questioner would like you to respond to first.

4. For vague, wordy, complex questions, ask for the main idea behind the question before you attempt to answer it.

SPEAKER: Okay, I understand the general idea of the question. What is the specific point you want me to respond to?

5. For open disagreements, state that there may be a possibility the person is right. You have not agreed by saying this, all you have admitted is that there may be a possibility, however, slim, that the person's view is correct. You have reserved the right to stick to your own opinion. After you have indicated the possibility, do not elaborate. Turn to the next question.

SPEAKER: Yes, it is possible that we may find bigger oil fields in the future—not likely enough, though, for me to want to bank on it.

6. For hostile or argumentative statements or questions, begin your response by indicating that you do not appreciate the way the statement was made but that you can understand how the person feels or why he or she thinks that way. For example:

QUESTIONER: That sounds like a bunch of bull to me!

SPEAKER: I'm not sure I like how you put that, but I can see how you would be skeptical, since this project has been discussed for a long time without anything being done.

7. When an audience member has made a valid point that contradicts you, or has stated a singular exception to your point of view, give the person credit for the perceptive insight before you attempt to clarify or explain why that statement does not destroy the basis for your point of view. For example:

QUESTIONER: But air bags are only good for head-on accidents and not all accidents in cars are head-on.

SPEAKER: That's a good point you have brought up. It's true that air bags are not as helpful in the side-on collision. However, we are concerned about saving as many lives as possible. Only 12 percent of auto accidents involve side collissions. If more accidents involved side impact, I would have to agree with you more.

ENCOURAGING THE AUDIENCE
TO PARTICIPATE

In certain speaking situations one of the goals of the presentation is to get listeners involved actively in controlled interchanges. At times, experienced speakers use these controlled interchanges to further develop ideas with the audience. As a speaker you need to be familiar with the types of questions you can ask to draw out the audience. After you have the audience members participating, you need to know what types of questions will ensure that listeners begin to see the relationships among the pieces of information as you've intended.

Three basic questions to get listeners involved are:

1. **Open questions.** These ask the audience members for their opinions or reactions, with no restrictions on what the answer does or does not cover. For example: "How do you feel about the plan?" "What is your reaction to legalizing marijuana?" "What do you think we should do?"

2. **Specific or follow-up questions.** These limit or narrow the range of acceptable responses in relation to a previous statement. For example, if a person has just given a description of his teenage years, you could ask that person "What was *your* high school like?" If a person has indicated that she didn't like the way someone else ran a meeting, you could ask: "Tell us what it is you didn't care for in her approach to running the meeting." And if a person indicates he does not like a proposed plan, you can ask: "What don't you like about the plan?"

   Specific and follow-up questions limit the area in which people can respond. For example, you could ask, "What are some of the advantages?" "Why did you choose to major in communication rather than business if you want to go into sales?"

3. **Reflective questions.** These summarize what you understand the person to be saying, in the form of a question that asks the person to indicate how accurate your perceptions of what he or she said are. Sample reflective questions are: "I get the impression you are not sure which field you want to go into?" "You seem to have some doubts about the value of this assignment?" "So you feel this class forced you to work on some skills you would not have tackled on your own?"

   It is important that reflective questions be asked in an open, inquiring, "am I right?" attitude. Sarcasm or implied judgment will

destroy their value. Reflective questions accomplish several things for you and the other person in the interchange:

a. The audience member knows you listened to and tried to understand his or her point of view.

b. The audience member can see how well you understand what he or she was attempting to express.

c. The audience member's response to your reflective question shows you how accurately you understand his or her comments.

This chapter has been developed on the premise that speaking exists on a continuum from conversing to formal public speaking. The communication skills that lead to effective conversational interchanges also have a place in public speaking if they are planned and well executed. Not all audience interchanges are as planned or developed as the speaker intends. For these moments the speaker needs to take steps to control the situation. On the other hand, the speaker may have to encourage or stimulate desired audience interchanges. The bottom line is that an effective speaker in today's environment needs to be skilled in more than talking. She or he must be able to listen, question, and respond to questions and comments in an appropriate manner.

WHAT TO KNOW

This chapter points out that the basic speaking and listening of everyday conversing and the formal speaking of public talks come together when the public speaker interacts with his or her audience through question-and-answer interchanges. These speaker/audience interchanges should be controlled by the speaker, and this takes planning. Controlling interchanges may mean handling hostile reactions or encouraging a reluctant group of listeners to ask questions. The speaker needs to anticipate the kinds of questions and comments he or she may get (or the lack of them) and be prepared to handle the interchange with poise.

WHAT TO DO

Meet the Press/Face the Nation   Make a special effort to observe both the questioning and responding techniques on television programs such as "Firing Line," presidential news conferences, and the like.

Questioning in Class   Focus on asking at least one of the three positive types of questions (open, specific or follow-up, or reflective) in class everyday. You may also wish to observe the types of responses your instructors use in the classroom situation.

Conversation: A Place to Practice   Everyday conversations, especially the more "heated" exchanges in the student center, are useful situations for you to ask questions and respond to others. These conversations will be particularly rich in interruptions, loaded and leading questions, disagreements, and credibility attacks, so you should have ample opportunities to try out your controlling techniques.

WHERE TO LEARN MORE

Downs, Cal, Wil Linkugel, and David M. Berg. *The Organizational Communicator.* New York: Harper & Row, 1977.

Downs, Cal W., G. Paul Smeyak, and Ernest Martin. *Professional Interviewing.* New York: Harper & Row, 1980.

Pace, R. Wayne, Brent D. Peterson, and M. Dallas Burnett. *Techniques for Effective Communication.* Reading, MA: Addison-Wesley, 1979.

Stewart, Charles J., and William B. Cash, Jr. *Interviewing Principles and Practices.* 3rd ed. Dubuque, IA. Wm. C. Brown, 1982.

Ross, Raymond S. *Speech Communication Fundamentals and Practice.* 5th ed. Englewood Cliffs, NJ: Prentice-Hall, 1980.

**THE
END**

12

IN CONCLUSION

Speaking never ends, but we are concluding this book. We are concluding the writing of this text and you, the reader, are probably finishing the reading of this text. We are happy with our writing efforts and hope that you are equally happy with your speaking success.

> *Speech is civilization itself . . . it is silence which isolates.*
>
> THOMAS MANN

As we stated in the beginning of the text, speaking is mainly a matter of getting listeners' attention, keeping listeners interested, and stimulating favorable responses in listeners. (Sounds like we are a little listener-oriented, doesn't it?) We reemphasize that the basic skills for public speaking already exist in our everyday talking and conversing. And that instead of having to learn something new and complex, we simply build upon previously acquired speaking experiences.

Notice how quickly in the following article the essence of being a "super speaker" is summarized.

Secrets from a Speech Consultant: How to Be a Super Speaker

Sooner or later, there comes a time when we're called upon to address an audience. Whether we are making a presentation at a sales meeting or addressing the garden club on how to grow roses, we want to come across in the best possible way. Here are some valuable tips on how to do it.

From the moment Charlotte Hardy got up from the dais and approached the lectern she did everything wrong. The 400 PTA members stared at her expectantly, but Charlotte, her eyes on the floor, could not have looked more terror-stricken had she been on her way to the guillotine. When she reached the lectern she realized she was too short for it and would look ridiculous to the audience. She spoke in a soft, apologetic voice, stared at the far wall and tried to get through her speech as quickly as possible. After 35 minutes, during 33 of which the members of the audience shifted restlessly in their seats, Charlotte retreated from the podium to a smattering of polite applause.

Charlotte has everything to learn about presenting herself and her ideas to an audience. Had she consulted Dorothy Sarnoff, she would have picked up all she needed to know in just six hours. Ms. Sarnoff is the author of *Speech Can Change Your Life* and founder of Speech Dynamics, a New York-based program that teaches people in all professions and levels of society how to give a speech,

make a board presentation, appear on a television talk show or succeed with any communications-related pursuit. Her clients include diplomats, senior executives of major corporations, and editors from the nation's top magazines. In addition to the private, intensive courses she gives in New York and the seminars she leads around the world, Ms. Sarnoff has just completed a library of 20 cassette tapes for speech improvement. Included are tapes on overcoming nervousness, how to chair a meeting, being a better conversationalist, and even one on how to lose a New York accent.

Ms. Sarnoff, the vivacious, model-thin former Broadway singer of *The King and I* fame, is an expert in treating jittery speakers. Why, we asked, are most people so deathly afraid of getting up in front of other people to speak? "They're simply worried about looking ridiculous to others," she says. "But there are two kinds of nervousness. One is what my friend Gwen Verdon calls 'racehorse' nervousness, which is the kind that makes you high and gives sparkle to your performance. It's positive. The other kind is negative. It fills you with anxiety and literally cramps your style. It's this nervousness which you must learn to overcome.'' In her Speech Dynamics course Mr. Sarnoff's clients learn how to prepare their speeches and present themselves with authority and confidence. And no one, she asserts, is ever nervous after the fourth hour.

Here, for *Family Circle* readers, Ms. Sarnoff offers some pertinent hints and techniques on speech-giving, so that you and Charlotte Hardy will be exciting, persuasive, and relaxed the next time you confront an audience.

Preparation

■ Make sure your speech is composed in "spoken" rather than "written" language. It should sound as if it's just conversation enlarged rather than an academic essay.

■ Keep it short. "Anything over 20 minutes is too long," cautions Ms. Sarnoff. "Edit, edit, edit! You can communicate a great deal of information in a very short time."

■ Do not start out with "It's a privilege to be here." Always begin with something that will relax you and your audience—a light touch, something local, an anecdote perhaps.In the body of the speech, ask questions, give illustrations, examples, things that involve the listeners and relate to their lives.

■ Be descriptive. Use images that the listener can see in his mind's eye.

■ End with something memorable—a quote, a startling fact, a call to action.

■ When you type your speech (or write it by hand) CAPITALIZE ALL THE LETTERS and triple-space the lines. Each line should contain one phrase spoken as you would normally speak it with one

exhalation of breath, not necessarily a whole sentence. Then mark the phrases for emphasis, color, pauses, and pace. In this form your speech will be very easy for your eye to scan.

Familiarization

Having prepared yourself, you must now familiarize yourself with your material. "If you memorize your speech you lack luster," says Ms. Sarnoff. "If you read, you lack luster. Make sure those lines are in your system, not just in your head. You should be familiar enough with your phrased speech for your eyes to be up 90 percent of the time, only looking down long enough to key another phrase in your mind."

■ Rehearse your speech aloud on your feet at least six times as though you were in the real-life situation.

■ Guard against speaking in a monotone, and also make sure the pace isn't draggy. Nothing will put an audience to sleep faster than a droner. Your voice should come not from your throat, which will give a soft, wispy sound, but rather from below your solar plexus. At Speech Dynamics, clients are given an exercise to make their voices come out as full and rich as possible: Press the palms of your hands tightly together in a steeple position at chest level, elbows straight out to the side. This causes isometric pressure which tightens the diaphragm. After holding the press position for three seconds, let out your breath in a long sh-h-h-h-h sound. This is the effort you should use to speak every line.

■ Give the last rehearsal of your speech an hour or two before you go on. If you can, use a tape recorder to check your delivery for pacing and energy.

■ If there is to be a question-and-answer period after your speech, quiz yourself on the most awful, embarrassing questions that you could be asked, and rehearse an answer for them. Anticipate and prepare.

■ Several hours before you speak, visit the room where you will be appearing. Familiarize yourself with the setup. Check out the lectern and make sure it is the right height for you—the bottom of your rib-cage upward should be visible to the audience. Anything less or more can look silly. If you are short, make sure a "riser" for the podium is available. If you are too tall, requisition a lectern "wedge."

■ Get to know the engineer in charge of the room. Learn his name, so that should anything go wrong while you are speaking—the room gets too hot, the microphone shrieks—you'll still be in control. Instead of looking helplessly around, you can calmly say, "John, could you please adjust the mike?" Bend the microphone toward you, so that you won't have to lean toward it.

■ If you really want to be thorough, check the lighting. Take out a pocket mirror and see what the lights are doing to your face. If your eyes look like two black holes, or your face drawn and haggard, request "three-quarter" lighting so you can be seen clearly. Complete control is the name of the game.

Presentation

According to Dorothy Sarnoff, all message givers—speakers, announcers, TV-talk-show guests—should give out three positive "vibes." First is the vibe of joy—"Im glad I'm here." Then there is the vibe of concern and interest in the audience—"I'm glad you're here." And finally the vibe of authority—"I know that I know." Before you approach the lectern, repeat this "mantra" to yourself:

"I'm glad I'm here. I'm glad you're here. I know that I know." This is what's known as psyching yourself up.

■ Go to the podium saying to yourself, "I *love* that audience," advises Ms. Sarnoff. "You have the ability to trigger the response that you want. If you speak out of love, and not fear, your audience will respond positively."

■ Stand with your chest up and your weight evenly on the balls of both feet. If you stand on one foot or lean on an elbow, you will lose your look of authority. Your whole style should be pleasantly assertive, and the way you hold yourself is an important part of your projection.

■ Do *not* look at just one person, do *not* look at the wall and do *not* look at hairlines. Instead, look *directly* into the eyes of the people in the audience as you speak. Glance from one to the other, linger for an instant to give each listener the impression that you wish you could speak only to him or her. You can judge the reception of your speech from the eyes of your listeners and act accordingly. Are the eyes glazed? Then accelerate your speech, animate your talk. There should be no unknowns by the time you step up to face your audience. Everything has been taken care of. You know the audience, your speech, the room, the engineer, yourself. There is nothing that should go wrong, no way that you can come across as ridiculous. You are well prepared and in control. Enjoy the moment. The times when you're the center of attention with a captive audience are probably too rare; make the most of it.

SOURCE: Reprinted from Nov. 1976 issue of *Family Circle* Magazine. © 1976 THE FAMILY CIRCLE, INC.

Opportunities for speaking surround us. The better prepared we are to speak, the happier we feel during those speaking moments. And the more that we improve our speaking, the more our opportunities for better living increase.

Do not be like the Born Loser! Remember always that public speaking is for listeners. Listeners must be stimulated in order to respond. So, our parting shot (advice) is for you to persuade them, impress them, entertain them, inform them, but do show up and take every opportunity to *speak* with them.

Boldness has genius, power and magic in it.

GOETHE

"Furthermore . . ."

From *The Saturday Evening Post* courtesy of Reg Hider.

APPENDIX

SAMPLE

INFORMATIVE

AND PERSUASIVE

SPEECHES

INFORMATIVE SPEECH

The Speaker and the Ghost: The Speaker Is the Speech

Carolyn Lomax-Cooke,
Communications Specialist, Cities Service Company

Delivered to the Tulsa Chapter of the
International Association of Business Communicators,
Tulsa, Oklahoma, October 20, 1981

Tonight I want to talk candidly about what makes a good speech, a good speaker, and a good speechwriter. Please notice that I am emphasizing "good" in each instance. We have all heard unimpressive speeches. But what we want to look at tonight is that special quality that makes a speech memorable.

My message is very simple—for the good speech, the good speaker, and the good speechwriter all center around one understanding of the speech occasion. And that understanding is this: the speaker IS the speech. The man IS the message. The woman IS her words. If the speaker and the speechwriter understand this fundamental of a good speech, all will go well. If the partners fail at this point, so will the speech.

But what do I mean—the speaker IS the speech? I mean that the listener cannot separate the content of the message from the character of the speaker. During a speech, the message itself and the vehicle through which it is delivered (the speaker) are so integrated that when the audience evaluates one, it automatically evaluates the other. The speaker and the speech are one and the same.

Since the audience responds to personality and character, the good speaker will take care that the speech truly reveals his character. Personality, life, conviction, excitement, or despair—these must shine through the speech as a reflection of the speaker. The audience recognizes such honesty and always responds to personal stories, anecdotes about the speaker's family, or a reference to a book that the speaker has read. Because let's face it, the audience came to hear the speaker—not to watch a human body mouth the words of a written treatise.

And I can tell you right now that if you are interested in being a speechwriter, you will face this same difficulty. Many corporate speechmakers simply do not want to reveal any hints about themselves as people. They want to strike all references to their outside activities, to their opinions, to their personal experiences. They honestly believe that the audiences want facts—not warm human beings. Also, these guys are just plain modest. They don't want to draw any attention to themselves. And, like all other speakers, they are nervous. I read in the *Wall Street Journal* that Maurice Granville, former chairman of Texaco, complained to his wife about his nervousness when speaking. Her advice for him was wonderful. She said: Look out there and just imagine all those people in their underwear, and that will make you feel better about it. Granville reports he tried it and it worked. But mostly executives just want to deliver the facts and get off the stage.

Every truly impressive speech that you can remember is memorable because of the melding of speech content with the speaker's character and life experiences.

Who but Barbara Jordan could have delivered her powerful keynote address at the 1976 Democratic convention? This black congresswoman, with her forceful voice, said: "A lot of years have passed since 1832 (when the first Democratic convention met to nominate a presidential candidate), and during that time it would have been most unusual for any national political party to ask that a Barbara Jordan deliver a keynote address . . . but tonight here I am, and I feel that notwithstanding the past that my presence here is one additional bit of evidence that the American Dream need not forever be deferred."

From that point on, the audience was hers. She was the speech and the message was hers alone. No one else could have delivered it.

If you think that you need a fancy platform or an impressive audience to deliver a great speech, you are mistaken. Peter the fisherman stood on an ordinary street in Jerusalem not too long after the crucifixion of Jesus and delivered one of the most effective speeches of all history. He had no podium, no microphone, no notes, not even an invitation to speak. But he spoke from his heart, with the simple honest words of his own experience when he told his fellow Jews that they had killed the Messiah promised by God and foretold by the prophets. His message: "Repent and be baptized." I characterize this speech as a highly effective action-oriented presentation, because 3,000 people were baptized into the Christian faith that day as a result of his word. Now, we have more than our share of ministers on the Tulsa Main Mall—but not one of them is getting this kind of response!

You can see through these examples that when the speech is good, it is because the speaker is the speech, the woman is her words. But if the speech must reveal the speaker in a personal way in order to be effective—what is the role of the speechwriter?

I said earlier that the speaker and the speechwriter are partners. They are, but the ghost writer is the silent partner. A behind-the-scenes person. In fact, almost an invisible person.

The speechwriter is a server—one who serves the speaker in a variety of ways. Foremost, the speechwriter must keep in mind the fundamental which I have harped on for the past ten minutes—that the speech and the speaker are one. The ghost writer must reach into the man or woman to find the message. The ghost writer must make the message come alive through anecdotes, testimonies, humor from the speaker's point of view. The executive will likely resist efforts to personalize his or her comments. Your job as a speechwriter is to encourage him and persuade him that the audience asked to hear his ideas—not yours.

Does the process sound time-consuming? It is. A reporter once asked Truman Capote why he could not produce a book in two weeks, as another writer claimed he could. Capote retorted: "That's not writing, that's typing!"

Speechwriting takes time, too—it's not a matter of "just typing." The final product is the speechwriter's reward: A speech occasion where the speaker is the speech and the audience responds warmly to the life of the message.

Finally, a word of encouragement. If you do not think you can tolerate ghost-writing speeches—become a mother or father instead. Then you can practice and deliver your own speeches to a captive audience! And if you are fortunate, you may even see some good results coming from your performances!

Reprinted permission of "Vital Speeches of the Day", Vol. 48, No. 4, December 1, 1981.

Three Career Traps for Women
(Caution: Your Career May Be Hazardous to Your Health)

Bonita L. Perry,
Communicator Psychologist, Sun Company

Delivered to the American Women in Radio and Television
Philadelphia, Pennsylvania, October 20, 1981

My comments today are aimed at women who are and have been engaged in careers. Women who are pursuing those careers full steam ahead; who are making sacrifices for those careers and who are paying the price of achieving power, climbing the ladder, and gaining influence in the business and corporate world.

I will speak from two vantage points: my educational background in psychology and my professional experience as a management consultant with Booz, Allen & Hamilton, and as a fairly high-level manager at the eighteenth largest U.S. corporation, Sun Company.

There are three career traps women seem to get caught up in. Hopefully by being more aware of them, you can minimize the risks of these adverse conditions so you can maximize the rewards of your careers. The three traps I will discuss today I have labeled the Perfectionism Trap, the Burn-Out Blues, and Seduction by Security. Along the way, I will give you a little quiz that I think you will find fun and helpful. Hopefully, I will spark some questions and comments for a discussion afterwards.

First, there is the *Perfectionism Trap.* Actually, men as well as women get ensnared by it, but women seem to be particularly vulnerable. This reflects, I think, our conviction that the pressure is still on us to prove ourselves and our capabilities in the business world.

What is perfectionism? It is not the healthy pursuit of excellence by men and women who take genuine pleasure in striving to meet high standards. This is necessary for quality life, marked by true accomplishments. Perfectionism is setting standards which are unnaturally high beyond reach or reason. It is straining compulsively and unremittingly toward impossible goals. It is measuring self-worth entirely in terms of productivity and accomplishment. It is a compulsive effort to excel in all things.

The second trap I see career women susceptible to is what I call the *Burn-Out Blues*. Again, it isn't uniquely a feminine problem. But women seem to be particularly vulnerable to it as we broaden our position in the work force today.

What is burn-out? In its simplest terms, psychologists say, it is a condition produced by working too hard, too long in a high-pressure environment. From another perspective, burn-out has been defined as the high cost of high achievement. In a book with that title, Dr. Herbert J. Freudenberger argues that society itself is the breeder of burn-out. It results from an incompatibility in the relationships of the individual to society. Society continues to dangle impossible dreams before us. But at the very same time, it is eroding the traditions and weakening the support systems and relationships that are essential in achieving goals.

Recognizing the early symptoms of burn-out can help to avoid serious problems later. Now it's time for the quiz. I will read fifteen questions. Please consider each of them in terms of how much change has occurred in you and your feelings on this matter over the past six months. Then jot down a number from a 1 to 5 scale for each question, with 1 representing no change or little change and 5 standing for a great deal of change.

Here are the fifteen questions contained in a test framed by Dr. Freudenberger.

1. Do you tire easily and feel fatigued a lot, rather than feeling energetic?
2. Are people annoying you by saying you don't look so good lately?
3. Are you working more and more and accomplishing less and less?
4. Are you becoming more cynical and disenchanted with things around you?
5. Do you often feel a sadness you can't explain?
6. Are you more forgetful—about appointments, deadlines, and your personal possessions?
7. Are you more irritable, short-tempered, and disappointed in the people around you?
8. Are you seeing close friends and family less frequently?
9. Are you too busy for even routine things such as making telephone calls and sending out Christmas cards?

10. Are you suffering from physical complaints—aches, pains, headaches, or a lingering cold?

11. Do you feel disoriented when the day's activities come to a halt?

12. Are joy and happiness elusive?

13. Are you unable to laugh at a joke about yourself?

14. Does sex seem like it's more trouble than it's worth?

15. Do you have very little to say to people?

Now, total the numbers you jotted down and I will give you the scoring to position yourself on the burn-out scale. If your total is from 1 to 25 points, you are doing fine . . . 26 to 35 points means there are some things you should be watching . . . 36 to 50 points identifies you as a candidate for burn-out . . . 51 to 65 points means you are to some degree now burning-out . . . and a score of over 65 is in the nature of a red alert, suggesting that you are behaving in ways that are threatening to your physical and mental well-being.

What can you do about it? Some suggestions:

First, limit—*really* limit—the amount of time you work. And set aside some special time for activities that *you* find relaxing.

Second, take vacations. Mini-vacations and weekend get-aways count too. Don't get involved in the "not having time to do it" trap.

Third, find support—other women or men with whom you can communicate or commiserate and with whom you can problem-solve.

Fourth, promote the team approach to work. Ask for help when you need it, delegate work to others, and trust your associates and subordinates.

Fifth, stop searching for the *Big Reward* that will somehow solve all of your problems and make everything worthwhile. Satisfaction really comes from the blending of many small rewards—a pat on the back from the boss, a complimentary handshake from a friend, a word of thanks from a husband—those are part and parcel of our daily lives.

Avoiding burn-out is largely a matter of perspective. And I like this perspective contributed by American humorist Kim Hubbard: "Do not take life too seriously; you will never get out of it alive."

I've labeled my third trap: *Seduction by Security.* In comparison with the other two, it might be considered a downside risk since it is concerned with attempting not too much but too little.

The problem arises because some degree of security is attractive to all of us. After working for a time in one job in one organization we build up a considerable degree of security in such things as pension benefits, high salary levels and expectations, seniority, and comfortable individual and organizational relationships. And that security is fine as long as it doesn't blind us to the change that is continuously taking place in us and around us.

I suggest we carefully monitor what's happening in our organizations and in our jobs and how we feel about it. And when the fit is no longer comfortable, we must face the facts and initiate a change. This in no way means that we have failed—or that our organizations have failed us. It simply means that a normal process of change is taking place and that we are aware of it and we are adjusting to it.

Thomas Carlyle summed up the importance of a vocational fit in a way that is meaningful to me. He said (and I have changed the pronouns), "Blessed is she who has found her work; for she needs no other blessing."

In closing, I suggest that we weave into our career perspectives these words from the courageous Helen Keller. She said:

> Security is mostly a superstition. It does not exist in nature, nor do the children of men as a whole experience it. Avoiding danger is no safer in the long run than outright exposure. Life is either a daring adventure or nothing.

I suggest that choosing between those two outcomes—a "daring adventure" or "nothing"—is not a difficult choice.

Reprinted permission of "Vital Speeches of the Day", Vol. 48, No. 3, November 15, 1981.

PERSUASIVE SPEECH

Can't Nobody Here Use This Language? Function and Quality in Choosing Words

Jerry Tarver,
Professor, University of Richmond

Delivered to the Connecticut Association of Professional Communicators, Hartford, Connecticut, February 21, 1979

I suppose we must begin by shaking our heads woefully over the sad state of language today, whether in formal speeches, casual conversation, or in writing. Most of us in this room no doubt agree with the generally negative tone of *Time* magazine's year-end assessment of 1978 which claims "our language has been besieged by vulgarities." But to preserve our sanity as professionals in communication, most of us would probably join *Time* in optimistically expecting English somehow to survive and even to prosper.

On the negative side, if I may use a vulgarity to criticize vulgarity, I am often moved in my own profession to paraphrase Casey Stengel and ask, "can't nobody here use this language?"

To generalize about the language ability of students, I would say far too many of them can't express themselves well, and they don't seem to care. The most significant hollow verbalization among students today is not "y'know." It is "needless to say."

On the positive side, *Time* finds our language "enriched by vigorous phrases and terms" from such sources as CB radio and situation comedies. The major bright spots I see are the writing in advertising and on the bathroom wall. Let me quickly add that the *worst* writing also appears in these two places. Some of the most crude and senseless tripe I have encountered has appeared in ads or graffiti. But when they are good, they are very, very good. Both the ad writer and the graffiti artist must work within a small compass. They must be concise. To the point. And each is moved, urgently moved, to communicate. Unfortunately for the motivation of the advertiser, I am one of those people who can enjoy the sizzle and forgo the steak. I don't smoke cigars, and I don't even remember the brand involved, but who can forget the classical commercial in which Edie Adams used to urge, "Why don't you pick one up and smoke it sometime?" I admit I don't have a Texaco credit card, but little I read of modern academic poetry moves me as much as the soothing jingle, "You can trust your car to the man who wears the star."

My favorite graffiti is the plaintive sort. A poor soul eloquently crying out to be understood. In the men's room just down from my office, someone in apparent anguish wrote with painstaking care in the grout between the tiles, "What in the hell am I doing here?" Weeks passed before someone undertook a reply. Whether done in a spirit of helpfulness or malice, I cannot say, but finally in different handwriting, there appeared, "If this is an existential question, contact Dr. Hall in the Philosophy Department. If this is a theological question, contact Dr. Alley in the Religion Department. If this is a biological question, take a look."

Years ago I saw a quotation printed on a little gummed paper strip which had been attached to the wall of a men's room off the New Jersey Turnpike. It offered a simple biblical text and had apparently come to the attention of a tired truck driver. The quotation asked the question, "If God be for us, who can be against us?" No doubt in despair, the truck driver had replied underneath, "The dispatcher."

I suggest to write and speak our best we need, first, a grasp of the function of language and, second, a sensitivity to the quality of our words.

My desk dictionary includes among its definitions of the word *function*, "The action for which a . . . thing is specially fitted or used or for which a thing exists." The concept of function reminds us that words act upon people.

Let me give you an example of a piece of communication which illustrates function. You may recall in *Catch 22* Lt. Milo Minderbinder at one point instituted an elaborate procedure for going through the chow line. It involved signing a loyalty oath, reciting the pledge of allegiance, and singing "The Star-Spangled Banner." But the entire system was destroyed one day when Major de Coverly returned from a trip and cut through the red tape with two words: "Gimme eat."

That simple, and quite ungrammatical, phrase shows language in action. Words at work. Expression that eliminates the unnecessary and gets down to basics.

A grasp of function causes a writer to think of results. Impact. Effect. Audience becomes important. Who will read or listen? Why?

Function calls for the communicator to examine the reason for the existence of a given communication and to choose words that will be a means of expression and not an end.

Next, as I said, we must be sensitive to quality. I know of no objective way to determine quality. But I agree with Robert Persig who insists in *Zen and the Art of Motorcycle Maintenance* that most people intuitively know quality in language when they encounter it.

Most of us have written material we knew was merely adequate. No errors. All the intended ideas in place. No complaints from the boss or the editor. But deep down inside we knew we had done a pedestrian job.

I use a chill-bump test for quality. For poor writing or speaking I get one type of chill bumps. For good language, a better brand of chill bumps. For most of the mediocre stuff in between, no chill bumps at all.

Quality does not mean fancy. When General McAuliffe reportedly answered a Nazi surrender ultimatum with the word "nuts," his language had no less quality than the declaration of the Indian Chief Joseph, "From where the sun now stands, I will fight no more forever." Either of my examples would probably not fare well in a classroom exercise in English composition. But anyone who used such language in that situation would be guilty of ignoring the concept of function.

Our language will not be saved by the exhortations of evangelists in the Church of the Fundamental Grammar. It can be saved by writers and speakers with a grasp of function and a sense of quality.

Reprinted permission of "Vital Speeches of the Day", Vol. 45, No. 14, May 1, 1979.

Good News about Failure: To Fail Is Not to Be Defeated

Eugene W. Brice,
Senior Minister, Country Club Christian Church

Delivered to the Downtown Rotary CLub,
Kansas City, Missouri, January 6, 1983

I think of two stories I've stumbled across in the last week or two. One was a newspaper feature about an unbelievably successful person for whom nothing ever went wrong. The article described a man who had made a fortune in computer hardware. On arriving home, he goes to his grand piano and plays Chopin while his attractive wife puts the finishing touches on the gourmet French cuisine she has been preparing. Sometimes the man's playing is loud enough to disturb their fifteen-year-old son who has set up his own meteorology lab in the basement, says the article. The couple's daughter is away, being in a beauty contest at a local school. The whole article reads like the mimeographed Christmas letter your brother-in-law sends out.

About the same time, I read about an incident in President Truman's life after he had retired and was back in Independence. He was at Truman library, talking with some elementary-school students, and answering their questions. Finally, a question came from an owlish little boy. "Mr. President," he asked, "was you popular when you was a boy?" The President looked at the boy, and answered, "Why no, I was never popular. The popular boys were the ones who were good at games and had big tight fists. I was never like that. Without my glasses, I was blind as a bat, and to tell the truth, I was kind of a sissy. If there was any danger of getting into a fight, I took off. I guess that's why I'm here today." The little boy started to applaud and then everyone else did, too.

And so did I, as I read the story, for it is a reminder that all of us experience failure in different ways. That's why Paul's words in Corin-

thians have always hooked themselves onto my mind. "We are afflicted in every way, but not crushed; perplexed, but not driven to despair;
persecuted but not forsaken; knocked down, but not knocked out"
(2 Cor. 4:8–9). Because such moments come to us, we acknowledge the
bad times failure brings, and we look for good news. Then let's make
some observations about failure.

1. Start by saying that *failure is something we can avoid*. That's
good news, isn't it? Or is it? Failure is something we can avoid by saying nothing, doing nothing, and being nothing.

Let me brag on myself a bit. I have never in my life choked up
while singing a solo. I have never lost a match in a tennis tournament.
I have never had a poem rejected by a literary magazine. I have never
been defeated in a race for public office. Inasmuch as I am one who
loves music and tennis and poetry and politics, that's an amazing
record. But you see, I have never sung a solo, or played in tournament
tennis, or submitted a poem to a magazine, or run for public office. I
have never failed at any of these things because I have never tried.

In life itself, the same options are open. Paul confessed that many
times in his life he was afflicted, perplexed, persecuted, and knocked
down. But many in Paul's day suffered none of these discouragements.
Safely living tight little lives, they never offered themselves for any
great new truth, and they lived and died with nothing more than
kitchen failures and backyard defeats. What small battles most of us
limit ourselves to: some successes, but at a very low level. Never any
great commitment. Never a hard promise made. Never a challenging
job taken.

2. Move on from there to note that *failure is a teacher*, the best one
we'll ever have. Consider this: the only way you ever learned to walk
was by failure. If your first step had waited until you were sure you
would not fall, you would still be wearing high-topped white shoes
with unscarred soles. The only way you ever learned to read, or add, or
play the piano, or run an adding machine was by trying it and failing,
and then trying again.

Last summer at Estes Park, in a court next to ours, some nine-year-
olds were trying to play tennis. It wasn't going too well for them. One
of the nine-year-olds swung at the ball and hit it clear over the fence
just as his mother walked by. "Throw the ball to us, will you, Mom,"
the boy said. The mother replied, "Why did you hit it over the fence?
You've had a tennis lesson!" It takes more than a lesson in tennis to
learn how not to hit it over the fence. It takes long practice and frequent failure. You don't learn to hit it in until you've hit it out many
a time.

Failure teaches us. If, in our work, something is going badly, something we need to learn is offering itself to us. There must be a better
way to do this. In this situation, I am failing! What am I doing wrong,

and where do I go from here? If, at home, things are going badly, we have the opportunity to learn, and to proceed stronger than before. Every marriage should expect moments of failure; the strong marriages are not those which never fail, but those which learn from their failures. Learning in marriage to treat all disasters as incidents and none of the incidents as disasters, the bond between husband and wife grows ever stronger.

Failure is a teacher, and it becomes an asset to us if we learn from it. We may learn that our present strategy won't work. We may learn that our goal itself wasn't good. We may learn that our inner problems interfere with our outer work. We may learn that we quit too soon. Whatever it is, failure teaches us if we will let it.

3. Therefore, *failure need never be final!* To fail is not to be defeated. Mary Pickford said, "If you have made mistakes, even serious ones, there is always another chance for you. What we call real failure is not the falling down, but the staying down." Someone tells of the young Methodist minister who went from seminary to his first church, and proceeded to fail miserably. The Bishop came out, talked with the laypeople, discovered that indeed, the young minister had botched the job completely. Invited to preach on Sunday, the Bishop publicly criticized the young man for his poor job. Everyone wondered what the young man would say the next Sunday, after having been publicly humiliated. He rose to the pulpit the next Sunday and said quietly: "I can sin, you can sin, and the Bishop can sin. I can make mistakes, you can make mistakes, and the Bishop can make mistakes. I could go to hell, you could go to hell, and the Bishop can go to hell!" No failure ever need be final!

In a bit of whimsy, Neil Postman quotes a letter written by a high-school senior who had received a letter of rejection from the college he wanted to attend. "Dear Admissions Officer," the student wrote. "I am in receipt of your rejection of my application. As much as I would like to accommodate you, I find I cannot accept it. I have already received four rejections from other colleges, and this number is, in fact, over my limit. Therefore, I must reject your rejection, and will appear for classes on September 18" (Neil Postman, *Crazy Talk*).

Crazy as it is, *I like that!* It may not have worked for that student, but it has worked and it works in many a life. That's just what Paul did. The world stamped "failure" on his hand, and Paul erased it. "Perplexed, but not despairing. Knocked down, but not knocked out." "I *reject your rejection!*"

Any one of us can say that, too. So many have said it, and have risen from failure to real achievement. In 1902, the poetry editor of *Atlantic Monthly* returned a sheaf of poems to a twenty-eight-year-old poet with this curt note: "Our magazine has no room for your vigorous verse." The poet was Robert Frost, who rejected the rejection. In 1905, the University of Bern turned down a Ph.D. dissertation as being irrelevant and fanciful. The young physics student who wrote the dissertation was Albert Einstein, who rejected the rejection. In 1894, the rhetoric teacher at Harrow in England wrote on a sixteen-year-old's report card, "a conspicuous lack of success." The sixteen-year-old was Winston Churchill, who rejected the rejection.

Go ahead and complete the list. "In 1982, John Doe failed in the effort to (and you fill in the blanks): keep a job, expand the business, make a good marriage, head a community project, be a good father." *Name your own failure.* How long the list might be! But John Doe rejected the rejection, and tried yet again. One of God's best gifts to us is the joy of trying again, for no failure ever need be final.

Then sum it up with this. A small boy had been looking through a stationer's stock of greeting cards when a clerk asked, "Can I help you find what you're looking for, son? Birthday card? Get-well card? Anniversary card for mom and dad?" "Not exactly," said the little boy, shaking his head. Then he added wistfully, "You got anything in the line of blank report cards?"

Life does; God does. Especially at the beginning of every new year those new report cards are available to us, and we ourselves fill them in by how we respond to the D's and F's of life. With God's help, we rise up from failure; afflicted but not crushed; perplexed, but not despairing; knocked down, but by the grace of God, never knocked out! And that, my frequently failing friends, is good news, indeed!

Reprinted permission of "Vital Speeches of the Day", Vol. 49, No. 8, February 1, 1983.

INDEX

Credits

Page 2, Jeff Albertson, Stock, Boston, Inc. Page 6, B.C. by permission of Johnny Hart and Field Enterprises, Inc. Page 10, (top) Jerry Howard, Stock, Boston, Inc.; (bottom, left) Art Stein, Photo Researchers, Inc.; (bottom, right) Vicki Lawrence, Stock, Boston, Inc. Page 11, (top) Sam C. Pierson, Jr., Photo Researchers, Inc.; (bottom, left) Kay Lawson, Jeroboam, Inc.; (bottom, right) Photo Researchers, Inc. Page 15, Parker, *The Saturday Evening Post.* Page 16, Peter Southwick, Stock, Boston, Inc. Page 17, (top row, left to right) Danilo Nardi, Freelance Photographers Guild, Bob Clay, Jeroboam, Inc., Bill Owens, Jeroboam, Inc.; (middle row, left, center) Fredrik D. Bodin, Stock, Boston, Inc., (middle row, right) Bob Clay, Jeroboam, Inc.; (bottom row, left to right), Joyce McKinney, Jeroboam, Inc., Laimute E. Druskis, Jeroboam, Inc., Anestis Diakopoulos, Stock, Boston, Inc. Page 20, Arthur Grace, Stock, Boston, Inc. Page 22, drawing: Futzie Nutzle. Page 23, diagram: Susan Boria. Page 25, B.C. by permission of Johnny Hart and Field Enterprises, Inc. Page 27, by permission of the artist. Page 34, Rose Skytta, Jeroboam, Inc. Page 35, by permission of Lundberg. Page 39, Beetle Bailey by Mort Walker, copyright King Features Syndicate, Inc.; World Rights Reserved. Page 40, Barbara Alper, Stock, Boston, Inc. Page 46, Charles Gatewood, Stock, Boston, Inc. Page 49, The Born Loser by Art Sansom, by permission of Newspaper Enterprise Association, Inc. Page 50, reprinted with permission from *Sales Meetings/The Magazine for Successful Meetings* (Oct. 1972), copyright Bill Communications, Inc. Page 52, Robert Llewellyn, Freelance Photographers Guild. Pages 60–61, The Wizard of Id by Parker and Hart, copyright Field Enterprises, Inc., 1983. Page 68, Ellis Herwig, Stock, Boston, Inc. Page 72, B.C. by permission of Johnny Hart and Field Enterprises, Inc. Page 80, The Born Loser by Art Sansom, by permission of Newspaper Enterprise Association, Inc. Page 88, Arthur Grace, Stock, Boston, Inc. Page 89, Hazel Hankin, Stock, Boston, Inc. Pages 93, 95, Phyllis Rockne. Page 98, (top) ad for Mission Viejo Company, client, by Cochrane, Chase, Livingston and Company (Irvine, Calif.), from *Communication Arts* (Nov./Dec. 1979), p. 40; (bottom) ad for Northwestern Bell, client, by Bozell and Jacobs, agency (Minneapolis), from *Communication Arts Annual* (1979), p. 101. Page 99, (top) ad for WCCO-TV, client, Carmichael-Lynch, agency (Minneapolis), from *Communication Arts Annual* (1979), p. 31; (bottom) ad for Michael Salerno Exercise, client, by Deborah Rodney, agency (Los Angeles), from *Communication Arts* (Nov./Dec. 1979), p. 38. Page 100, ad for People for Boschwitz, client, by Bozell and Jacobs, agency (Min-

neapolis), *Communication Arts* (Nov./Dec. 1979), p. 38. Page 101, Phyllis Rockne. Page 104, Van Bucher, Stock, Boston, Inc. Page 107, Salo, *The Saturday Evening Post.* Page 109, Marcus, *The Saturday Evening Post,* permission by Jerry Marcus. Page 111, by permission of The Wella Corporation, Englewood, N.J. Page 115, Richard Bermack, Jeroboam, Inc. Page 128, Frank Siteman, Stock, Boston, Inc. Page 131, Tom Henderson, *The Saturday Evening Post.* Page 136, The Born Loser by Art Sansom, by permission of Newspaper Enterprise Association, Inc. Page 144, Campus Clatter by Lewis, by permission of Newspaper Enterprise Association, Inc. Page 145, The Born Loser by Art Sansom, by permission of Newspaper Enterprise Association. Page 151, Peeter Vilms, Jeroboam, Inc. Page 152, Anna Kaufman Moon, Stock, Boston, Inc. Page 153, (top) Elizabeth Crews, Stock, Boston, Inc.; (bottom, left) Jean-Claude Lejeune, Stock, Boston, Inc.; (bottom, right) Richard Bermack, Jeroboam, Inc. Page 154, Don Ivers, Jeroboam, Inc. Page 155, George Bellerose, Stock, Boston, Inc. Page 162, Catherine Ursillo, Photo Researchers, Inc. Page 176, Michael Hayman, Stock, Boston, Inc. Page 184, Owen Franken, Stock, Boston, Inc. Page 186, Peanuts by Charles Schulz, by permission of United Feature Syndicate. Page 191, Campus Clatter by Lewis, by permission of Newspaper Enterprise Association, Inc. Page 192, Art Stein, Photo Researchers, Inc. Page 204, Peeter Vilms, Jeroboam, Inc. Page 206, The Born Loser by Art Sansom, by permission of Newspaper Enterprise Association, Inc. Page 208, Shoe by Jeff MacNelly, by permission of Jefferson Communications, Inc. Page 210, Jeffry W. Myers, Freelance Photographers Guild. Page 214, George T. Kruse, Jeroboam, Inc. Page 218, B.C. by permission of Johnny Hart and Field Enterprises, Inc. Page 232, Chon Day, *The Saturday Evening Post.* Page 238, Stock, Boston, Inc. Page 241, Hagar by Dik Browne, copyright King Features Syndicate, Inc., 1978; World Rights Reserved. Page 242, Gregg Mancuso. Page 246, Suzanne Arms, Jeroboam, Inc. Page 249, Anestis Diakopoulos, Stock, Boston, Inc. Page 254, Jerry Berndt, Stock, Boston, Inc. Page 258, The Born Loser by Art Sansom, by permission of Newspaper Enterprise Association, Inc. Page 259, *The Saturday Evening Post,* courtesy of Reg Hider.